THE DEVIL PREFERS

By: Edward Jamison

IMPORTANT: EVERY PICTURE, AUDIO OR VIDEO CLIP SHOWN OR MENTIONED IN THIS BOOK CAN BE VIEWED IN CHRONOLOGICAL ORDER AT WWW.THEDEVILPREFERS.COM/BOOKEXTRA

WE HIGHLY RECOMMEND THAT YOU OPEN THIS LINK ON YOUR MOBILE DEVICE AS YOU READ TO VIEW HIGH RESOLUTION VERSIONS OF THE PHOTOS IN ADDITION TO BEING ABLE TO WATCH THE VIDEOS MENTIONED OR THE AUDIO CLIPS MENTIONED THROUGHOUT THE BOOK.

Edward Jamison Esq.
848 N Rainbow Blvd. #2305
Las Vegas, NV 89107
www.thedevilprefers.com
media@edcontracts.com

ISBN: 979-8-9850181-0-3

CONTENTS

PART 3 - The Triads

PART 4 - Black Magic Battle

INTRODUCTION

What I am about to expose and write about in regards to the criminal underworld in Asia has never been written or talked about before, at least publicly anyway. This story is a 100% accurate account of what happened to me while in Macau and Vietnam from 2009 to 2011 and again in 2014 & 2015 and what has continued to happen to me due to this criminal underworld since I moved back to the United States. Once you see the dark details and cloak of secrecy revealed how these criminals operate, you'll feel lucky to live in a Western Society. The disregard for human life, abuse of women, and the level of deception these criminals employ in their daily lives are shocking, and as you'll learn, deadly too if you're unlucky. Although these criminals prey upon their own people, Westerners are the preferred choice; they also like to have the young girls they enslave and rape from the time they are children do all the dirty work in the numerous scams they run against their victims. I currently live in America with my son that I had with a "now deceased" Vietnamese Girl in Vietnam while living there in 2010 that was "unbeknownst to me" a soldier for the Triads, whom she was sold to at age ten by her evil parents that were also in on the plot against me since day one. Let's go back to 2009 to see how it all started.

PART 1 - HOW IT ALL STARTED

1 – My First Time in Asia

I visited Macau in July 2009 and got lured into falling in love with a girl enslaved by Triad Godfather Luis Lui that worked at one of Luis' 50 Saunas in Macau called the Eighteen Sauna, which is located inside the Golden Dragon Casino in Macau. Three weeks later, I willingly gave the girl $4600 US Dollars as a gift as I said goodbye due to me starting to have strong feelings for her and not wanting to love somebody 8000 miles from home. This money was to allow her to return home to Vietnam. However, at the time, she told me she wasn't enslaved and that the $4600 was just money she owed people to repay getting her brother released from jail for killing somebody while driving his motorcycle drunk in Vietnam. I didn't care if it was true; I just wanted to help this poor girl that I was starting to love but also saying goodbye to at the same time. She cried and went into the bathroom for 10 minutes and then came out, threw the money on the floor, and walked out! I was stunned; I never saw any girl give me cash back, especially when I said goodbye. That was the first strategic move of many that were done to lure me over to Asia to ultimately take everything I had, including the son I had with her after moving there. This dark story happens all the time in Asia, but you won't find too many accounts of it because the enemy behind these scams is patient and calculating in ways never seen in the Western World. If you want to see pure evil, look no further than Luis Lui, #4 in power for the Macau Triads. The things I learned and experienced as I escaped the Macau Triads have led more than ten people to say it's a Hollywood movie, the only difference being that this is 100% true. I escaped several of the clever scams they executed against me that ranged from:

- Trying to get me to sleep with a Triad Boss's Wife so they could extort me
- Framing me as a drug smuggler by planting drugs on me in flight from Hong Kong to HCMC Vietnam
- Attempting to murder me when all previous scam attempts failed

Hong told me that in Vietnam, all of the Police are corrupt and that when somebody dies in a situation like drinking and driving, the accused will get arrested, but the reporting of the crime won't go into the system for at least 24 hours. After 24 hours, it is harder to bribe your way out because the Police are scared that the Government will find out and they'll lose their job and go to jail. The families of the victim know this too. Even though the victim's family is distraught, they figure it's better to have money than punishment for the accused because sending the culprit to jail won't bring back their child; so they quickly negotiate a deal between the families and the Police and the guilty person's family will pay off the victims and the corrupt Police and the whole thing will be recorded as an accident or as an unsolved crime with no suspects in the event it is a murder.

Before I go right into these scams in detail, let me first go back to the beginning in 2009 when I visited SE Asia for the first time, so you understand the history leading up to how I came into the crosshairs of this Secretive Criminal Empire.

I admittedly did the craziest thing any guy has ever done for love, which is moving to Vietnam to be with a girl that I thought would be the perfect girl aside from her apparent misgivings regarding her past. Before I tell you the story about the move that almost ended my life, let me tell you why I moved there and what attracted me to Asia and Asian Women in the first place.

I was always good at making money, good at losing it also, lol. I was always much too generous with women because money was just money; I could always make more after giving it away or spending it. I have since changed my viewpoint on that and don't give money away as I used to because I have a sweet little boy to worry about that only has me to rely on since his mother never had his best interest in mind.

Anyways, before I ended up in Vietnam, I was an Attorney in Los Angeles for ten years; with the final few years, I started to develop software and transitioned away from lawyering once that business started doing well. During my ten years' stay in Los Angeles "L.A." I went through two long-term relationships where I gave everything to those two women only to have them steal more and complain that they were owed six figures because I took them off the market for a few years each, whatever. Without boring you with the details of that, let's say that I had a pessimistic outlook as to where L.A. dating would lead me. I also got to a point where I completely lost faith in the legal system (due to a corrupt Judge that allowed admitted perjury to go unpunished because he was in cahoots with Plaintiff's Attorneys. I discovered this after hiring a private investigator only to be ignored by the regulatory agencies that police judicial corruption when I blew the whistle. This experience left me thinking our system is smoke and mirrors at best and that American women are a nightmare. I must say now that I was 100% wrong because I judged American Woman based on "L.A.," which is not representative of the typical American Woman but just representative of "L.A." ... That said, I had a friend who always asked me to go to Macau for over a year and told me it was a guy amusement park with thousands of beautiful, submissive women that just loved Westerners and made you feel like no American woman ever could. At the time, I was going out on three dates a week with the same type of L.A. woman and was burned out; I figured this different experience might be the thing I needed to break the monotony.

If you haven't heard of Macau, it is a 1-hour Ferry Ride from Hong Kong and is the Las Vegas of Asia. It makes two times more gambling revenue than Vegas, and most Vegas Casino Brands have a casino in Macau, i.e., Wynn, Venetian. None of the American Casino brands have Saunas in the Casino. However, a majority of the Asian-owned Casinos also have a Sauna somewhere inside the Casino. You can go hang out all day and get every kind of body treatment you can think of in addition to getting your haircut, and finally, you can pick a girl from "Showtime" to take to a private room.

The Casino does not own the Saunas in each Casino. The Saunas are all owned by the Triads, who lease the space from the Casino. The businesses are not connected; they only occupy the same building. Many patrons don't realize that and feel secure in these Saunas since they are inside a multi-million-dollar Casino. I remember when I asked the front desk if they had any coupons for the Sauna and the Lady was quick to say that they have no affiliation with the Sauna as though I just accused her of a crime.

When you go to any Sauna in Macau, every 30 minutes to an hour (depending on the Sauna), a bell would ring, and the ladies doing the regular sauna services would all start shouting "Showtime, Showtime," where they coerce you towards a room blasting loud music. Once you enter the room, you will see over 100 beautiful girls wearing dresses with a number on them, and you can pick a girl by her number and go to a private room for an hour and do whatever.

Prostitution is legal in Macau and has been pretty much since The Portuguese colonized Macau in 1557. I was told by a friend (whom I now think was completely wrong) that prostitution is normal and not taboo in Asia and that the girls are very grateful that they can help their families with the money they make. At that time, I wasn't aware of the real dark substance behind this industry, and the human trafficking and advanced scams aspect were not even crossing my mind or apparent from what I observed while there initially. My naive assessment almost got me killed more times than once, and escaping Asia once the bottom-feeding underworld sunk their teeth in left me with a story that is a cross between "Catch Me if You Can" & "Constantine." Asia is different from the Western World; deception is mastered in ways the Western World is not akin to.

Before going further, let me say that I feel bad for visiting the Saunas in Macau now that I know that these girls are not thankful and happy

like my friend led me to believe, but instead smiling to keep from being beaten if they don't. I am trying to make the wrong decisions I made right by fighting against the people that enslave these girls. Even though these girls scammed me, I am trying to help them because they have no choice. I haven't visited a Sauna since early 2010, even though I had plenty of opportunities in addition to the approval of my ex. The last five times I did go to a Sauna, I only got regular services like a massage and was just there to relax even though "Show Time" was one room over. Please keep that in mind before you decide to judge me. It takes courage to admit that I was even over there, let alone stand up to an evil organization like the Triads in Macau; so, try to remember that before throwing criticism my way.

MY 1ST DAY IN MACAU

The date I first visited Macau was July 25th, 2009. I arrived in Macau around 1 AM, upon which I was greeted at the lobby of the Wynn by my friend the moment I arrived. My friend then introduced me to his friend and asked me if I wanted to check out a few hotspots, but he couldn't join us because he already had a girl meeting him at the hotel. I said yes even though I hadn't slept in 24 hours, and it was 1 AM already. After taking a quick shower, I met him in the lobby, and we went to a place called the "Racetrack" in the Lisboa Hotel where about 100 girls walk around the halls and wait for you to come to say hello to negotiate a price and take them back to your hotel. These girls are independent, and they must keep walking, or they will kick them out of the hotel since this is done in the public hallways of the hotel and is not an official business like the Saunas in Macau. I approached a Chinese girl who looked at me like the Night Stalker and said no as she quickly walked away. I said WTF to the guy I was with, and he told me that he never saw that happen, but two minutes later a girl did the same thing to him, so we said screw this place and went to the MGM where he said there is a pick-up bar with tons of girls hanging out. The bar ended up being dead, so we almost called it a night when he asked if I wanted to go to a famous Sauna called the Eighteen Sauna inside the Golden Dragon Casino.

We arrived at 2:20 AM and sat in an area where they offer services like manicures, ear cleaning, thigh massages, and body scrubs. I got my ears cleaned which is a scary thing if you never had it done before. It makes you think they will pop your eardrum the entire time, but luckily, I was OK. The guy I was with was perplexed at why Showtime was taking so long to start (I now know why; it's because they were delaying it to make sure their best English-speaking girls were available since Western Guys were there). After pondering for a moment, I said, "what the hell," why not. We were there for an hour and 10 minutes before they rang the bell, and the guy I was with said it always happened every thirty minutes. Around 3:30 AM, a bell started to ring, and the woman that did the massage and ear cleaning services started saying "ShowTime, ShowTime" and motioned for us to go to the other area of the Sauna where you could hear loud music playing. The guy I was with lit up like a Christmas tree and said, "come on, let's go"! I walked into the room and was stunned by the number of beautiful young women walking around in Evening Gowns with a unique number pinned to the top. Holy Shit! I exclaimed as I laid eyes on Hong for the first time.

At that time in my life, I liked to save lost souls; However, even though it wasn't my plan originally, after falling in love with Hong, I decided the concept of being with a girl I met at a Sauna long term wasn't a deal-breaker because I know these girls came from nothing.

It wasn't their fault that they ended up since their families pushed them towards it. I believe everybody deserves a second chance and figured that a girl like that would be 100 times more grateful than the average girl, but I now know I was wrong only because of the horrors their families and the evil men who own and control them have subjected them too. This harsh environment effectively reduces them to a learned helpless state where Evil Men that respect nobody completely control them.

Anyways, I noticed Hong right away and was stunned by her beauty. I picked her immediately, and the Manager called her number, and she was whisked away to a room downstairs as I waited for the other guy I was with to pick who he wanted since I didn't want to leave right away and be rude. He took ten minutes to pick his girl, and I almost changed my choice because I almost forgot how beautiful Hong was as I stared at the other 100 women for ten minutes after she left. I ultimately decided not to change my pick. I got Hong's phone number before leaving. I proceeded to call her every day without an answer or a callback, but in the meanwhile was visiting other Saunas throughout Macau and met a striking girl at "Darlings 1" named Phuong that went by the name Hanna and was #301 at Darlings 1 (There is a Darlings 2 also). The video below is of the "18 Sauna" and "Darlings 1."

View the video by clicking "**Section 1**" at **www.thedevilprefers.com/bookextra** which is a webpage that contains all the images, videos, and audio snippets in the order they appear in this book. This page is meant to be open while you are reading the book to quickly allow you to watch and listen to video and audio snippets without having to type in a link for each one. We will also put the actual link next to each video and audio snippet for the first 20 to get you accustomed to using the website while you read. After the first 20, we will only refer to the section where you can listen or watch. Hearing and seeing the videos and audio is very important because nothing adds credence like the videos and audio of the referenced events.

18 Sauna Video

See https://bit.ly/dprefer1 or keep Section 1 open from **www.thedevilprefers.com/bookextra** on either your laptop or mobile device and click each video or audio file in the order they appear in the book in order to not have to open each link one at a time. This media page has 5 sections that contain every video, picture and audio file at one place. Start with Section 1 and go from top to bottom to view all media files in the order they appear in the book.

Darlings 1 Video

See https://bit.ly/dprefer2 or view this video at **"Section 1"** from **www.thedevilprefers.com/bookextra**

I started to like Phuong "Hanna" a lot and went back to "Darlings 1" once more that week in addition to paying to have her come to my hotel and decided to pursue her when suddenly Hong calls me the day before I went back to America. I liked Hong a little bit more, so I went to see Hong one last time before leaving and proceeded to communicate with both of them via phone and email for the next three weeks. I planned on returning to see both of them for five days each without disclosing that I liked two girls, not one like I led each to believe. Being the multi-tasker, I would send a message and just copy and paste the same message and send it to the other to save time. Statements like "you are beautiful" and stuff like that, but little did I know, there was a Vietnamese girl named Nhan translating the messages for both girls. I thought I was playing them, but they were scamming me from day 1. BUT, after spending five days with Hong on that second trip, the guilt I felt was overwhelming. I decided to tell her everything and said that I am starting to feel love for her and cannot love somebody 8,000 miles away, so I wanted to say goodbye to her and Phuong forever because it is too hard loving somebody so far away. I told her I wanted to pay off the debt she owed so she didn't have to work in a sauna anymore and gave her $4600 US before I left and said goodbye for the last time. She was crying and went into the bathroom and called somebody while I continued to talk to an interpreter that I hired to help us talk since Hong's English was bad at the time. Ten minutes later, Hong walked out of the bathroom, threw the money on the floor, threw the iPhone on the bed that I bought her, and walked out crying. I was shocked! Never have I seen any girl give anything back when I was saying goodbye. Did I just lose an amazing girl???

I still had five days in Macau, so I decided to stick to the plan and spend it with Phuong even though I told her the same thing. I only gave her $1400 though, and she kept the money and the iPhone I bought for her also, which was fine because it was a gift. The second day after telling Hong goodbye, while with Phuong, Hong kept calling and texting me saying Why Why Why!!! Phuong kept telling me to look at my phone when a text message would come in; I now realize that she did it to help forward the scam, which was to get me to love Hong since Hong was the better option to assure success since they all realized that I liked Hong the most. After about a day of sending me messages, I couldn't take it anymore and agreed to see her even though Phuong "acted as though" she was angry. The second I saw Hong, I was floored. Hong looked so innocent and heartbroken that I quickly thought to myself the possibility of moving here to be with her since I knew it would take over a year to bring her to America. I decided within 2 minutes. I quickly realized that I could still run my business from Asia and was tired of all of the bullshit in America, so it wasn't too hard to make the decision based on love since I wasn't scared of the unknown either. I shot the video below just three days later as we waited for me to go to the Airport. Look at how convincing and sincere she looked. Now you see how I got pulled in; I thought this girl would take a bullet for me by the way she seemed as though she loved me. She was diabolical.

Hong the Day I Was Leaving.

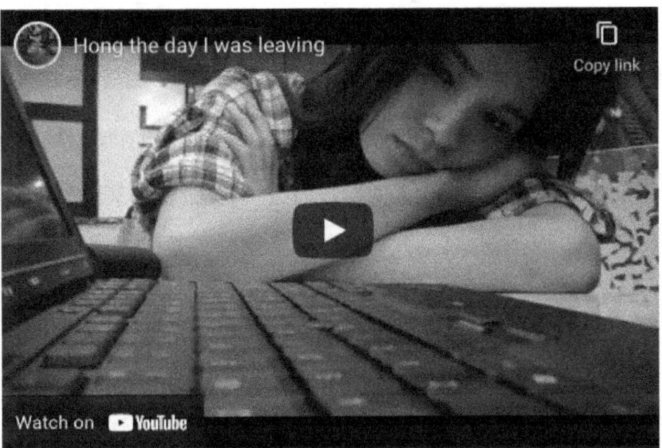

See https://bit.ly/dprefer3 or view this video at **"Section 1"** from www.thedevilprefers.com/bookextra

Hanna "Phuong" (Darlings 1)

After going back to America on September 2nd, 2009, from my 2nd trip to Macau, within a week, I already had a 7-week trip planned

from October 10th, 2009, to December 2nd, 2009, where I planned on staying with Hong in Vietnam so we could look for a place to live and so I could make sure I was ready to make such a big move. □The plan was to go back to America and close shop from December 2009 to February 24th, 2010, when I would move my entire household and my two dogs to Vietnam for good. □At that time, I was intrigued by Asia; even though I couldn't speak the language, I liked the simple way of life and was burned out on L.A. Women and American Materialism. As far as I knew, I would live with Hong in Asia for the rest of my life. □The cost of living was next to nothing, and being in love was enough to keep me from being too homesick. □Even though Hong went back to Vietnam, I had her meet me in Macau for eight days from October 10th through the 18th□to see my friends before we left Macau together for my first visit to Vietnam on October 18th, 2009. □On the second day in Vietnam, Hong suggested we go to Cangio, nicknamed "Monkey Island," a 2-hour drive by motorcycle from HCMC. □Hong's sister Tuoi, her cousin Muoi "Kiwi" and two guys that were supposedly their friends came with us.

I now know that the two guys were Triad Soldiers meant to study me for any weakness, etc., to fleecing me for everything I had in the future. □Hong always told me how her friends were amazed that I lasted almost two years in Vietnam and that most Westerners tire and want to leave within three months. I now know that she was statistically speaking from experience due to the hundreds of scams her people and the Triads pulled off against unsuspecting Westerners. I didn't see those guys again for over a year because a friend of mine had his Vietnamese friend meet us for dinner later that night, and that guy saw their tattoos and warned my friend that they were "Banditos" (a slang description of Asian Gangster) and that he thought I would end up dead one day and disappear. □I told Hong that, and she must have told the guys not to come around because it was blowing their cover and jeopardizing the scam.

RANDOM FACT: On the 2-hour ride to and from Monkey Island that day, I kept singing the song "Rooster" by the band "Alice in Chains," but I only knew two verses to the song, and I just kept singing those two verses in a silly loud way, and Hong and I laughed the whole time. I didn't even hear the song recently, but it popped into my head for some reason. I never even listened to Alice in Chains other than hearing them occasionally on the radio. I didn't have any of their songs in my 22,000-song iPod either. □I never sang a song to Hong for more than 15 seconds the whole time we were together, but this song I sang for at least 90 minutes between the rides there and back. □I didn't even know what the song meant. I thought it was about a real Rooster being slaughtered for dinner; it wasn't until I had moved back to America in early 2012 that I heard the song and listened to the words and realized it was about an American Soldier in Vietnam. The only song I ever sang to Hong repeatedly was a song about an American nicknamed "the Rooster "surviving his Vietnamese enemies during numerous attempts where they tried to kill him. □What are the odds of that? □I don't know even one other song that describes an American surviving over in Vietnam; the odds must be more than a million to 1. □I think God planted that in my head as humor! □I didn't realize how meaningful that song was in describing my future until long after leaving Vietnam. The lyrics to the song are below; the real "Rooster" was" Alice in Chains" Band Member Jerry Cantrell's Father that survived death on many occasions while in the Vietnam War. □I highlighted the verses that hit home the most, even though I only knew two verses at the time.

Two Triad Soldiers at Monkey Island

Rooster Lyrics

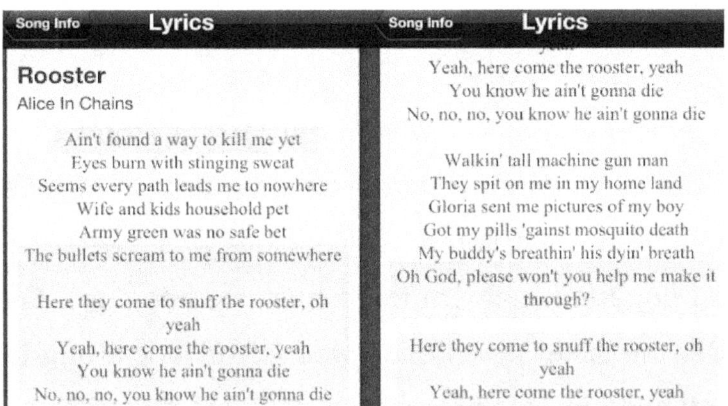

During the rest of October and November, I toured Vietnam with Hong, rented a house, bought furniture, and was the best man in her friend "7's" wedding of 400 people since her Chinese Triad husband didn't have anybody at the wedding. Even though their marriage was legitimate, the fact that they asked me to be the best man was a last-second ploy to make me feel loved, so I would continue to put my guard down more and more as they dug into what was initially supposed to be my murder but then switched to frame me as a drug smuggler when that got sidetracked due to Hong feeling guilty since I was the father of our son born on December 2nd, 2010 (exactly one year after I left Vietnam for the first time on December 2nd, 2009, which was three months before moving there permanently on February 24th, 2010. □I got her pregnant the first week after I moved there, around March 3rd, 2010). □ I ended up leaving Vietnam for the last time on my son's one-year birthday "December

2nd, 2011". □This 2nd day in December was very significant the whole time from 2009 to 2011.

Let's go back to December 2nd, 2009, when I returned to America. □ I found the picture below when I ran forensics software on Hong's hard drive that recovered deleted items. This picture was taken less than 12 hours after I departed Vietnam to go back to America. □On December 5th, 2009, my ticket to America was from Hong Kong to Los Angeles, but I stopped in Macau for three days before my flight. As you can see in the picture, Hong (pictured on the right of the picture three seats down from the guy in the red shirt) was out with her husband Cuong, who is sitting to her left. Hong's sister Tuoi was with the guy sitting next to Hong and is pictured directly across from that guy wearing the brown striped shirt

I spoke with Hong every other day, and yahoo messaged her several times a day for the 3 and 1/2 months from December 2nd, 2009, to February 24th, 2010, when I moved to Vietnam for good to be with her. □I took my dogs too, which was a pain in the ass. I got them into the country without a hitch though, and was greeted by Hong, her sister Tuoi and her Cousin Kiwi. □I could see that Hong was sad when we made eye contact; she was also sad when I first saw her in Macau previously when I went there for seven weeks in October 2009. □I now know why. □She did love me to a degree, and she was sad knowing that my fate would be so grim once her "owners" decided it was time for me to go.

Starting in April 2010, I tried to take Vietnamese Lessons, but the progress was too slow, and I gave up after four months. □I hung out all day with Hong and watched T.V. or went to get a foot massage which was $3 for an hour in Vietnam. □Hong encouraged me to go to Macau and hang out with her friends that were still there and hang out with my friends that came into Macau every five weeks or so. As a result of me exposing the Triads, I have lost touch with that group after they distanced themselves from me out of fear that the Triads will retaliate against them just for knowing me. I understand why they did it, but the good news is that they were a group I met in business and were not my core group of friends, so it wasn't a big deal. I mostly hung out with her friends anyways when I went to Macau. Hong said she wanted me to have fun and felt terrible that I was so bored in Vietnam. I thought she was a dream girl, but little did I know, it was all part of the scheme.

Little did I know though, Hong originally only called me back before I returned to the USA during my first visit because her Boss realized I liked her and Phuong and that I would be a great "Mark," so they all colluded to play a deadly game on me to ultimately try and steal all of my money, which they do all of the time in Macau and across the globe.

After I returned to America with my son in late 2011, I was able to get Hong to admit to certain events that took place while chatting with her on Yahoo Messenger. This only lasted for a few days before her "Owners" found out and put the fear of God in her, and she didn't give any admissions after that time. I chatted with her in broken English because she understood better, which should explain my incomplete sentences in the messages as I conversed with her.

Below on the top left, you will see where Hong admitted that she only called me at the end of the week because her friend wanted her to play a game on me. On the right is a chat session where Hong admits to giving the money back because her friend told her to.

Hong's friend & Boss went by the nickname "7" and was married to Luis Lui's underling Guang Lin that went by the "AKA John Lam." Hong rarely ever told the truth; these moments were few and far between where she owned up to what she did. □These chat sessions were about August 2009 when I met her for the 2nd time in Macau but took place in early 2012.

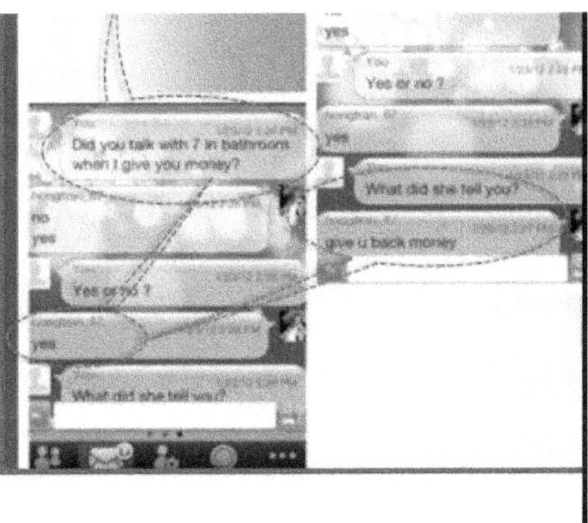

Even though I received several warnings from people who know about how Macau runs behind the scenes just before moving there, I was imprudent; I never thought something like that could happen to me even though I was told that this was a regular practice of the Triads. This started an array of deception that was patiently played out over the next 20 months until they kicked their scam into high gear with the Airplane scam on April 14th, 2011, that I narrowly escaped only to be vigorously pursued to this day by an evil enemy that cares about nothing but themselves. In hindsight, I counted over 100 people that played a part in one of the several scams, the actual number I'll never know.

2 - Moving to Vietnam

I arrived in Vietnam with my dogs with plans on staying for good on 2/25/2010. I remember lying in bed the first night thinking, WTF did I do? I snapped out of it the next day thankfully, and tried to make the best of it. The first month was uneventful until I found out that Hong lied to me about being in Singapore just before I got there.

Hong attempts suicide

In late March 2010, Hong said she wanted to visit her mother after I was there for a month and said it was better if I stayed home since the power always was out down there in the jungle where her family was from. □I had a weird feeling because Hong had her sister and her cousin's passport in our dresser but not hers, so I started snooping and looked at her computer while she was gone and saw that the I.P. Address, she sent an email from just a week before I came to Vietnam for good was an I.P. address in Singapore. □I said WTF? She never told me that she went to Singapore; what was she hiding? □I called her while she was at her mother's and asked her where her passport was so I could see if she was in Singapore. □ She kept saying that she didn't go to Singapore and wanted me to wait until she returned to show me where the passport was. □I was pissed; why did she lie about going to Singapore? □Before she returned, I was able to run a low-level analysis on her hard drive that pulled up deleted cookies that showed she had a Facebook account which I also didn't know. □I was able to find the username and reverse engineered a way into the account by guessing what the password was from other passwords she used and saw that she was talking to some guy in Singapore that was proclaiming his love for her. □□I acted like her and chatted with the guy to find out what they had done or how serious it was. I was able to gather that she only kissed the guy (Long story as to how I did it, but I know how to manipulate, and this guy seemed like he was a virgin, so I assumed it wasn't anything other than her having a Plan B in the event I decided not to move there). □□I was beside myself though, because she lied. Who knows what else she was up to while there, so I told her that it was over. □She returned in tears and finally showed me the passport, and I saw that she was in Singapore for three weeks just before I moved to Vietnam. □I told her that I wished I had picked the other girl Phuong, and that she was "no good," etc. □I went to get a foot massage and came back to find her lying in bed when she told me that she took 24 sleeping pills. □WTF... □I quickly took her to a medical place that only spoke Vietnamese, and Hong said to me that they said she would be OK as long as she went to a hospital within 24 hours. □They said they couldn't help her there because they were just a small clinic. □I was up for two days and tired and returned home wanting to go to sleep, but it didn't make sense to me why a pill overdose is OK for 24 hours, so I angrily told Hong to get on the motorcycle so we could go to the hospital 10 miles away. □It was 2 AM now, and I drove like a madman and screamed at Hong the whole time for taking those pills.

The fact that I drove like a madman kept her awake and saved her life. We walked into the hospital, and it looked like a warzone. People were lying everywhere on the floor because all of the beds and stretchers were full. Every other person was in a motorcycle accident since 99% of all vehicles in Vietnam are motorcycles, and many were riding while drunk since it was so late. □Guys were lying on the blood-soaked floor with their intestines in their hands; another guy had his eyeball hanging from his head. All you could hear was anguish and moaning. I quickly got the attention of the intake nurse that spoke some English, and he asked why I was there. □I showed him the empty box of pills she took, and his eyes about popped out as he quickly went to get a doctor to come and take Hong's pulse. As the Doctor took her pulse, I could see he was scared, and even though there was a bloody mess of people waiting, he took her immediately and put her on a gurney and wheeled her outside on the sidewalk since there was no room in the hospital. □

They began to pump her stomach within 5 minutes of me walking in the door. □The Doctor told me that she would have been dead in 20 minutes had I not come. □Little did I know, she was also one week pregnant with our son. □I saved two lives that night. □I now know from being told by Hong's friend that Hong took the pills out of fear that the triads would sell her off as a lifelong slave since she messed up the scam against me by going to Singapore.

The picture below was the picture I took at the hospital. The hallway she is in has an open wall to the right that is an outside courtyard. They left her in that hallway for three hours until they got a room for her, where she was admitted until the next day when I took her home.

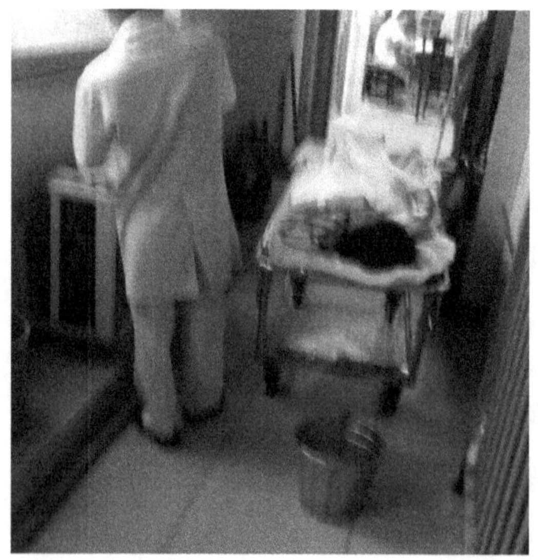

The route I drove from point A to Point B from my house to the hospital that night is pictured below. I lived at the spot the arrow points to on the top of the map and the arrow on the bottom points to the hospital we were at. I didn't know how to get there; if Hong had passed out, we would have been screwed, and she and my unborn son would have died for sure because I had no clue where to take her.

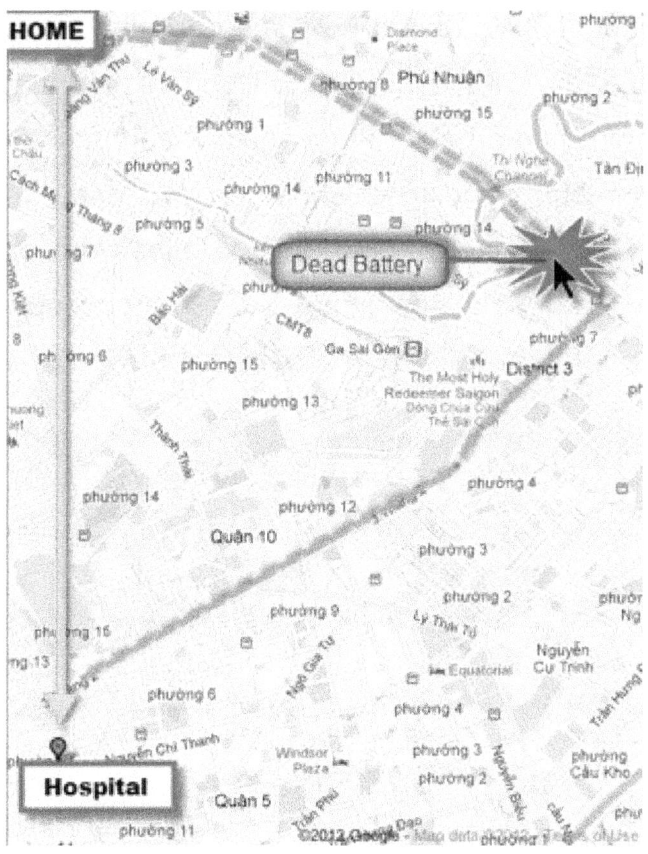

Hong and I reconciled while she was still in the hospital, and I tried to move on from the whole thing, but no matter how hard I tried, I always had it in the back of my mind that she was dishonest, and I always felt like there was something else that I didn't know. □I was right in more ways than I had ever wanted to know, but time would deliver the details bit by bit; it wasn't going to come overnight. □So basically, I was bored in Vietnam and occasionally went to Macau to hang out with Hong's friends. □We ended up finding out that Hong was pregnant a month after the pill overdose, and Hong told me that she would be shamed if she had a baby out of wedlock and pushed me to marry her "in a shotgun wedding of sorts you could say" in only two months in Vietnam. □I knew that the United States wouldn't recognize the marriage, so I said yes since it was supposedly important not to shame her family by having a baby out of wedlock. □

3 - The Bogus Wedding

There were close to 450 people at the wedding throughout the day, and I had only my knucklehead friend Yanni that I flew in 3 days prior, LOL... □I practiced a Vietnamese Toast for over a month and thought it was strange that Hong quickly left right before I said it. □I now know it was because she felt terrible and didn't want to stand there as everybody secretly laughed inside since they all knew it was a scam. □Only my friend Yanni and I thought it was legitimate, but they do it all of the time in Hong's family; I was just another sucker very close to getting hung out to dry. □The wedding was beyond Crazy, it was in the jungle at Hong's Parent's house, and Hong hired 7 Ladyboys to perform. □They were taking off their tops with 4-year-old kids looking on. □It was a night to remember for sure. □

The fact that they go All-Out on the wedding is part of the scam. By making sure it is professionally videotaped and comes across as genuine, it is done to erase any doubt that the marriage wasn't legitimate so they can keep your money once you get arrested or killed. □ They have this scam down to a science. □Hong even told me that there are a few Americans in the remote jail by her father's house. □No Americans live within 100 miles of there, and it's not like America where they transfer prisoners far away to do their time. They are there as a result of being set up by girls like Hong. □They steal more than the money you have though; Hong told me that their families send money from America to get better food and living quarters. □Hong's family gets residual income off the scam. I am pretty sure that the guys in there probably don't even realize that the one they loved was the one that set them up because they do everything behind the scenes with exacting detail and always make sure that they can point the finger at one or two other directions when the time comes.

Below on the right is a map that shows where Hong's family lived in Vi Thanh, Vietnam. □The "1" arrow was her father and Uncle's houses and where we had the wedding. The "2" arrow is the prison where Hong said Americans are and the prison where the Warden is also good friends with Hong's Father, who once scolded Hong for not framing me sooner, which I found out six months later. □The other two yellow blocks are where her other Aunts and Uncles live.

The Wedding (watch at bit.ly/dprefer4 or at **"Section 1"** at **www.thedevilprefers.com/bookextra**)

Wedding Location

Wedding Afterparty (watch at bit.ly/dprefer5 or at "**Section 1**" at **www.thedevilprefers.com/bookextra**)

July 2010- After the wedding, Hong and I regularly argued due to several more lies I caught her in about her past. She had her friend "7" come to the house and invite me to stay in Macau at her place for five days which is when my every 5-week trip to Macau started to happen. □This was in August 2010. □Hong always said I could have fun if I didn't fall in love with anyone. □I was very lonely over there, and the change of scenery every five weeks was fun, not to mention that all her friends doted over me the entire time I was there. I was the only guy there with 6 to 8 girls around me at all times unless "7's" Husband was there, but he never went out with us because he was too busy hacking my computer back at the house whenever the girls would get me out of the house for that sole purpose by taking me to the Disco. □Little did I know it was all part of their master plan to destroy me after my guard was completely down and after I trusted them like family. □

Kieu is on the left below, and "7" (real name Ngoc My Linh) is on the right. "7" told me that she got the nickname "7" because she ran away from home at 11 years old and didn't return until "7" years later when she was 18. Hong said that wasn't true and that "7" had to go make money for the family and that she didn't leave until 14. 7's mother seemed to be very sweet, but their father was evil; I remember one time I went to their parents' house and "7" started crying and screaming out of nowhere, and her father kept saying "Du Me" which means "Fuck your mother" in Vietnamese. The reason "7" cried was that she just found out that her father stole $5,000 U.S. that was meant to buy property for "7" and "7" gave the money to her mother to hold a few months prior, but her father forced the mother to give it to him, and he blew the money on his mistress and gambling. 7's father used to rape her older sister Nhan when they were younger.

"7" was the leader and Boss to all the girls; as I stated previously, she ended up marrying a Chinese Triad named John (his AKA) that lived part-time in Hawaii and liked computers like me, so we hit it off pretty good. □John would do things like ride with me in the Taxi back to the Airport when I went back to Vietnam, insist on paying for the Taxi and even walk me inside to make sure I got checked in OK. They have a way of making you feel special. □I also think it was done to assure they knew where I was and who I always talked to to ensure their scam would never be discovered. The fact that he was a Triad was quickly forgotten and overlooked since I genuinely felt like they cared about me like family. □I'm not entirely naive; I knew that they liked me for my money and what I could do for them, but that was OK with me because I didn't feel like it was the most important reason. □They know how to make you feel loved, especially when you can't speak to 99.9% of the people you meet, and all your friends and family are 8000 miles away. They know that you are lonely and feeling out of place. That dynamic makes you a prime target for their scam technique. □Below is a picture of John and "7" at their wedding

Another detail that I think speaks volumes was when I was at John and 7's wedding they had a guy singing, and the guy came to my table and was singing in my face but he didn't realize that the guy sitting next to me was my interpreter that lived in America since he was 14 and was also naïve about how things go down in Vietnam since he moved away long ago and lived in Saigon before leaving. My interpreter came from a good family. His grandfather was an American Soldier who got his grandmother pregnant but had to leave Vietnam at the end of the war. They haven't seen the grandfather since because the grandmother had to burn all evidence of the grandfather's existence out of fear that they would be killed if it was discovered by the Communist Party at the time who were raiding and pillaging Saigon after the end of the war. His father didn't look Vietnamese at all even though he was 50% Vietnamese and to this day only speaks Vietnamese. My interpreter's family were good people that were not discriminatory towards Americans since they had to endure how badly his father was ostracized and tormented while growing up in Vietnam, looking like he was an American. My interpreter told me that the guy singing to me at 7's wedding was singing a traditional Viet Cong war song as he and the crowd laughed. □My interpreter didn't even realize it until later, but the guy was mocking me in front of everybody. □He sang a song that says, "we will kill you and be victorious," in front of almost 400 people.

4 – The Drugs

I was never a big drug guy and didn't even drink alcohol until I was 28 due to getting gravely sick from drinking half a bottle of Peppermint Schnapps when I was 15, which turned me off on alcohol for 13 years until I started drinking red wine when I was 28. All of Hong's friends smoked what I was told was Designer Ephedra even though it was "ice." □They would always come up to me and put it in my face and offer it to me constantly with their cute little smiles to go with it. □Hong told me that they do that when they like you and want you to feel special (whatever!). But keep in mind that I wanted to fit in since I was a fish out of the water over there, so it was hard to resist after a while, and I eventually relented. □I wanted to connect on any level since the language barrier and culture clash isolated me in a way I never knew could exist. □Once the drug hits, you feel a bond with the people you are doing it with, and they would give me massage after massage, and several of her friends came on to me one after the other. □Remember, Hong said I could have fun and fun I did have. □Ignorance was bliss as they molded me into their evil web, with me being none the wiser the entire time. □I would buy all of her friends' gifts, help them with their iPods, go to Discos with 8 of them and only me; I felt like a Rock Star, and I thought life was amazing, but looking back, I can see that they were gathering information and executing their scam the entire time. □

Typical Day at 7's in Macau

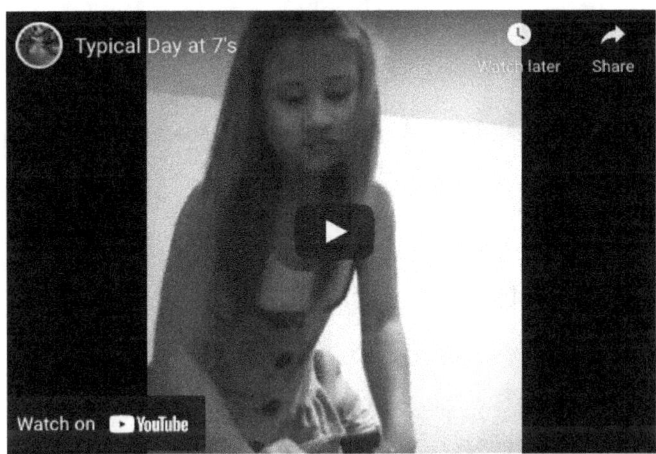

Watch video at bit.ly/dprefer6 or at “Section 1”

Watch video at bit.ly/dprefer7 or at “Section 1”

This video was taken by me when I was with her friends at the DD3 Disco in Macau. My hard drive on my brand-new MacBook broke the very next day, which I now know resulted from 7's husband hacking it while we were at the Disco. That was the whole purpose of getting me to stay at 7's house, so they could access my computer when they took me to the Disco or test my bravery to determine what scams to execute. 7's husband John seemed like he was faking sleeping before we went to the Disco, but I didn't overthink it at the time.

Watch video at bit.ly/dprefer8 or at “Section 1”

I went to a Disco a total of four times with her friends in Macau and almost got into a fight three of the four times. □I now know it was staged because they wanted to test my bravery to decide what kinds of scams they could do to me. □Every time I didn't back off an inch and showed zero fear. The three episodes had 1, 2, and 3 guys that I almost got into a fight with. □If I flinched or showed fear on these three occasions, they were going to try and scam me by getting me to sleep with 7's Husband's Boss' Wife that did come onto me, but she wasn't my type. □She never tried to come onto me again because they realized that I wasn't a coward, and their plans to have me sleep with his wife and then act like he found out and wants to kill me if I don't pay money wasn't going to get them very far with me. The two Discos in Macau that they took me to, which I was told they take all scam targets, were called "DD2" and "DD3". □DD3 was safer than DD2 because 99% of the people in DD2 are Triads. □I had two of the three skirmishes at DD2 and one at DD3. □The picture to the left is of 7's friend Yuri and her Triad Husband that I never met in person. □Notice how he has a few guys in the background always watching his back. □This guy has four Wives and can't even go to the bathroom without several Goons shadowing him for protection. □I guess he worries about retaliation from the hundreds of people they have already scammed.

Yuri with her Macau Triad Husband
2010/05/17

5 - Criminals in Asia

Hollywood's Portrayal of the criminal underworld in Asia is inaccurate. The criminals in Asia all approach you with a smile. □It's not like the movies where there is a cocky Asian Guy with tattoos acting tough. □They dress nice and come off as legitimate businessmen and run legitimate businesses too. Still, the crimes they plot and commit behind the scenes are eviler than anything you see in the movies. □They try to not only steal everything you have; they try to take your heart and soul too. □They are evil, hateful cretins; it's no wonder women are so abused in Asia when a specific class of guys exercises pure evil so easily and with no remorse whatsoever. The good Asian men are not much help either since Asian culture is so tight-lipped that nobody will say anything or rat anybody out even if they disagree with what they are doing. How can you expect women to be treated well when many of the guys are so entitled and evil to the core and are not being challenged or exposed by the good Asian Men over there? □I am referencing the criminals over in Asia, not Asian men as a whole, but let me say that there is no shortage of criminals over there, and the criminal's constant practicing of the art of deception makes it hard, if not impossible, to tell who is who. You need to expect the unexpected but can even the playing field if you stand up to them with zero fear. □They can't easily overcome that; they need you to cower with your tail between your legs before pouncing, or they won't have the courage to attack you. □I had 5 to 6 guys sitting outside my house at a coffee shop 8 hours a day, six days a week for almost two months from May 2011 to July 2011, using smartphones to control my computers that my ex helped them infect. Still, I always stared them down every time I left my house, and they would always shy away because deep down, they are cowards. □If given a chance, they will slice your throat and not lose a blink of sleep over it, so you need to be prepared for anything over there. It's not like America, where you can tell if a person hates you; their deception skills are unlike anything you'll come across in America. I was, of course, dealing with the worst of the worst when I was in Asia. I have tons of respect for all Asian cultures and people. I will be the first to say that Asians commit the least crime of any demographic in America, but that shouldn't cause you to put down your guard over there because, like all countries, Asia has plenty of dogshit also.

As previously mentioned, I was warned by several Americans that either lived in Asia for many years or go there regularly that I was being scammed. □They told me that the girls who work at the Saunas are trained to get Western Men to love them and convince them to move over there for them. □Relocating there is not required for them to scam you though, most of their scams are blackmail executed on men that only visited there but got their computer hacked while there upon which the Triads studied the victim for a way to extract money from him. Regarding the ones that do move there, they told me that they try to get you hooked on drugs in hopes you'll become detached from your family. At the same time, they spy on you and try to isolate your assets until they feel like the time is right, and then you disappear. Your family just assumes you went off the deep end since you already weren't calling that often because you were in a drug-induced depression and just a lost soul that forgot everybody and went to God knows where. I was very close to having that fate, but God smiled on me, and my son came along to sway things in my direction too.

Love in Return

Even though all the girls ultimately joined in to scam me in the end, it seemed a few of them started to love me (which I believe because I look back and see how the girls were sabotaging each other in their efforts to try to help me at different times in attempting to warn me). I wanted to save them all at the time, and they could feel how I cared about them in ways their own family never did. □It took its toll on them, and Hong's friend "7" warned me that Hong was a bad person and even told me that when I first met Hong and gave her $4600 that it was "7" that Hong called when she went into the hotel bathroom crying, and "7" said to give the money back because it would make me love Hong and want her. □"7" was right. □

Hong also helped me from time to time and betrayed her conspirators, but I was too naive to heed the warnings and just shrugged it off. □Hong warned me that 7's husband was jealous of me and that I need to think about why he would be happy with a guy coming over and taking all the girls' attention away from him and making him less important. Hong also warned me not to go anywhere with 7's husband the one time I was in Macau in October 2010 when there was a big blowout where Nhung told "7" she loved me and didn't want to work in Macau anymore. □I now know it was her saying no to scamming me anymore, which made 7's husband John irate because if Nhung left Macau, it meant less money for him since he got a cut of what the girls made at the Sauna. □Hong told me that John thought I was playing games, and Hong and Nhung thought John was taking me to a place 5 miles away to ambush and kill me. I was still confused and thinking they were my friends, so I didn't believe Hong, but at the same time, I said no to him when he asked me to go with him. □John ordered food an hour later and was adamant that I ate and ignored me when I said "NO" and just kept telling me to eat. □It was a surreal moment; I think he laced the food with something that would have put me out, but I never took a bite. Hong thought that maybe John was going to have me and Nhung

killed. □I now know that she was right because now that I know Nhung wanted to leave Macau because of me, John was scared Nhung would tell me the truth, so he planned to kill us both to protect the Triad's dirty secrets since he knew killing only Nhung wasn't enough since he also didn't trust Hong and feared she would tell me too. □At the time, I thought Hong was still wrong though even though John was giving me weird vibes with the food so I told John that Hong thought he was going to have me killed possibly and I could see the look of astonishment on his face that one of the girls would go against his trash organization like that. □This was October 2010, which shows me that Hong and Nhung loved me at least for a short time. □"7" was always angry with John, and the very next day before I returned to Vietnam, she threw something at John after her older sister Nhan cried in front of John and me and angrily called him a snake that smiles the whole time while he is stabbing somebody.
□

I was later told that it was not only because they found out that John wanted to kill me the day before but that he still planned on having me killed soon. □This showed me that 7 and her older sister Nhan loved me like a brother (I was never intimate with either 7 or Nhan, which is why I say love like a brother, but I was intimate with 7's younger sister Kieu and their friend Nhung). Four months later, in February 2011, "7" told me that her younger sister Kieu loves me as she told me about Hong being evil. "7" told me that her younger sister Kieu loved me and kept trying to say that Hong was not a good person. I was very generous and sweet to all the girls, and they felt that I cared, I guess. □Usually, much older guys go to Macau that only care about having sex with these girls. I think that helped the stars align in my favor and tested their loyalty to the Triads and their families also since I was probably the first guy that showered them with gifts and love with no strings attached that was also under 40 and in good shape. I showed them I cared about them constantly. □ I didn't judge them, and they knew that; it tore at their hearts over time. □I remember how Kieu called me crying one time and said that I am so good, and she just kept crying but wouldn't tell me why. □I now know she was forced to execute the scam on me, but she loved me and felt trapped. □□I cared deeply about all of these girls, so you can only imagine my fall from grace on the day 7's husband John told me that they were all scamming me from day 1. □

Below are pictures of Nhung, 7's older sister Nhan and 7's cousin "Baby." □I know that Baby cared about me because she cried in front of me one time out of nowhere, and towards the end, she was never happy like she always was when I first started hanging out with them in Macau. □I also remember when Kieu called me crying, saying that she has problems with Baby about something she wrote in her diary. □I now know it was pertaining to her being sad about what everybody was doing to me, and Kieu felt terrible because she was starting to care about me. She felt horrible for being involved in the evil plot to bring me down. Still, she was being pressured by her Father, John Lam, and the other behind-the-scenes Triads who do this all of the time but probably never fail due to their absolute patience and attention to detail.

NHUNG

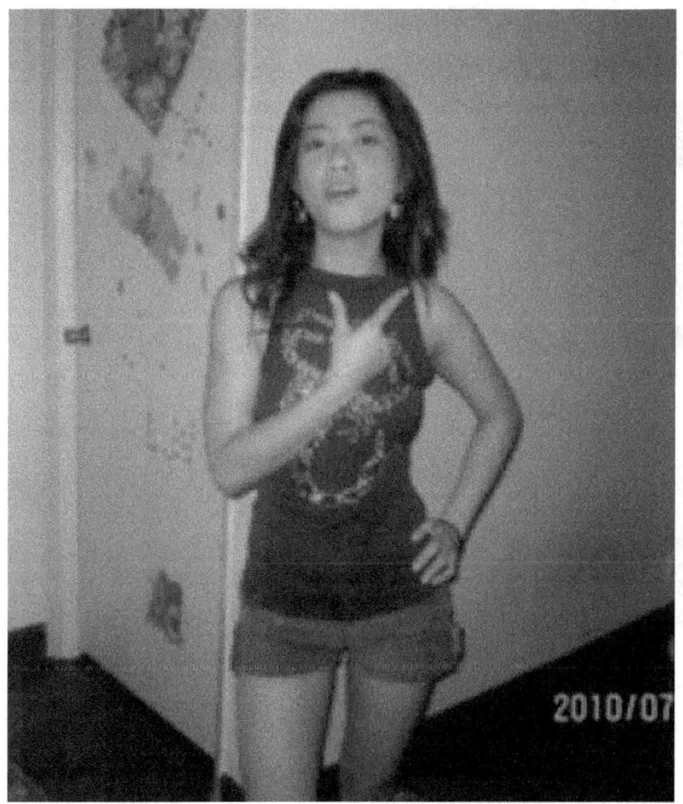

NHAN & BABY

7 AND CREW

(7, Yuri, Nhan & Kieu (from left to right)

Back to the beginning of the story, there was also Phuong that I met the same time I met Hong. I stopped communicating with Phuong when I decided I would be with Hong long-term until I ran into her again in Macau in April 2011, over a year after I moved to Vietnam. Phuong called me the day after I got there and tried to warn me, but I didn't understand what she meant at the time. □She told me not to take iPhones that belong to other people, which I now know was about the iPhone that "7" and John had me take to Vietnam on April 14th, 2011 "The Airplane Scam," which was a clone of my iPhone with other things added to it, like fake text messages to a number in China making it look like I was a drug smuggler or something else illegal! I guess Phuong cared about me in the end also. □

Phuong

6 - My Son is Born.

Given that Hong got pregnant around the time I arrived in Vietnam on February 24th, 2010, Hong didn't know if I was the father or if it was her Vietnamese ex Cuong Nguyen. She wouldn't let me be in the delivery room and even had her cousin take me to get Baby Formula the second my son was born on December 2nd 2010 at 11:43 PM before letting me see him. She wanted to make sure I was the father. If my son had looked 100% Asian after they cleaned him off, the plan was to attempt to kill me before I returned to the hospital. Hong's cousin had me driving in circles for a half-hour, acting as though she didn't know where the place was to buy formula when she received a call from Hong during that time, and within 30 seconds, she knew which way to go. Hong didn't even open the formula; she breastfed our son from day 1. I didn't figure this plot out but was told by a friend of Hong long after moving back to the United States with my son. She said to me that Hong had people lying in wait for the order to kill me and that Hong's cousin was going to lead me there and act as though it was the direction we needed to go for the formula, but after Hong called and said the baby was mine, they called it off.

Hong later slipped and told me that Cuong Nguyen went back to America two days after my son was born, which I now know he did because he was hoping the baby was his and angrily left Vietnam once he realized the baby wasn't his. Cuong Nguyen came back to Vietnam five months later, on April 15th, 2011, only one day after the Airplane scam. He was in the air the same time as I was. Cuong planned to be with Hong since I would now be in jail forever, but as you'll learn, they counted their chickens before they hatched, and I escaped that plot. Hong and Cuong started to reconcile sometime in February 2011 and secretly chatted while he was in America as the plot to take me out unfolded. If my son weren't mine, I would have been killed if I couldn't escape the thugs lying in wait for me to arrive. My Son and I took turns saving each other's life as you'll discover later in the story. □I have spoken to two Korean guys who frequently traveled to Vietnam for business since my return to the United States. They both were very knowledgeable about how these scams play out in Vietnam, and both were shocked and kept saying they couldn't believe I escaped once they latched on because nobody escapes once they target you, according to them. They noted that scamming Americans is very common, but any ethnic race gets targeted if the opportunity arises. The Triads help lure wealthy targets to Vietnam, like in my case, by using the women as bait. These scams are a big business for these dirtbags.

New Year's Eve December 31st, 2010

The picture below was taken on December 31st, 2010, at 11:45 PM, just one hour before Hong and her conspirators started to put the plot into motion.

One hour after this photo was taken, we left the nightclub and jumped in a taxi, and Hong claimed that her brother got sucker-punched in the backseat as he was getting in. I didn't see a thing even though I was in the front seat, and I didn't hear a fight either, but Hong called her friend Giang without telling me and then told me what happened when we were almost home. Hong knows I'm fearless and would have helped, but that's not what she wanted.

When I first moved to Vietnam, Hong did love me even though the initial plan was to scam me. She would tell me how she distanced herself from her previous friends because they were all bad people that only wanted her money. Hong even said that Giang was evil and that I never met him because she was worried he would scam me. Since she already said that, when her loyalty shifted away from me, she needed to have a good excuse as to why she invited Giang to come, so calling him to defend her brother against a gang of alleged attackers was the best way to do it. Giang showed up with three friends within 5 minutes of her calling him at 1 AM on New Year's Eve! This guy was a drug addict also, which makes me know for sure that it was a staged fight with her brother because there is no way you can get four guys to drop everything they are doing (drugs too) to be somewhere in 5 minutes at 1 AM for a girl they haven't seen in over a year. It takes that long to piss first, let alone get somewhere. Giang lived more than 5 minutes from our house by the way, so this was obviously a game they were playing.

I just brought the $1.5 Million of Chinese Yuan into Vietnam 2 weeks prior also. Add that to the $100,000 of Yuan I already had plus around $50,000 US, the temptation was too much to resist, and they decided it was time to move against me.

I went with Hong and those guys back to the nightclub, but the supposed attackers were obviously not there. In the future, Giang wimped out on killing me two times after that night, so there is a chance that he was supposed to kill me that night with his friends also, but since it was the first time he met me, maybe they were scared because of my size. I'm 6'3" 225 pounds; that's a Giant in Vietnam. The other possibility is that this night was supposed to only be an initial meeting where they could size me up and make me feel indebted to them for running to my wife's request for help, which would make it easier for them to get me to invite them in my home in the future. Whatever the two possibilities, it was the first time Hong made a big move towards betraying me to steal my money eventually.

The picture above is significant because it shows you how masterful they are at deception. Hong looks 100% normal and loving in this picture even though she was trying to get me killed in an hour or, at a minimum, betray me to jump the scam into high gear. How can she look so sweet, calm, and normal when she was 1 hour away from doing something horrible to me? Like I said. These people wrote the book on complete deception. This poker face makes them very dangerous. I've searched her eyes in numerous pictures and couldn't detect deception ever.

7 - The Calm Before the Storm

From January to March 2011, I look back and can see that Hong loved me at that point and was trying to prevent her family and the Triads from scamming or killing me. □She must have felt bad because our son was born, which only lasted a few months before the absolute nightmare began. I had to go with Hong to a Vietnam Government office to apply for my son's birth certificate when I snapped the picture above. Little did I know that the image was about to come true in more ways than I could imagine.

The Corrupt Local Police

Even though I had lived in the same house for ten months already, the local Police at the end of our street never came to my house one time. Still, within two weeks of me bringing the Chinese Yuan into Vietnam, they visited soliciting donations for something I donated to and then seemed to be at my house every few weeks from that point on. I couldn't understand what they were talking about, but my wife even brought me to meet them outside the house on occasion also. I now know that they were probably discussing how to set me up the entire time so they could take all my money. I remember how I would only go outside once every two days, but when I did, the same police guy would just so happen to be taking his neighborhood stroll past my house. The timing was astonishing and more than mere chance. It was meant to put me off guard and worry me as part of the psychological warfare aspect of their scam. They didn't start playing those games until Hong successfully stole my custom declaration, preventing me from taking my money out of the country. The fact that the Police were always there the moment I left the house told me that they were monitoring my inside security cameras that my wife helped them hack by getting me to leave the house long enough for their people to come into my house and hack my surveillance system. A few weeks after the Airplane Plot, I microwaved my security system's hard drive for 5 minutes after realizing they spliced into a port. The following day, I saw that same cop, and he looked at me very angrily, put his hand up to his mouth, and made a smoking gesture that was meant to imitate the way the drug ICE is used. I realized this afterward because I was still trying to take in how people that smiled so much for over a year could be so evil and hateful on the inside. I didn't realize the significance of many things I observed until sometimes days or months afterward. Once I realized that Hong was 100% involved, I had to go back and reanalyze everything I could remember from the very moment I met her going forward, which made the most innocent of events give a whole new meaning.

Outside of the Police visits from January through March 2011, those few months were uneventful for the most part; I think Hong was protecting me and resisting her conspirators since I was the father of our son that was just born a month prior on December 2nd, 2010. But that all changed at the end of March 2011.

The Pig Roast Farewell

On March 27th, 2011, even though we were already at her Parent's house three times with our Son, Hong told me that her father wanted to kill a pig in my son's honor, so we had to make the 5-hour drive down to the jungle where they lived. □I asked her why he didn't kill the pig in his honor the last three times we were there, but she didn't reply. □

We were just there two weeks prior when a weird thing happened as we were getting ready to leave. Hong's father's friend, the Warden at the prison near her house, called Hong over to speak to him. I could see she was angry when she got in the car, so I asked her why. She said that the guy said, "Aren't you Le' Daughter?" to which she replied, "Yes, but I have a mind of my own," to which he then replied, "I didn't know Le's daughter was so outspoken." I now know that he was scolding her for not framing me and referencing that she is her father's daughter because that is what they are expected to do, Scam Americans. This event must have been the straw that broke the camel's back and caused Hong to give in and bend to their will because not even two weeks went by, and Hong came up with the pig story and used my son as an excuse to get me to go there one last time before my demise.

That trip was weird; her uncles wouldn't look me in the eye, and I could see that a few of them looked ashamed. □I now realize that they all knew I was getting set up in a few weeks, and they felt bad since I did just buy them all new motorcycles a few months back. Hong also told me how her father and uncles talked about how brave I was and how they would live their lives more like me if they had a chance to do it again. □I now realize that it was a goodbye party for me; they even asked me to do the honor of killing the pig, something they don't even let their kids do until they are well into their twenties. I said yes and killed the poor thing. □I figured that he was going to die anyway, and I didn't want to offend them. □

WARNING, the video below is graphic; it's me killing the Pig "in my son's honor" on March 27th, 2011.

Watch video at bit.ly/dprefer9 or at “Section 1”

The Midnight Snack

Three days after returning from the pig slaughter, on 3/30/2011, Hong got a call at midnight, talked for 10 seconds, hung up the phone, and then said she wanted to get something to eat. Hong never wanted to eat after 10 PM and was also scared to go outside past 10 PM because the criminals prowl the streets looking for people to rob. I said OK, and we went to the garage, and even though I heard nothing, Hong said, "OMG, did you hear that Moto stop in front of our house? I said no, and Hong asked me to go in the direction of the Moto "motorcycle" even though that direction had a very dark alley with no lights. I thought that was very strange but went that direction anyway, and we pulled up to those two guys riding the one motorcycle, and they laughed as they looked at us and I laughed back and sarcastically said Hello in Vietnamese. I could tell Hong wasn't happy about the whole thing and was being forced now that I look back and analyze the whole thing. Two weeks later, after they failed with the Airplane Plot, the same guy on the back of the motorcycle that night tried to come inside the Massage Parlor I bought for Hong's sister after it was closed. Even though the door was locked, I could see it was him before he walked away. I didn't realize it was the same guy for about five more minutes, but I later found out that this guy was one of Giang's goons (Hong's

Criminal Vietnamese friend Giang, not to be confused with the Triad Guang Lin "AKA John Lam") and he was supposed to scare me I guess. Of course, it had no effect, but this proves to me that Hong got a call from Giang to lure me outside a couple of weeks prior so they could either size me up or maybe they videotaped me going that direction and this was a piece of their drug smuggler framing plot meant to go down in 2 weeks on April 14th, 2011, in the Airplane. □I know Hong's personality, and she never wanted to follow a potential problem and would never have me do that at midnight, which shows she was involved and helping these losers.

This email in the picture to the left was sent to me by Hong while I was in Macau 2 days before the Airplane Scam, which was also the same time she was sending a celebration message to her friend 7 thinking I was going to prison forever, which I discovered two days after escaping the Airplane Plot. □Hong sent this to me after telling me on the phone that she was leaving my son and me forever to join a monastery to help disabled people. She never even brought up the fact of ever leaving me and always thanked me for how I helped her whole family. □This was the first time Hong said this to me and was done in preparation for me getting arrested, to have one less thing to deal with when that happened. □I think it was also done to make sure I was visibly upset on the Airplane on my return two days later, or maybe she hoped I would change my flight to come back to help me since the scammers were already set to go on April 14th, 2011.

□

I would assume that she tried to help me except for the message I discovered two days after the Airplane where she said "Cheers" in Vietnamese to "7", which obviously would have been in celebration of my downfall. Still, she never hit send, and it remained in the outbox, so I don't know what to think as to if she was happy or sad about it.

To: Edward Jamison <info@jamisonsystems.com>

Anh Yeu I love you .

I thinks in 2day and I wait you come home I wait you happy and tell you. My English no good I can't talk all my mind I want you know and understand anything I want talk with you.

I not lie you about cuong. Cuong Nguyen not my ex boyfriend . I feel bad anything because you come Vietnam for me you love me. You have anything in merica.

you are in a position and a very high position many peple know about you . Here you go to a foreign country the language barrier you do not talk to people just because miss love a girl like me . Your sacrifice is too great for me and I always tell myself not to do anything for you to be sad and sorry for you.

I take it all and forgive scolding anger adultery unfaithful I feel your pain and shame your abger most recent. I always remember everything you made for me sacrifice your great for me. sometimes I want to tell you we farewell and return your life back to your country with your full.

you have given me a great gift that our son that all from me.

I know you want to live in Vietnam, I will live with you until you have a passport and nationality Vietnam Vietnam .

I'm gone and will never bother to your new life will not take money or anything you from me when you have nationality Vietnam I go change anything to your name moto oto and paper married . I tell you sally salon and give you back money. And I want you take care B give B love . I can take care myself and take B good . You give B life full but I can't .

I want we talk when you come home I want you happy time in Macau. We live together for what ? We all sad no happiness

most importantly, respect and mutual trust. your love is now turned into sadness and depression

I always worry and fear of your anger I do everything you are not happy and feel good. I worry all the time . I'm tired very tired if you really love me give me go aways don't keep me . Keep your love to me forever .

we love each other but with no debt coast. we broke up, but in my heart always love and think about each other

let me leave your consent. then we will forget each other and happy again when we find new love. We alway be friend a goodfriend forever . Come see me when u feel sad.

I really want and determined to say bye bye. Let me go I will die in worry scared , suffering in love . You don't want see me sad and cry much right? Me too I don't want see you cry and sad I scared your anger it's kill me soon and kill our love . I love you and our son .

You and B can come see me anytime u want but me never come see you and B

The Triad Party Invite on April 12th, 2011

Hong is on the left, and 7's cousin Yen is on the right in this picture. Yen has a rich Triad boyfriend that lives part-time in Vietnam and the remainder in America. Yen's boyfriend was in Macau and part of the airplane scheme on April 14th, 2011. Yen invited me to a party on April 12th that I didn't go to at the Golden Dragon Casino. Why would she ask me to a party where her boyfriend is? Not only that, but her boyfriend also spoke English and was the one to call me from Yen's phone. He called me several times and kept inviting me even though we had never met, and he had no reason to want me there other than to help forward the scam. It was a staged party meant for me to be sized up and possibly create false witnesses while still in Macau before they executed the Airplane Scam two days later.

8 - THE AIRPLANE SCAM - PHASE 1 (The Purchase)

The ATM Machine Setup on April 13th, 2011

An ATM machine service in Asia called "UnionPay" allows you to insert cash and send it to somebody with a UnionPay account number even if you don't have a UnionPay account yourself. □The two months leading up to the Airplane Scam, "7" and John kept complaining that they had their friend Rocks send money for them and that he stole some of it. □They even went as far as having the Triad Boss's wife Yuri come to 7's house on April 13th, 2011, and call Rocks on speakerphone "meant so I could hear" and accuse him of stealing the money, which he played along and denied it because I now know he was in on the scam too. □After Yuri hung up the phone, "7" asked me if I could send $90,000 MOP ($13,000 US Dollar Equivalent) to her husband that was in China using UnionPay and that she would give me the money to send but asked if I would do it because she was on a work permit that showed that she made minimum wage. If there were cameras, she was scared she would get questioned. □I said, "Sure" I wasn't suspicious at all; these were my friends, "so I thought," and I was happy to help. □7's sister Kieu came with me and was holding her phone towards me the entire time. □I now realize that she was taking video of me sending the money, which I now know was being sent to somebody to purchase drugs, and they were making sure they had me framed in a way that I could never get out of. □The day was April 13th, 2011, the day before I went back to HCMC.

Rocks Cheng played the untrustworthy friend to pull me into the position to send the money via UnionPay so they could video me making what they would claim was an illegal purchase as far as the payment's purpose.

THE AIRPLANE SCAM - PHASE 2 (Make sure I'm high)

On the day that I left for the Airport from Macau on April 14th, 2011, all the girls were doing the drug "ICE" more than I ever saw them do it and kept blowing it towards me and trying to get me to take it every two minutes even though I didn't want more. □I was confused but still didn't overthink it because these were my friends, right?

THE AIRPLANE SCAM - PHASE 3 (Assure I was rattled in flight)

The day before I went to the Airport in Hong Kong, just two hours after asking me to send the money via UnionPay, "7" went to China to meet her husband, John "Guang Lin." They told me they would meet me at the airport the next day in Hong Kong since we were supposedly flying together to Vietnam. □The next day when I went to the Airport, John called me after I was on the Ferry for 10 minutes to tell me sorry and that he and all the girls were scamming me since day one and that he and "7" were not meeting me at the airport because they got into a fight. □He said Hong and her entire family were in on the scam and that they do this all the time but that he only helped on this scam against me but felt terrible and wanted to clear his conscience. □I didn't realize it at the time, but they were already tracking me by GPS since they had my iPhone cloned and could access it remotely. □I even got off on the wrong Train Stop to the airport after exiting the Ferry but didn't realize it since I was going crazy after what John told me that they all did to me and was arguing with Hong on the phone and not paying attention to my stop on the train. □John asked me if I was at the airport and I said yes, thinking that I was, to which he replied, are you "really" there already? □I now know that he knew precisely where I was and was scared I would miss my flight.

I barely made the flight and was the last person to board the airplane when I saw two people sitting in the seats meant for John and 7. The guy sitting next to me instantly started talking to me and asking me questions. □He asked if I was seeing the girls in Macau; I knew he was a conspirator right away because only 5% of the flights out of Hong Kong are people coming from Macau, most are leaving from Hong Kong as the place they visited plus he was sitting in the seats reserved for "7" and John. □I could see that the guy had an earphone in his ear and was squinting as he tried to listen to somebody that was telling him what to say. □I then proceeded to tell him how I knew how he was involved, upon which he just laughed. I then asked him if he was a powerful guy, to which he replied "Yes" with this evil smirk on his face. □I then asked him how much it would cost to let one girl go free to which he replied, "$1200 US". □This guy was a snake; you could see the evil in his eyes. □I then began to tell him that I may be naive and have a big heart but that when I know I have an enemy, I will win 100 times out of 100. □I told him to fuck off and proceeded to take my suitcase into the bathroom, thinking that they already planted drugs on me, which was an idea that just popped into my head as I talked to the guy. (Phase 3 of the scam to frame me... Make sure I was visibly rattled to assure that more than one person could say I was acting strangely to give the Police good cause to arrest me and find the drugs on me that they could not plant yet). The problem with this phase here is that they never prepared for the possibility that I would cause such a huge scene and make everybody, including the flight attendants, watch very closely. This heightened scrutiny made them hesitant to execute, knowing somebody other than me was suspicious of them.

Below is a picture of the receipts for United Flight 0869 on April 14th, 2011, that I purchased for John (Real name Guang C Lin) & his Wife "7" (real name My Phan) & myself, along with a seating chart that shows you how we were seated together. The Triads needed to make sure they had their people sitting next to me to forward the scam. Hence, they had John and "7" act like they wanted to fly with me to keep those two seats open to allow their conspirators to sit there who were ticketed with different seats since the ones next to me were reserved for me John and "7".

See a larger pic of the below image at bit.ly/dprefer11

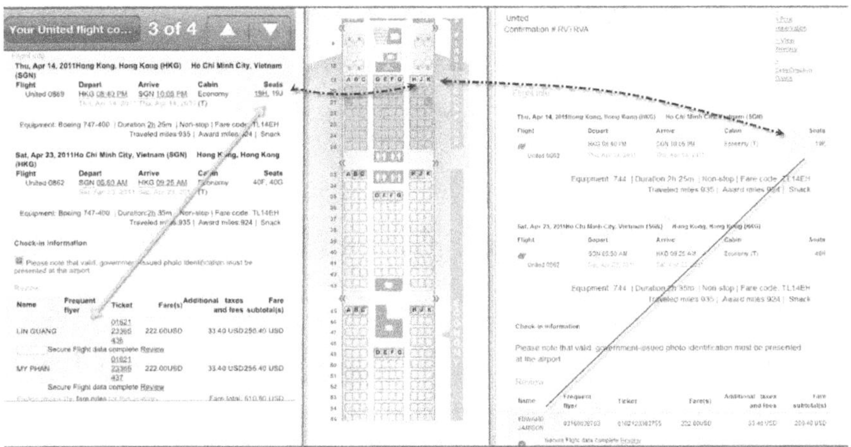

Within 30 seconds of entering the bathroom, a flight attendant started knocking frantically on the door, asking if I took my suitcase in there because somebody said they saw me enter the bathroom with my bag. □I said "Yes" and that I would be out in a minute. □We were in the air for about 10 minutes at the time I went into the bathroom. □They kept banging on the door as I frantically searched for drugs that I assumed they already planted in my bag. □I couldn't find any though and finally exited the bathroom after 3 minutes. I quickly apologized to the flight attendants and explained that I was being set up and then told them about everything that happened in the past day. They were very friendly. □I asked them to have the

Police waiting in Vietnam, and they said they already called because they were required to in situations like this. □

THE AIRPLANE SCAM - PHASE 4 (Strategically plant witnesses)

The flight attendants told me to stay in the back of the airplane to keep me away from the guy sitting next to me, but a strange thing happened, and three guys gravitated towards the back of the aircraft and sat around me almost as though they were plotting something. The Flight Attendant even mentioned that he thought it was odd and agreed with me that something was going down, although he couldn't say precisely what. □When the airplane landed, the flight attendant told me to wait until everybody exited the plane, but two guys dressed as Phat Giao Monks waited in the exit row for me to go before them. □I could tell they were involved; why would they be waiting in the exit row with no luggage or any other reason to remain behind? □I told them to get the fuck off the airplane, and they angrily looked at me and then exited before me. Phase 4 of the scam to frame me was to have conspirators behind me as I left the airplane that could say they saw me take something out of my pocket upon which the corrupt Police could have even planted it once they took me to a private room. I essentially foiled that part of the scheme by forcing the fake monks to go in front of me.□□ Hong also admitted afterward that they were Triads and were in on the scam. The fact that I forced the guys to leave before me in full view of the flight attendants prevented them from bearing false witness, and they knew it. □

THE AIRPLANE SCAM - PHASE 5 (Assure I took the cloned iPhone)

(Phase 5 of the scam to frame me... Make sure I take the cloned iPhone that most likely had fake text messages between me and somebody in China telling them I am sending the money to buy the drugs etc. □I know the phone was cloned because a week later John was at my house trying to say he was innocent when I glanced at his phone and saw my contacts. □I said, what is that? and he quickly tried to think of a reply and said it must have happened when he used my iTunes account, which I let them use to save money and not have to buy programs I already bought)

I wasn't in the clear yet though. □15 cops were waiting for me as I exited the airplane, and I proceeded to tell them what happened, and the one cop kept telling me that I needed to take the iPhone and money that I left behind on the airplane.

Anyways, I told the cop no and that it wasn't my iPhone, and I think it's part of a plot to set me up. □He kept insisting that I take it, but I remained adamant and even told him to fuck off as the other 14 cops laughed since their colleague was not bending me to his will. □I now know that the cop was involved in the plot and wanted me to take the phone as additional evidence to support the fake monks' observations and complete the scam so they could take me to jail forever and walk into my house and take all my money. □Hong would have tried to make me think she was innocent and that the crooked Police took my money. □But, given the fact that I made the fake Monks exit first, in addition to the fact that I wouldn't take the iPhone and the money along with the considerable scene I created that made the airline very aware of a suspected plot against me, it must have been too much. They decided to abandon the scam since I effectively knocked out all five branches of the plot they planned to execute in framing me. □I was fortunate to get out of there that night. □They planned this thing for months.

AIRPLANE SCAM OVER (Now I'm home and know my wife is evil)

Hong and I got into a huge fight when I got home, and I threw her across the room, and she started to bang her head off a concrete wall on purpose because she was angry and said she wanted to die. The whole time this was happening, Hong's sister Tuoi watched and looked at Hong with hatred. She didn't try to help Hong and didn't even stop her from smashing her head off the wall until about the 10th time. About a month before that night, Hong talked with Tuoi upstairs, and Tuoi was crying and moved out of the house a few days later. I now realize that it was then that Hong told Tuoi of my fate, and Tuoi cared about me and couldn't live near me anymore because it hurt her too much.

9 - Here Come the Psychics

About a week after the Airplane Plot escape, Hong started having different people come to the house that were specialists in predicting the future or expelling spirits from the home. She had a guy there for almost 5 hours, walking around the house lighting candles and standing there with an intense look on his face. Hong told me that she keeps seeing Ghosts and that even the dogs saw them and that my big dog wasn't scared, but my little one was petrified. The crazy part is that my little dog stopped going up the stairs and would sit at the bottom of the stairs and shake in fear until you carried him upstairs. That started the day after Hong told me that the dogs saw the ghosts too. Coincidence? I don't know, but what happened with the card reader blew my mind.

Hong had a guy come and give everyone in the house predictions of their future, which he did by reading the cards from a tarot deck after the person he was reading about cut the deck three times. So, I sat there and cut the deck three times and watched as he laid out the cards and started telling me what they meant. The first thing he said was that I was a good guy and that he was surprised by how much I will do for my family. Then he said I would be the most important factor in my son's life by far. I was a little skeptical when he said that. At the time, Hong, her sister Tuoi, the nanny Co Hai and

Hong's four cousins that lived with us were more involved with my son than me. I was very depressed from living there and would spend all day in my office on the computer doing drugs. He said I was very good at making money, but I don't like to make money too much, so I limit myself on purpose. Now I know why I got lazy when the money started to pile up, ha-ha. He then said that out of everybody living in the house, I was the only one that had a spirit protecting me and that the spirit was a guy around my age that likes it when I went to play with the girls and be bad. Whoa, now he had my attention.

My good friend Jett was my age and died from Leukemia in January 2009 and loved to go out and have fun. I made a memorial site for him that is still up located at http://www.forjett.com. He was a good friend and would be there if you needed him, so I thought this guy was onto something if there is such a thing as Ghosts. He then told me that I would have two family members that I am close to dying before the end of the year. I thought, wow, bold prediction given nobody died in my family for five years now, and he predicted two would die in less than eight months. Ok, I thought, we'll see.

He then did a reading for our nanny Co Hai, and Hong wasn't happy when she said that the guy said Co Hai would help me the most in the future. I thought it was odd that she was not pleased hearing I would be helped by our nanny, plus I could see that Co Hai was scared and had a look of denial on her face as though she was caught stealing. I now know that it was because they were all scamming me, and it wasn't good to have a trusted fortune teller predict you will help the enemy! Co Hai did help me when she tried to warn me of danger outside a few weeks later; the guy was right.

But perhaps the most convincing reading of all was the one he did for Hong's Aunt when he told her not to build her house this year or her husband will die. Her uncle was 41 years old and healthy; I don't know why building the house would be a reason for him to die, but that's what the guy said, and Hong's Aunt still built the house over the next few months and before the end of the year in November 2011 about a month after they finished building the house, he died. Not only did he die, but my grandmother and her sister died too in 2011 just like he predicted, and I left Vietnam with my son and became the most important part of his life by far, just as he predicted. Can you believe it? WOW

Hong sent me these pictures when she went down to her uncle's funeral while I stayed with my son in Mui Ne because I didn't want to make the 8-hour bus trip with him.

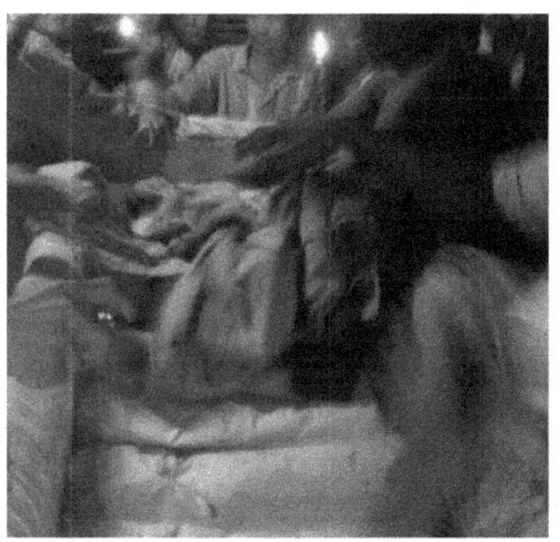

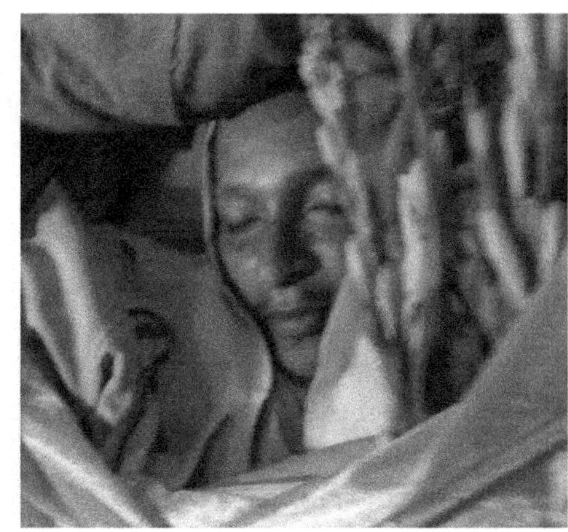

Time to Murder Me

Let's go back now to where I left off, which was about a week after I escaped the Airplane Plot and Hong had the fortune-tellers and ghost people coming to the house. In Vietnam, they place a very high value on these psychic predictions and consult with them before any big decisions they make in their life for insight and guidance in how to proceed. I now realize they wanted to find out how they lost against me and what weaknesses I had for them to exploit and make sure they didn't lose in the future. They didn't wait long to try to take me out; the next three months following the Airplane Plot were a living hell. □Within two weeks, Hong had her friend Giang act as though he was having marital problems and was supposedly arguing with his wife that was close with Hong, and he wanted to vent to Hong, but I now know that the purpose was for him to kill me. To supposedly thank me for allowing him to hang out at our house while he fought with his wife, Giang brought me 2 Japanese swords as a gift, but while he stood in my office, he was breathing heavily as he gripped the sword in front of me. □I now know he was trying to get himself psyched up to chop off my head, but he couldn't do it. □I was still naive and believed Hong's story that her friends from Macau were jealous and trying to set her up too, so I didn't suspect Giang at the time. The sad part is that Hong showed me extra affection just before leaving the room when Giang was gripping the sword. □She never showed love in front of people but did this time which shows me she was saying goodbye, fully expecting me to be dead in the next 10 minutes.

Below is a picture of the Swords Giang supposedly gave me as a gift. Giang really brought them into the house to kill me. □□

That same evening after Giang failed to kill me, he came back with three friends, and Hong asked me to go into the living room and not be rude. Hong once again was overly affectionate to me, but this time it was in front of four guys before she left to go upstairs for 20 minutes. I could see that the guys were nervous and arguing with each other, and two of the guys wanted to leave and got up and walked out. I had my 100-pound American Bulldog with me the whole time, and I think that was what made them scared to attack.

After Giang failed to kill me a second time, it was back to framing me within a week. I started to suspect Giang the next day and told Hong that I didn't want any more of her friends coming over. Hong still had her friend Hanh come around not even a week later and said she was staying with us for three days even though I told her I didn't want anyone at the house. She said she would stay with her and the baby at a hotel if I refused to allow her to stay, so I eventually relented.

The next day Hong told me how Hanh never used a computer and didn't even know how to create an email address on Yahoo and asked if I would do it for her. Hong was up to something, but I let it go and made the email address upon which her friend disappeared upstairs for 3 hours. I happened to check my DNS settings in my media server and noticed that there were custom settings somebody put in that routed all Skype traffic back to the media server. That's when I realized that they were capturing audio from my computers via Skype and had it stored on my media server where they could grab it later in the event the internet wasn't working. I immediately had a weird feeling and went to see what Hong's friend Hong was doing and saw she wasn't using Hong's computer because the battery had died, so I took the laptop she was using and went and plugged it in. The drained battery caused the laptop to hibernate, and her windows and everything she was doing came back on the second the screen turned on. I could see that she was doing a search that specifically included hidden files that contained the word "Trasp." Hanh also had a free SMS Service open and running in Firefox that allowed you to send complimentary text messages in Vietnam and was also reading help files of specific programs that were hundreds of pages long.

(A Trasp device is a spy device that changes the electronic DNA of an electronic component but is indistinguishable from the actual component it replaces. I'll talk more about how it pertained to me later.) Trasp devices are helpful in re-routing internet traffic, deploying malware, and many other things depending on the kind of Trasp Device it is.

I said, "WTF," as I looked and saw that the page in the help file she was reading wasn't the original help file but a slightly changed file that had a message on the 80th page that said, "I need 20 Soldiers in Tan Binh now". It was meant to get a reaction from me because it was in English, and this girl wouldn't be writing this in English. I was told she didn't speak English at all by Hong, but who knows if that was true. This message was located inside an Apple Help file for iMovie and wasn't part of the original text. These Cretins have a clever way of communicating where they place an encrypted message at a predetermined place. They look for the key to unencrypt the text embedded in an HTML5 movie's source code located at this YouTube knock-off site in Vietnam. Hong showed me how they send messages by picking the video that is out of place on the page as to the first frame and within that video's HTML5 code is an encryption key for the text they have saved in the help file which the person uses the key to unencrypt the help file to read the message. It's a clever way to not leave a trace as to your communications with your other conspirators. This slick method was thought up and taught to them by the Triads and implemented as the preferred way to communicate to avoid capture. Hong admitted to this after I kicked Hanh out of the house, but the Triads were listening and sent people to kick her brother and cousin off their motorcycle as they rode to send a stern message to Hong to stop revealing their plot. I never got Hong to admit to it again after that day. I was too upset to pay attention to how they did it in detail because at the time she admitted it, there were people throwing bricks off the side of my house. I thought I was getting attacked at any moment due to the brick barrage, plus the video below where I discovered her friend was talking to several people in a chat room right before I took the computer from her. I started to video the computer screen, and all 50 people in the chat room still logged on started to log out. I told Hong that she was evil and that I know they are setting me up, and then all of a sudden, they all started to log back on. Still, nobody said anything for a few minutes until a guy said in English, "Is anybody from China here?" to which another guy replied, "Why do you need China? Isn't Vietnam good enough?". They were trying to scare me because I still had 1,500,000 Chinese Yuan in my house. They wanted me to freak out and leave the house with it since I caught on to their scheme, and they knew they couldn't attack because I was on full alert and ready for them to come, so they were scared to rush into the house that I now had on complete lockdown.

The Interpreter that I trusted just so happened to be visiting Vietnam and stopped by to calm me down after I told him what was happening. As he was there, Hong's phone rang, and I could see it was Giang. I told Hong to say hello normally and not say that my friend Tan "the interpreter," was listening. I answered the phone on speakerphone, and the first thing Hong said before Giang could say a word was, "You are on speakerphone, and Eddie's Interpreter Tan is listening. As soon as Tan told me that, I wanted to kill Hong. I told her I was calling the Police; within 5 seconds, a brick slammed off the side of my house where my office was located. Tan looked at me utterly perplexed because he thought Hong was sweet and the fact that she was involved and doing this to me had him at a loss for words.

Hong's friend Hanh was also using Tuoi's iPad that Hong took to her upstairs a few hours prior, so I asked Hong where Tuoi's iPad was, and Hong said Tuoi came and got it. I knew she was lying, and I searched everywhere for it and discovered that Hong hid it inside my office under a basket with the iPad strategically placed, standing up, so they could hear everything I said. I forget the name of the program that was running when I checked the iPad. Still, at the time, I researched the program and saw that it allowed sending and receiving files which I am assuming had something to do with not only recording audio but also sending computer commands via Bluetooth to control the computer I was using. Once I found the iPad and explained to Hong that she couldn't lie anymore, Hong knew she was cornered at that point and had to fess up to something. I got her to show me the secrets on how they communicate with the encrypted messages that have keys hidden in plain sight on the internet that only her organization knows where to look for them. It only took a few hours though for her criminal organization to send a stern message, and Hong once again clammed up and became an impenetrable wall that I couldn't get to admit to anything.

A considerable part of their scam is patience. Hong took care of me like no other girl. They do that for several reasons. The main is so you rely on them for everything, so when they decide to attack, you are helpless. I couldn't even get food unless it was a U.S. Branded Restaurant like Pizza Hut, and over time, I allowed myself to become dependent on her for everything but the money, of course. They also make sure you rely on them to assure you won't quickly decide to leave once things go wrong to ensure they have enough attempts to take you down should something go wrong in their initial plot. They are the polar opposites of who they proclaim to be, which also gives them an element of surprise that is monumental. If you are self-sufficient and robust enough to try to escape once they make you completely reliant on them, they secretly set it up so they can instantly cut off your communication to the outside world should you call for help. The worst part is that you will think you successfully called somebody when you didn't. You'll be shocked when you see the next clever thing they did to assure they were successful in taking me down.

The picture located below shows my iPhone screen, which was already hacked unbeknownst to me at that time. The iPhone Configuration Utility application allows Companies to administer iPhones of their workers, which was designed for corporate America and used by the Triads for their criminal purposes. This application is extremely dangerous because they can install any icon they want to and have that application open in full-screen mode and go to a web URL of their choosing. □All they need is for you to click on a link to take over your phone, and your phone doesn't even need to be jailbroken. Hong had access to my iPhone and asked to use it a few weeks before the Airplane plot and asked me for my password so she could play a game. She claimed her iPhone's battery was dead. I now realize why she wanted my iPhone. Hong needed to click on a configuration file to allow the Triads access to my iPhone from that point forward. They could send push updates to my iPhone and make changes without the need for anybody clicking any more links once they clicked the first. In the other picture below, you can see a Skype icon that doesn't have an "X" on the top left to allow me to delete it like the other Apps that don't come pre-installed on the iPhone. They installed a web app that I thought was Skype but was a fake Skype icon that went to an html5 website address controlled by them that mimics the Skype program where they could either connect my Skype calls or not.

Verizon
3:12 PM
52 %
Settings
General
Auto-Lock
3 Minutes
Passcode L
On
Restricti
On
NO
PROFILE
Date & Time
Keyboard
International
Accessibility
Reset

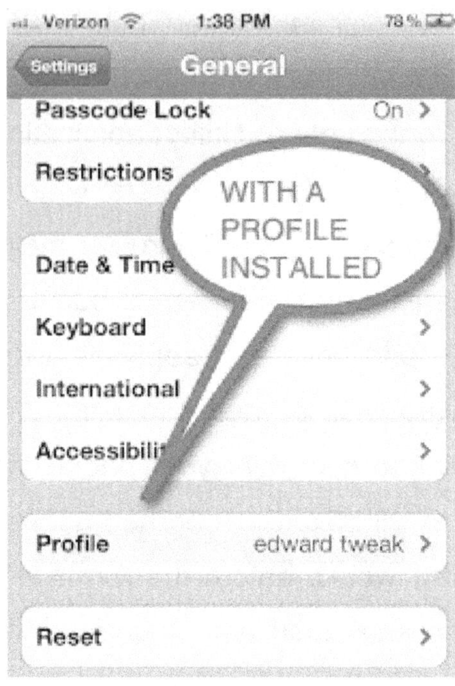
Verizon
1:38 PM
78 %
Settings
General
Passcode Lock
On
Restrictions
WITH A
PROFILE
INSTALLED
Date & Time
Keyboard
International
Accessibili
Profile
edward tweak
Reset

Verizon
1:42 PM
81 %
Skype
G-Whizz!
Phone
Mail
Safari
Apple

Now I know why they were eavesdropping and recording my audio for so long. They needed time to record copies of everybody's voicemail so they could set up voice messages that were identical to the ones of the people I called, except for the fact that my recipient wasn't going to receive the messages because it was left on a server controlled by the Triads. I figured this out when all my outgoing calls were going to voicemail for days in July 2011 when things got nasty. I don't know how I thought of this, but I decided to dial my mother's number directly on the keypad after it went to her voicemail three times in a row after ringing six times each call, which made me know her phone was ringing and not without service. Rather than press on her name in Skype to call her cell, I dialed it from the keypad, and suddenly, she answered on the first ring. I asked her if her phone rang before, and she said no and that it was beside her the entire time. □They took the time to record everybody's voicemail in my contact list to prevent me from calling for help since I would be leaving a message on their server and not with my mother as I thought. They had me completely isolated. They also had other programs I used automatically crash when I tried to open them if they didn't want me to use them. They had all my email routed through their servers to look at it first and decide if they wanted to allow it to send. I also sent several emails for help that nobody ever got.

Trust me when I tell you that these bastards probably never lose. I truly needed and got help from God to escape them; I know what my skills are. I can fight wars better than anyone I know. One of my exes screwed me over once and was scared and told my friend she was worried because most people think two steps ahead, but I thought eight steps ahead on everything, which she said she learned by living with me over three years. Well, let me tell you, these evil bastards were thinking ten steps ahead. I ran out of options several times, and sheer luck (I now believe God) nudged me toward the right direction to escape or foil the plots when I wasn't even logically close to figuring out what was happening. □

The Criminal Chat.

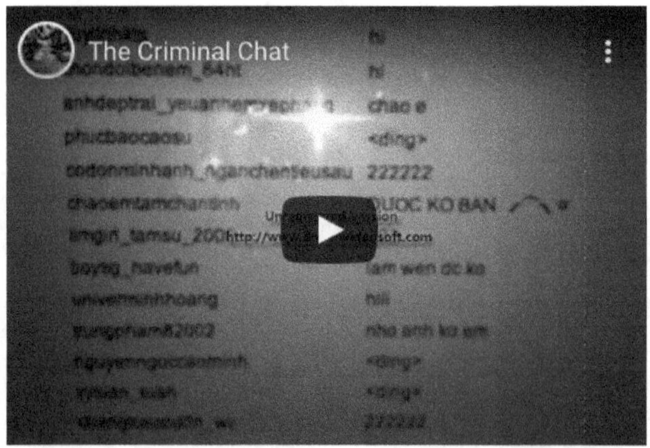

Watch at bit.ly/dprefer12 or at "Section 1"

In the messages below, Hong admits that Giang came to the to kill me.

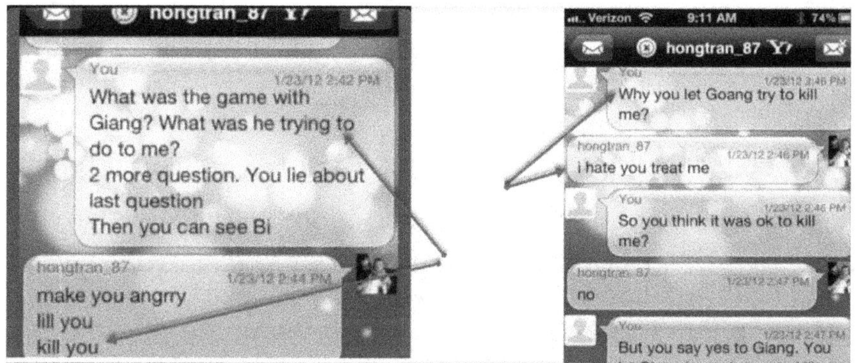

10 - The Dogs are at the Door

The next few nights after I kicked her friend Hanh out of the house were brutal. Hong and her family kept unlocking padlocks on the doors and windows every two hours (like the one pictured below) and acted innocent when I would scream at them. I would find more Windows unlocked and had to keep locking them. Hong's sister was going to take my son to visit her mother for a few days, and when I came out of my office to say goodbye, my son saw me and started screaming and reaching for me as though his life depended on it. I went for him and hugged him, and he squeezed me with a grip that was so hard that I could have pulled my hands away, and he would not have fallen off me. He was only five months old at the time. I watched as Hong's Aunt buckled over as though somebody hit her in the stomach because she knew what the plans were for me, and the fact that my son sensed danger and was trying to help his Daddy was too much for her to take. She ended up leaving our house for good the very next day even though she stayed with us for five months to help the nanny with my son. She had enough, but all the while, Hong stood there stoic with her poker face on as usual. I said, "FUCK YOU," nobody is taking my son anywhere, and I wouldn't let them take him. My son effectively accomplished his plan and caused me to prevent them from taking him, and he calmed down immediately. I think they would have come in for sure that night if my son wasn't there. Still, I believe Hong stalled them after that since my son was in the house. Still, it didn't stop them entirely because at 1 AM, even though the neighborhood is usually tranquil due to everybody sleeping, motorcycles were driving by every few minutes with guys screaming like some sort of war cry.

I tried to call the Police that night from all three cell phones I had with three different providers that all had full bars, but every call dropped. I now realize that they were outside of my house with a cell phone jammer pummeling my house, which prevented my phone from connecting. I kept every light on in the place and stayed up all night. Even my dogs helped that night because they slept in spots that they usually don't sleep at that had perfect vantage points of the garage and staircase. Every time I walked out of my office, they were sitting there and keeping guard and never moved all night, nor did they ever sit at those same spots ever again after that night. They sensed the evil. I needed help from my son and my dogs to make it through that night.

I took the video below while lying in bed that same night on May 5th, 2011, with Hong just one day after I kicked her friend out of the house. At the time, I was still confused about what was happening and thought that maybe I was being set up as somebody who talked bad about the Vietnamese Government since the guy on the airplane also told me that he hated the Communists and asked what I thought of them. I didn't know what was going on, but you'll see that I was pretty much onto their scheme but wasn't sure exactly what they were plotting. I now think the Communist bashing set-up was just one more layer to assure I wasn't helped after they arrested me with Police that weren't corrupt since I would have been somebody talking bad about their Government.

The following day, I had the neighbor kid, a 14-year-old kid that I trusted, buy me all new locks. I trusted him because he was visibly sad when guys would say things to me in Vietnamese that I'm sure were insulting. He was a good kid and wanted to learn English too. The packages of the locks were unopened when he gave them to me, so I knew copies weren't made, plus he came back within 15 minutes, which I timed as being just about how long it would take to buy the locks and return. There wasn't time to make copies of the keys, so I felt that I was safe.

I replaced all the locks on every window. The windows all have padlocks like the picture above. I didn't give anyone in the house a key. You couldn't leave the house without a key since every door, window, and garage door had these padlocks on it. I was finally able to sleep, which I did in my office with the door locked. I kept the keys with me and told Hong to let me know if anybody needed to leave and that I would open the door for them.

Not even a day went by, and the bricks barrage started again, but now with more frequency than before. I called the U.S. Embassy several times, but they just kept telling me to go to a nice hotel and that they couldn't help me other than that. After a few days of the brick bullshit, I was up for almost three days. I felt that I wasn't safe enough in the house even to sleep anymore, so I decided to make a 5 mile run in my car to a 4-star hotel in District 1 with my money and safely made it to the Caravelle Hotel. I dead bolted the door and slept for 14 hours before going straight to the airport to take my chances at smuggling my money to Singapore. The route I drove that night from my house to the Caravelle is illustrated in the picture below. I left $50,000 US in my safe before going to the Caravelle Hotel just in case my Chinese Yuan got stolen or confiscated as I tried to get to the hotel or as I left the country the next day. I made it through airport security without being stopped, only to have two cops walk up to me at the gate asking me to get coffee with them because they saw my money as it went through the x-ray. I bribed the guy with $1900 U.S. and was able to get most of the money I had safely to Singapore before returning to that nightmare in Vietnam, where I fought every day to protect the $50,000 U.S. and close to $70,000 U.S. worth of Chinese Yuan that I also left behind in the ceiling.

Once I returned from Singapore, I noticed several guys outside my house that I never saw before across the street at a coffee shop six days a week using handheld smartphones to control my computers that Hong helped them infect. □ Over the next month and a half, I came within minutes of either getting killed or arrested by the corrupt Police in my neighborhood that were also in on the scam. This continued until I left for America on July 14th, 2011, when my Buddy came to help me move my belongings and my Dogs back to America. I would have to leave my son for now but returned within three weeks with only three suitcases and an ATM card ready to fight for however long it took to get out of there with Hong and my son. This ended up being another five months before I left with only my son on his 1-year birthday.

May 5th, 2011. (Watch at bit.ly/dprefer13 or at "Section 1")

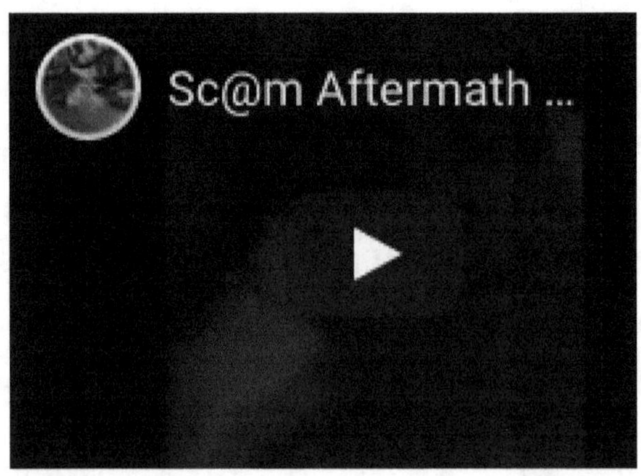

The Locks I Bought

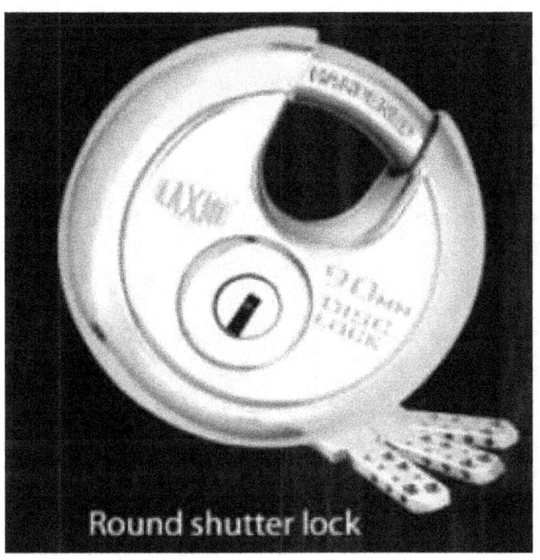

Round shutter lock

The Money Route

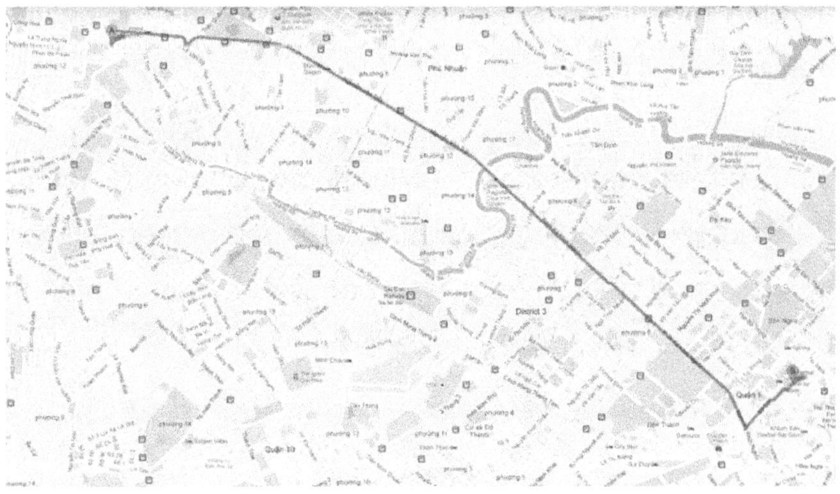

My Dog Ginger Posted in Front of My Office Door!

I took this picture when I was under attack to send to my friend to show how my dog knew I was at war, and she stayed in this spot for almost a week and slept there too.

Below is another rare admission I got from one of Hong's family members. She admitted that Hong used to be a bad person but lied and said she was good after my son was born. Bi means "baby" in Vietnamese. We were talking about my son.

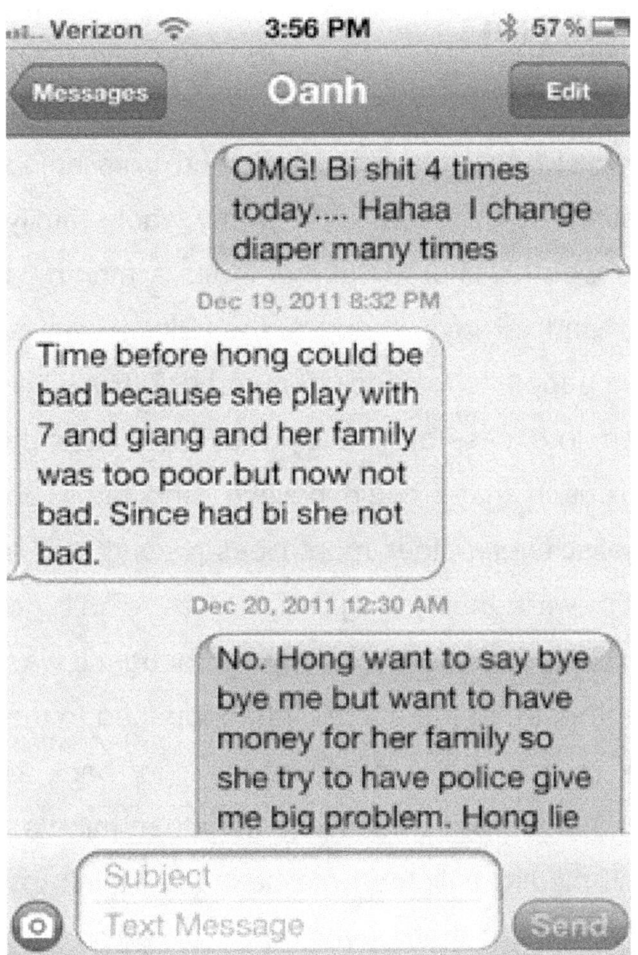
Verizon
3:56 PM
57%
Messages
Oanh
Edit
OMG! Bi shit 4 times today.... Hahaa I change diaper many times
Dec 19, 2011 8:32 PM
Time before hong could be bad because she play with 7 and giang and her family was too poor.but now not bad. Since had bi she not bad.
Dec 20, 2011 12:30 AM
No. Hong want to say bye bye me but want to have money for her family so she try to have police give me big problem. Hong lie
Subject
Text Message
Send

11 - THE GOD FACTOR

It wasn't until I moved back to America that I switched from being Agnostic to being a Christian "sort of" even though my whole family was always Christian and went to church several times a month. I never bought the story and always thought the Bible was a marketing tool that allowed people to feel included and "Big Religion" to extract money from them in excess by abusing their trust. Nobody ever gave me a logical reason that I could believe, and the High Rolling Television Evangelist every other month being caught in a scandal plus the Priest's with the young boys sure didn't go unnoticed in my mind. I wanted to believe, but inside I thought it was bullshit until I had time to process all the events that happened to me in Asia, which didn't sink in until three months after I got back to America. If anybody knows of a more convincing story than mine as to why I know God is real, please enlighten me because I think my account makes the best argument that I ever heard of for proving God exists when amongst the company of people that doubt.

Let me give you a few preliminary concepts that I believe even though it departs from conventional wisdom. Once I concluded that even though some things were way overinflated regarding Christianity, I realized that it is still authentic, and most concepts stay intact. That helped me logically conclude God and Jesus are real.

Here's what I'm saying: First off, I don't think God is as powerful as organized religion makes him out to be. But God is good, and yes, he does care, but I think he is only a little stronger than the devil "Evil," and every day is a struggle. Just like my battle with these losers, you win some; you lose some. Do you think God would allow evil to exist if he could wipe it out like that?

I saw a movie that made me think that the truth is probably like the plot of this movie. Watch "The Adjustment Bureau" with Matt Damon if you haven't seen it already. I can see how I was helped in subtle ways over in Vietnam, where it would lead a logical person to believe that God can only sway things so far here on Earth and must pick and choose where he will put his energy in his never-ending battle to fight evil. Even when I was growing up, I escaped certain situations that could have led to my downfall had God not got me out of it through his subtle orchestration he can apply to our lives. I believe that God, unfortunately, can only interject into our lives so much, and even though I'm sure he wants to save us all, he can't and has to use his intervention powers wisely. I believe God helped me more than many people because he knew I would fight against evil and take some of the burdens off him for the battles that need to be fought on Earth. If you want to worship and love God more, try praying less and asking him for things and put that energy towards making God proud of what you are doing on this Earth. It's like dating; nobody wants it too easy; God doesn't need a billion lapdogs; he needs a few million "at least" people that really want to serve him and proactively fight evil. I saw the devil in Asia; God would not allow evil at that level to exist if he could help it. He needs our help. You have no clue what it's like over there when you live amongst them as I did. I could feel the weight of their eyes as they started to close in on me. People that smiled at me for a year turned into heartless zombies that only cared about getting my money no matter how long it took. Anyways, back to my journey to Jesus and God.

From the time I had my first pager when I was 16 years old, a popular thing to do with your girlfriend when pagers were around was to send the digits 143, which stands for "I love you" since "I" is one word, love is "4," and you is "3". The strange part is that I do not watch the clock or cares about time unless it's work-related, so I rarely glance at the clock, but if I do glance at the clock 20 times in 1 week, I swear that at least eight times out of 20 the time is 1:43 AM or PM. I have noticed this since I was 16, and it always was in the back of my mind, but I didn't overthink what it meant if anything for that matter. But recently, even though I have always had Cinemax, I never watched it even once, but my son was playing with the remote and changed the channel recently. It switched to Cinemax, and the movie "The Adjustment Bureau" was starting. I was relaxing on the couch and didn't feel like getting up to grab the remote and change the channel, so I just left it on, which is an example of how God can intervene in our lives. I don't think he can part seas as the Bible says, but I think he can nudge us like a steering wheel driving on a snow-covered road; he can only steer our direction so much before the forces of human nature hold and keep us going toward whatever path we are conducting ourselves. God's hands can only run so many steering wheels at one time, which means he needs to choose based on what will help assure the survival of "Good" in its never-ending fight against "Evil."

I was never an angel, but I never tried to hurt people and always met injustice head-on, whether for me or somebody else's benefit. I think God forgave my quirks for what he saw in me on my strengths that benefited the cause of protecting good against evil. I'm not just pulling crap out of the sky; I mean, I am the first person I can find on the internet that is going after the Triads monumentally, but that isn't an accident. God knew my fearlessness and absolute hatred of injustice long ago and everything that has occurred and every situation I escaped, both leading up to Vietnam and after, was meant to give me the ability to do what he knew I would do once confronted with and exposed to pure evil. This is why he chose to help steer my wheel more than most people, in my opinion. I have many examples, but here are a few that stuck with me over the years:

When I was 28, I got into a fight with a guy that ran into an alley and grabbed a gun he had planted there and started to chase me with it. I stopped and stood there as the guy began to pull the trigger, and I could see his face change from pure determination to absolute fear as he dropped his arm down and fired just as I jumped. The gun was a huge .45 caliber that would have blown apart whatever it hit, but he missed and then ran off. The part that always puzzled me was his face and how it changed from aggressive and determined to frightened in a split second. I know how emotions work, and they don't change in a split second like that; they move along a scale and slowly change unless somebody is unaware and gets startled or finds out they won the lottery, which the complete changing of circumstances can explain. Still, this guy was already chasing me with a pointed gun; there wasn't anything that monumentally changed that explains how he went from one extreme to the other in a split second. I think he saw something meant to startle him and change his mental state, which was a spirit or angel doing God's work to assure I lived on to fight the more significant battles ahead.

Another time was when I was 28, some asshole ex-boyfriend of my girlfriend was making threats to her and calling her constantly. I didn't put up with that shit and saw him in a bar, kicked his ass, and got arrested, although I got the charges dropped later. My luck wasn't good that night because this guy had a few friends that were cops, and they made sure they took their time on my paperwork. I ended up being in jail for 24 hours, even though it should have been 8 hours. The way jails work in Pittsburgh is that nobody goes out until the following day once they do a shift change at 11 PM. I knew my Buddy was upstairs bailing me out, but the guard told me that it was too late and nobody ever gets out after 11 PM. I was going insane and was ready to start punching everyone when suddenly, I hear a guard on the intercom asking if I was down there, to which the guy said yes, and the guard on the intercom said, well, get him up here, his bail is posted. I don't know why I was supposedly the only person ever to get released after 11 PM, but let me tell you, I was about to explode, and I was really into lifting weights with my testosterone levels higher than ever at that point in my life. I guarantee you I would have possibly got in a huge fight and caused myself to get in a position I couldn't quickly fix later. I think God nudged that guard upstairs to call for me even though it was past the time of complete lockdown.

A year later, I was still a fitness fanatic, and the supplement that was supposed to release Human Growth Hormone called GHB was still legal and sold in Health Stores everywhere. If you know anything about GHB, you would know that it is essentially the same as the "date rape" drug if you take too much, and no matter how hard you try, it is impossible to keep yourself from falling asleep if you take enough to fall asleep. My girlfriend and I took it a few times, and both fell asleep at the same time while having sex, Ha-ha. You can't fight it; you can operate on somebody without waking up if they fall asleep from taking too much, which is why it is used as a date rape drug. Anyways, one time I took it and decided to go driving, and I fell asleep at least five times and woke up just as I was ready to smash off a wall without a second to spare. God was busy that night, that's for sure.

The age of 28 and 29 were two crazy years for me, that's for sure. I gave God a break after that for a while. I didn't require his help too much until I moved to Asia. In 2006, God did try to help me believe in him in a big way, but I found a way to logically dismiss it even though the writing was on the wall. My Dad died in 2006 at 4:301AM, and precisely one week later, at 4:31 AM, I was having what seemed to be a dream but was much too intense and real to be a dream. My Dad was on one knee and looked weak as my mother (who is still alive but was in the dream) talked and said, "all the years of gambling and drinking took their toll" (My Dad drank six beers every night and was good at handicapping horses, which was a full-time Hobby for him, but a stressful one since winning and losing money was a daily part of the hobby. He made money over the years, though, not much, but he was ahead in the end). The dream instantly changed to where my Dad was standing directly in front of me and was strong as he held out his arms and said, "My Life with Jesus Christ," as he leaned forward and hugged me. I could feel he was strong like he was before he got cancer, and I could smell him and everything. I instantly woke up with my heart beating like a drum, and my dogs were going crazy the moment I woke up. My ex was sleeping next to me and told me that she felt the wind in her ear just before I woke up and that she rubbed her ear from the wind hitting it because it caused her hair to tickle her ear when the wind blew. The windows were closed, and the furnace was off, so nothing could have caused a breeze. I couldn't get that out of my mind but still denied God's existence by thinking that people die and go to another dimension of sorts and that the people that believe the same as them get grouped similar to a Country and its better to be with a big group to defend against whatever is over there, so my Dad wanted me to believe to assure I wasn't an outcast after I died when I entered this other world. That's how I logically concluded the meaning of what happened until after I came back from Asia, where God showed me many more examples of proof that a hard head like myself needed to believe since I was a natural skeptic and strictly adhered to logic on the topic of whether he exists or not.

God Shows

Here are examples of things that happened in Asia that I believe God either did to help me or prove to me that he is real since he knew I struggled with that.

-The first thing that happened in Asia that I think God's hand was involved in showing me he was real was when I kept singing "Rooster" by the band "Alice in Chains," which I discussed earlier.

-The Airplane Plot has God written all over it to successfully guide me through all 5 phases they had set up in that extremely clever set-up. Their mastery of deception over in Asia is off the charts; God knows that and he knew I needed powerful evidence to prevent me from getting sucked in and believing Hong, so he made sure I saw a few things that would always stick with me whenever I was weak and started to believe her lies. God made sure I saw Hong's sister Tuoi's hatred towards Hong after the Airplane Plot to let me know that Hong could have done more to protect me because if Hong didn't have a choice, her sister wouldn't be angry at her for helping scam me. Other aspects that are too many to name are laced throughout this book, where too many coincidences of dumb luck add up to be something that dumb luck cannot explain.

-When my son screamed for me and wouldn't let go to get me to say they couldn't take him anywhere. God knew they were going to attack me, and he knew I needed another day before I would be ready to admit it was more than I could handle and go somewhere safe, and he knew Hong would stall her conspirators for at least a day if my son were still in the house.

-A few weeks after that, there were only two friends of Hong's that I didn't think were involved, and Hong wanted me to come to say hello and hang out, but I couldn't leave the bathroom because I was constipated for 5 hours. I never get constipated, and nothing happened as far as me eating differently that would have caused it, but I wasn't constipated anymore as soon as they left. I later found out from the girl who did love me, who told me all the dirty secrets on how the Triads run things in Asia, that they were involved. She told me they were going to say they bought drugs from me while the Police waited to storm the house, but they couldn't do it since I never left my office. So, you tell me, was my first constipation episode in history a coincidence? I don't think so.

-I had a strange feeling about my video surveillance system. I felt I needed to destroy it due to suspicion that they hacked it and were going to use it to set me up at any moment, so I grabbed it and put it in the microwave for 5 minutes, to which Hong came and asked me what I did. When I told her, she went crazy and kept asking me strange questions which I could tell were meant for me to answer so they could use it to set me up, but I just stood there and looked at her. The girl I mentioned before that told me everything confirmed that they were going to arrest me the next day because they had a guy come up to my house and act like he was handed something from inside the gate where the camera couldn't see but that he was going to claim he bought drugs from me. She told me he did this every day for a week and that they had all the visits recorded on my security camera that they had hacked. Only God could have got me to fry that system because I didn't think anything about why I was worried except that they hacked it to watch me only and not to set me up even though I guessed this later and then had the girl confirm I was right. She told me the whole plan they had, which I foiled by frying the security system. The following day, that Corrupt Cop looked at me angrily for the first time when he made the smoking gesture as he peered straight through me with a frustrated, angry look on his face.

-One night in early July 2011, I had a strange feeling and felt like I had to go down to the garage at 2 AM even though I never did that before. Within 30 seconds of me standing in the garage at 2 AM, I heard a window open, and keys drop on the street, and a motorcycle picked up the keys and drive off. I ran upstairs and started screaming at Hong. Hong first said she dropped them to her brother, but once she realized that made zero sense since we always physically let anybody in the house because you need keys and a garage door remote to let somebody in and the keys wouldn't be enough by themselves, so she instantly changed her story and said the neighbors must have dropped keys for somebody. I couldn't believe that she so blatantly lied and changed her story like I was a complete moron that would believe it. The keys could be used to open upstairs windows where they also could have got in the house. I had to stay up all night listening to see if somebody was coming, and the whole time, I would press the button on this Taser Stick I had that made a loud noise when pressed to let any would-be attackers know I was awake and ready. I went to a hotel again the next morning since I knew I wasn't safe there.

-Before I went back to the United States on July 14th, 2011, with my dogs for three weeks before I returned alone, I had a moving company come to pack my entire house to ship back to the United States. This company was anal about packing every item and wrapping every item. They even wrapped disposable pens and half-used toilet paper rolls, and the house was completely empty when they left. Still, I went through to make sure they didn't miss anything, and there wasn't anything in the entire house but garbage except for the room directly above my bedroom that Hong used to say she heard pounding from late at night and would say it was the Ghost. I did hear banging upstairs once at three in the morning, so I believed her. In that same room, the banging came from there was only 1 item which was the only thing left in the entire 7-bedroom house. The cross pictured below that my grandmother gave me as a gift that I told her not to buy me any more religious gifts because it wasn't my thing. Still, since it was from my grandmother, I kept it along with the Bible she gave me even though both items were always packed and not out on display. This cross obviously was a nice item and wasn't meant for the trash, and it was already packed in a box somewhere in the house but somehow made it out of the box and ended up in the same room that Hong said the Ghost occupied that scared her and her family. I remember looking at it and thinking that I still don't believe, but I'm sure as hell not leaving you with these evil people, so I picked it up and put it in my backpack and took it home with me to America. I think God was trying to test me and ask me if I will still deny him after everything he has done to shield me from this pure evil I was facing. Thank God I protected the cross even though I didn't believe it yet.

- My friend Jett that I did the memorial site for at http://www.forjett.com had a favorite hat his mother gave me after he died. My grandmother gave me this ugly camel a long time ago that many girlfriends I've had through the years have tried to throw away more than once, but I always saved that stupid camel for some reason. While I was in Vietnam, Hong and I stopped at a place to eat while driving to her mother's, and they sold Displays with Cobras inside them posed in different ways, and I decided to buy one. It just so happens I bought it on the way home from the visit when I killed the pic, which was meant to be my goodbye party and just 2 ½ weeks before they attempted the Airplane Plot that sent my life into a tailspin. Other than what I just mentioned, there wasn't any meaning to these items other than the first two were sentimental, and the third one was cool-looking. After I turned to the United States for Good, I was trying to clean my house. Still, I couldn't find a place to put those three items, so rather than box them up, I just put them on top of the refrigerator the way you see them in the picture below, and it has remained that way for months since I never moved them. Then one day, I happened to look on top of the refrigerator and stared at those three items when something hit me. Remember how the fortune teller guy said that I had a protector on the other side that was a guy about my age that I assumed was my friend Jett? You can also see that I protected and kept that camel since it was from my grandmother, and only me and my grandmother liked that camel.

Well, my grandmother died in late 2011, and I still had to escape Vietnam when she died and couldn't come back for two more months when I finally got out of there with my son. The Snake display made me start to think, and I began to believe this whole display was symbolic of my situation in Vietnam and epitomizes the big picture of my entire struggle. Look how two giant cobras are trying to kill the little snake, but the little snake is still alive. You need to look closely, but there is a little snake in the Cobra's mouths. I think this arrangement shows how my friend was on top of things and protecting me, which symbolizes the hat, plus the fact that Hong heard the Ghost upstairs. My grandmother symbolizes the camel watching over me too, as I defy the odds and battle the Triads on one side and Hong and her family on the other. They represent the two snakes trying to destroy me, obviously, but I'm still alive. I thought that was amazing, even though some of you might think I have too much time on my hands to ponder into what it all meant.

- The hidden file that was being used by the Triads that was 666MB and erred out at 69%, that has God written all over it in the sense that he is trying to tell me who the devil on Earth is and the forbidden fruit that lured me over there to see firsthand!

- In September 2011, I was trying to get Hong a Visa to come back with my son and me to America when my Vietnamese Lawyer said it would be best if Hong had $20,000 US in her own account in Vietnam because the U.S. Embassy would see that she had assets in Vietnam and would be less likely to stay in America and violate her Visa. It made sense to me, so I had $20,000 wired to Hong's account. The day the wire took place, Hong and I were fighting, and I told her no less than five times to not screw it up and make sure she got the correct account number. The wire was rejected because the account number Hong gave me was wrong. Hong later admitted that she planned on taking my son somewhere in Vietnam and hiding forever if she had that money. I think God prevented that and made sure the account number was off a digit or two. I can't stress enough how I badgered Hong that day to make sure she got the correct account number because I was frustrated since I knew they were still coming after me at the time. I wouldn't have my son right now if the account number were correct.

- In November 2011, while in Mui Ne, I was in the bedroom alone, and Hong was in the kitchen on her computer when a girl I haven't talked to in almost a year sent me a message on Skype. I was tired and didn't feel like getting into it about the story when she asked how I was doing, so I quickly thought of a reply that would let her know I'm not doing well but at the same time give me a reason not to elaborate when she asked for details so I said to her that I couldn't talk on Skype about further information because the FBI told me not to. Within 2 minutes, Hong burst into the room saying, "Who were you talking to" while screaming at the top of her lungs. The girl I spoke with was through Chat, not a voice call, so I realized that Hong was involved in the plot and that they have my communications wholly hacked. I think God got that girl to contact me, knowing I would reply with a white lie. I called that girl a few days later and told her I lied because I didn't feel like getting into it, and she was shocked when I told her my ordeal.

- A week after the Skype incident, I had a stupid moment and thought once again that Hong was innocent, and her friends set her up. I called my mother while Hong was there and told her that I believe Hong is innocent. Hong left the house a few minutes later and came back in when I told her I had an awful feeling and thought we had to go to a hotel. The internet wasn't working, and my sim card was out of money even though I just added $30 U.S. that morning and barely used the phone. Hong said that she ordered me food and we need to wait because she felt bad since she already told the lady to get it. I told her that I didn't care, and we needed to leave. The front gate was locked, and I asked Hong for the key, to which she replied she doesn't know where she put it even though she just had it 5 minutes before when she left the house. I kicked the gate open as I noticed the neighbors sitting quietly on their porch, watching in the dark as the drama unfolded. I think they all had a front-row seat and were all aware that my end was near. Hong went outside to call the Calvary once she heard me tell my mother she was innocent. She didn't waste a minute before calling in the troops. My money was in Singapore, and she could have got it if I died, and she wasted no time. I think God made me have a stupid moment because he needed me to see who she was without any doubts whatsoever. After that night, I decided I was going to America without Hong, and just me and my son would be going, so I fought her over the issue for a few days until she relented and said yes. God didn't want me to bring Hong to America; he showed me what I needed to see. The next day I called my mother and told her I was wrong and that Hong was involved 100% as I told her about every plot in detail that Hong and her people did. That saved me because Hong backed off since she knew my family would protest her getting my money if I died since they knew she was involved. That was the straw that broke the camel's back and caused Hong to give up and silently admit defeat. She helped me a lot in getting my son's Visa to leave the country. She was tired and couldn't battle me any longer.

- After I moved back to the United States, I met a girl that I dated a few times before becoming friends with her since I moved away from Florida. This girl was very religious, and at the time, I was Agnostic, and we would have civil conversations about the whole thing, and she got the chills and said, "OMG, I don't know what it is when I'm around you, but my spiritual energy goes crazy. I asked her what she meant and if she meant something as far as physical attraction, and she said it has nothing to do with that, but it's her spiritual energy she feels when she is in touch with God. She then told me that God has huge plans for me. I started to think, wow, why is she predicting God will have huge plans for a guy that telling her he doesn't buy the whole God story I thought. Well, about a month after that, I came through the fog after piecing together everything that happened in my life and made a few core tweaks regarding the facts that I think may have been a little exaggerated regarding religion, and I saw my purpose and now believe in God and Jesus Christ 100% in addition to Buddha ...

I admit I have rough edges and blaze my own trails on almost everything in life, but that's who I am, and I will do what I think God would want me to do to help him while I'm here. As I said, God is Good, but he needs his people to do his work here on Earth because he can't just press a button like many people are taught to believe to scare them into believing as a shortcut rather than truly convince them. I asked my family why they believed many times, and the only answer I ever got was "I just believe." Or "it's in the Bible." Well, that wasn't enough for me, and I thank God for giving me concrete proof. As of 2013, I didn't know what his overall hopes were for me; maybe it's for me to explain how I came to believe in him because I think my story is more convincing than any I've heard as far as getting a skeptic to convert goes, or maybe its multiple purposes which I'm meant to struggle and expose these evil men in Asia and save the poor girls that are treated like livestock. I think God is Good, and the way they treat their woman is anything but good, so I guess it's safe to say God would be thrilled I'm doing this. I have so much more to write about God but need to keep the theme of this book going, so I'll go back to 2011 in Vietnam.

12 - Nowhere Was Safe

Starting in June 2011, Hong's cousin Oanh cried almost every day when she looked at me, and Hong would say that she is having problems with her family and that it wasn't about me. One time in early July 2011, I was going to go to a 4-star hotel (the only safe place in Vietnam) with the $50,000 US I still had in Vietnam because I could sense they were going to attack soon. Hong left the house with our son when I was sleeping and wouldn't tell me where she was, which I interpreted as her not wanting my son to witness a war unfold when these cretins attacked. As I was getting ready to leave, Co Hai, the Nanny, and Hong's cousin Oanh told me not to go and had tears in their eyes. I asked Oanh if guys were waiting for me outside, to which she replied, "Yes." I said how many, and she said "three." I told her that I could handle that no problem and proceeded to leave with the money as I was chased the entire time by three guys on motorcycles. I lost two of them, and once the third guy realized he was alone, he stopped chasing me. This chase happened about two months after the Airplane Plot. The picture below illustrates the route I drove from my house to that hotel, which was closer than the Caravelle. Still, I just sold my car and had to go by motorcycle, so I chose that hotel even though it was a little less reputable than the Caravelle. I made a loop because I stopped at the massage parlor to make sure Hong wasn't there with my son first, plus I wanted to double back and see how many guys were following me.

I am still amazed at how evil Hong's family and friends could be. □I know all of them are not like that, but an alarming percentage were. I watched old ladies help in the several scams against me, and it seemed to me like they are secretly stalking Americans when they feel they can get away with it undetected.□I could tell that they didn't hide the scam from each other and shamelessly did things without hesitation that made me know anybody within hearing distance would know a scam was happening. Like the old saying goes, "When the Cat's Away, the Mice Will Play," in this sense, it brings out their true colors when they think they can score unnoticed. □I always smiled and said hello to anybody I made eye contact with and treated Hong and her family like Gold. I can't believe they could be so evil and greedy after everything I did for them, in addition to the fact that I never gave any of them a reason not to like me either. Here are a few examples of the things I did for Hong and her family:

- Built Hong's family a house
- I bought all her uncles and her father new motorcycles (9 in all) and bought her father a second motorcycle when the first one got stolen.

- I bought her sister a Beauty Salon / Massage Parlor for $5,000 U.S. Dollars which I didn't know at the time, but it was a scam to help Hong's ex-husband Cuong Nguyen since he got all the money and Hong never showed me a sales contract even though I asked her for one many times.
- I financially took care of her entire family, even her uncle's children.
- I bailed her brother out of jail by paying a $1,000 bribe to the police, which was probably all a scam to get the police some money and share it with them.
- I offered to give Hong's Mother's family 5 million Dong each "$250 US equivalent" so they wouldn't feel bad since I bought motorcycles for her father's family, but Hong said no because she didn't like her mother's family, but she liked her father's family even though they molested her as a child. If she liked them, I could only imagine why she didn't like her mother's family.
- I gave Hong's cousin Kiwi 10 million dong "$500 US" when somebody stole her money in Hanoi so she could give money to her mother and come back to HCMC and not be lonely.
- I paid for half of her sister Tuoi's Vespa and gave Tuoi an iPhone, among the many other things I did for her.
- I offered to pay for Hong's cousin Oanh to go to school and give her money to live on so she could fulfill her dream of

finishing school and make her family proud, but Hong told me not to.

When it came time to scam an American, even large electronics stores quickly jumped in on the plot. In late June 2011, I wanted to buy a new computer since all of mine were hacked, so I went to a huge electronics store near my house that is the size of a city block and six stories high. I later discovered that they gave me a new computer that they pre-hacked before giving it to me. After choosing the laptop I wanted, I had to wait 45 minutes as they installed Windows, which was a hacked version of Windows 7 that gave them access to my computer at the early boot state before the bios even loads. The way I discovered this was through pure chance. I plugged in an external keyboard and used that to type in the bios password when I changed the bios password from not having a password (default on all new computers) to a password of 88888844, which I chose because they are Google's two DNS servers and easy to remember.

I still think God nudged me to use the external keyboard because I never used an external keyboard on a laptop before. After all, you don't need one unless you hook up the laptop to an external screen which wasn't the case with me that day. Anyways, the keyboard I used, for some reason, would do a backspace when you pressed the 4 on the num-pad to the right rather than type a 4 as it should have.□ I don't know why I thought of this other than it was divine intervention from God, but I had the idea that maybe they had me hacked at the Bios level and decided to experiment with my odd acting #4 key on the right num-pad. Before hitting save while in the bios, I backspaced the password I entered and reentered it as 88888844 using the Numpad on the right, which essentially made the password 8888 because the fifth and sixth "8" were backspaced and deleted when I pressed the "4" two times and then I hit save and rebooted the computer and hit the escape key to enter the bios which now had a password that I needed to enter before I could proceed. This time I used the keys at the top and entered 88888844, which entered all numbers pressed since the "4" key up top worked as it should. As soon as I hit enter, I saw a confirmation that said, "Password Correct," a split second later, the computer blue screened and never turned on again. The hack they had set up was serving me fake screens that they controlled between the screen I was seeing and the computer's actual screen. Their program incorrectly read the 4 key on the right side and passed it to the bios as a backspace unbeknownst to them, so when I entered the same thing the second time, but with the working "4" up top, they assumed it was the same password and gave me a success confirmation before they passed along the password to the real bios, which caused the computer to do a blue screen. The picture below on the top left is a satellite view of the electronics store, while the top right is the store viewed at street level, and below that is the keyboard I used on the laptop.

The next day I took the computer back and accused them of hacking it, but they of course denied it. I then went to buy a MacBook Air without telling Hong or anybody that I planned on doing that; while I was still there, I told the salesman that I wanted to buy a MacBook Air, but I didn't want them to open it. His manager kept coming over and trying to turn it on as I filled out the paperwork, but I said no and stood firm that I didn't want them touching it. I said I would turn it on to show them it worked. As I was paying, the guy said he just needed to write down the serial number and stood out of sight and handed the computer to somebody else that quickly took it to the service desk where I glanced over and saw he was holding a MacBook Air, so I hurried over there but was too late. I saw several small windows loading as though Windows drivers were being installed, but this was a MacBook, not a Windows computer. I was pissed and demanded a new computer, but they said it was the last one. While arguing with the service guy, I realized that I left my bag at the counter where I paid and had to get it since a 3G Wi-Fi Dongle I bought the day before was still in there. As I walked over to grab it, I saw a guy getting off the escalator just next to that counter and noticed him put what looked to be the 3G Wi-Fi Dongle back in my bag. I don't know if he replaced it or just had to go write down the Mac ID to give to the corrupt cops that were working with the Triads, but I couldn't believe how brazen they were and how normal it seemed for them to work together and sabotage an American quickly. The picture of the 3G Wi-Fi Dongle I'm talking about is below. I haven't used it since buying it because I didn't know what they did with it and didn't want to risk using it.

Even the cable company installed a hacked cable modem with DD-WRT already running on it the moment they installed it. □They wouldn't give me a new modem at the cable storefront even though I could see a stack of them near the wall but said they would send one over in 45 minutes to my house because they didn't have any there. □I now know it's because they wanted to hack it first to spy on me since the local police were in on the deal, they probably just called them and told them what to do, and they complied with a smile. □The same thing occurred with a different Internet provider a few months later in Mui Ne when the guy didn't want to give me the password to the Wi-Fi router because he said it would provide me with access to their company servers. He was installing DSL, and the Wi-Fi router was separate from the DSL Modem. I told him he was incorrect and that the Wi-Fi router doesn't show me anything except my local network and the I.P. address I am connecting to. He knew he couldn't bullshit me, so he finally relented, but before giving me the password, he went into the router for a few minutes, which I'm sure was done to erase the settings they had that allowed them to snoop on my internet traffic which they do by using something called a loopback.

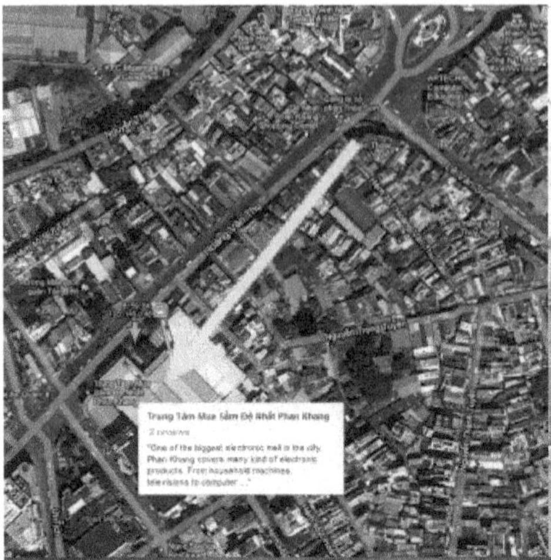

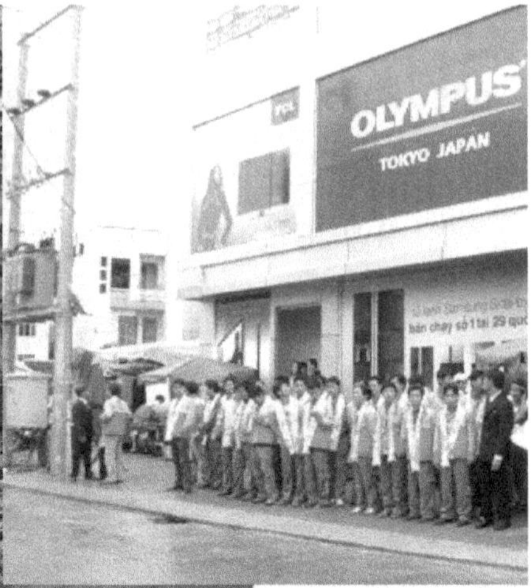
OLYMPUS
TOKYO JAPAN

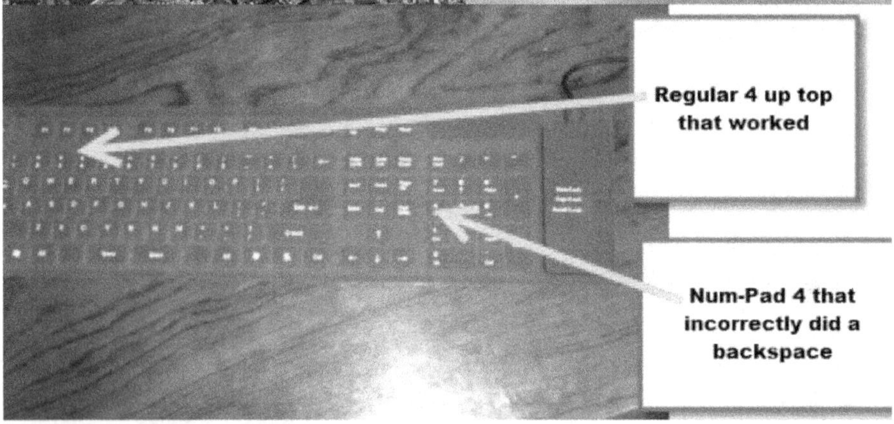
Regular 4 up top that worked
Num-Pad 4 that incorrectly did a backspace

CONNECT

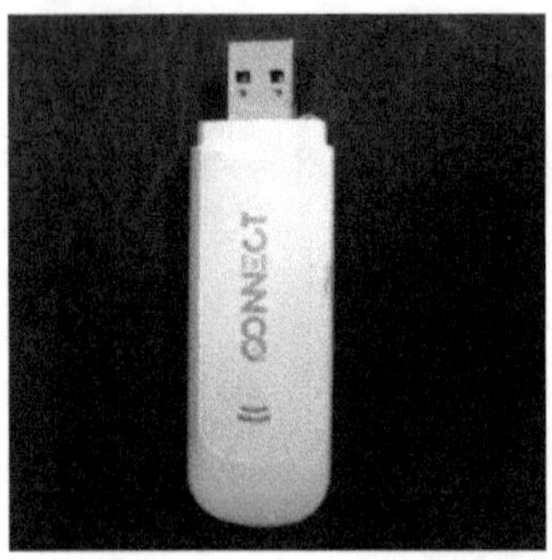

BETTER TRACKING THAN UPS

They knew everywhere I was going to go because Hong would tell them, or they'd hear me talk about it to Hong as they eavesdropped. Even if they didn't know, they could track me from my iPhone that I took everywhere. One time I went to make a Police report when Hong wouldn't tell me where my son was just before I left Vietnam in July 2011. Even though I called Hong 10 times that day, she didn't call me until I walked into the Police Station. This wasn't the police station near our house where the cops were involved, but a different one a mile away that was run by the North Vietnamese Government. She quickly pleaded with me and said sorry and that I can come to pick up our son. I knew immediately that they must have been tracking me in real-time because why the sense of urgency when I picked up the phone? I had already been telling her for two days that I would call the police, but she didn't care until she saw that I went to the Police station, not the one where they were in on the scam. Below is a copy of Hong's I.D. that I took to the Police Station, where the Police Officer wrote his name, phone number, and my report #

Perfectly Timed Anger

July 13th, 2011- LIES, LIES & More LIES- I remember that before I left Vietnam the first time in July 2011, I went to meet Hong's supposed ex-friends that she hadn't spoken to in over two months at a hotel that was 45 minutes away by motorcycle. I could feel something was not right as I sat there, so I left within 5 minutes. They said that they wanted to see me and say goodbye before I left. Even though I told Hong I was going to meet her friends, she didn't say anything or call me until 5 minutes after I left the hotel, and she was furious on the phone, telling me that I only love her friends and stuff like that. I then realized that her ex-friends were always her friends. They were trying one last attempt to frame me and set me up before I left. Once her friends called Hong and said that I left the hotel before they could set me up, Hong realizing there was no other way to get me before leaving and had a temper tantrum. She vented by calling me with anger that suddenly appeared over 2 hours after telling her where I was going. Hong is so easy to set up. I did something similar, on purpose, to prove to myself that they were all still friends when I first brought my son back to the States. I called her friend and told her Hong was trash and that I left Vietnam forever with our son. This call was at 5 AM Vietnam time. Guess who called me angry about something trivial only 4 hours later? Hong...

If these girls are supposedly her enemies, they sure seem to communicate quite a lot. It was apparent to me that all their fights were part of the plot. As I said, Hong and her friends were the most dishonest on the planet!

After my friend came to help me get movers and get my dogs out of there in July 2011, I had to come back in August 2011 because I couldn't leave my son with that evil family. □I also stupidly thought I could still save Hong if I could get her away from Asia. I was ready to die to bring them back, and I wasn't going to take no for an answer. I kept going back and forth on believing Hong because I didn't want to think the girl I loved, that was also my son's mother, was that evil, but in the end, the truth was obvious.

After getting back to America with my dogs in mid-July 2011, I decided to rent a car and drive cross-country from Los Angeles to Pittsburgh to prevent my dogs from having to fly again and give me time to clear my head after the nightmare I just went through. After being in America for only a week, I started to get sucked into Hong's lies and bullshit. We began to talk again civilly as I planned my return to Vietnam on August 1st, 2011, with only three suitcases and a debit card. I missed my son so much already and didn't care about the danger I would face by returning. I was only in Vietnam for one day, and Hong kept bugging me to get coffee in the morning and bring my computer. We weren't even at the coffee shop for 15 minutes when I noticed a warning on my screen saying another computer has the same I.P. address as me. I looked around at the five tables that had people sitting there and saw two guys with two phones apiece. Vietnam is a developing country; people don't have two phones, so I knew they were the guys trying to hack into my computer that Hong led me there for them to do precisely that. I told Hong that the guys at the table next to us were hacking me and said it's time for us to go. We had my son with us, or I would have probably spit in their face. Hong played dumb like she always did.

A RARE TEAR!

About a week after the coffee shop hacker incident in mid-august 2011, I was riding somewhere with Hong (whom at that moment I believed was possibly innocent even though common sense and proof showed otherwise). I reflected on the extent of what they planned to do to me on the airplane (which at the time I thought was to frame me as a drug smuggler or kill me). I said to Hong, "OMG! I can't believe people could be so evil; they didn't care about me, my son, or my family and only cared about their greed". Hong started crying very hard and wouldn't stop for ten minutes. I thought that was strange since I was at the time thinking it was only her friends, but I now know that she felt horrible for participating in trying to destroy her husband and the father of her child for money and greed even though they forced her hand to a degree. She never cried after that day.

Mui Ne Vietnam – 5 hours by motorcycle from HCMC

In September 2011, Hong, my son, the nanny Co Hai, and I moved to Mui Ne, a beach town about 5 hours from HCMC. I noticed that I was still being hacked and wanted to get away from HCMC. We stayed at a hotel as we looked for a place, and the first day we went to look, Hong, out of nowhere, told me to stop at this fruit stand to buy food for her cousins that came with us for the first week. Hong never stopped to buy food for her cousins before, but I didn't overthink it at the time. The place didn't even have much to choose from. Hong purchased some fruit and talked to the lady there who miraculously happened to have a rentable place just up the street that was brand new and ready to move in. I now know that Hong wanted to stop there as part of the plot. The lady was connected with the Triads. I told Hong I wanted to go to a different beach before we went to Mui Ne, and she kept telling me that she and her cousins want to go to Mui Ne, so I gave them their wish. I now know why they wanted to go to Mui Ne. Initially, the beach I wanted to go to is ten times nicer than Mui Ne but had tons of Westerners and would have made it harder to scam me since I would have probably made several friends and got schooled about how many Vietnamese feels about Westerners.

I told Hong to make sure she got the fast Internet, and the guy that installed the Internet didn't want to give me the password to the Wi-Fi router, as I mentioned earlier, because they had it set up to spy on me already.

I did become friends with a few westerners when I lived in Mui Ne from September 2011 to December 2011, and both guys warned me and said that the locals would rally to scam you, and that is why he is always very low key and minds his own business and lives like he has no money. They both drove a crappy motorcycle too, not to attract attention. Hong and her conspirators were opportunists like no other, but they are scared and not aggressive, so they have to make sure they are 100% sure to be successful before they strike. After being in Mui Ne for only two weeks, I saw a guy that seemed to be super drunk, and two young Vietnamese Guys were helping him, and I thought nothing of it as I entered the only modern convenience store I ever saw in Vietnam. When I came out, Hong told me that she almost came to ask me to help the guy because they were scamming him, but the people who drove him away were long gone by now, so I couldn't. I think I was wrong when I said he was drunk because he couldn't even stand, which seemed excessive. I now realize that it was probably a date rape drug of sorts that they spiked his drink with at the bar because my friend Yanni got scammed like that while out alone in HCMC on July 13th, 2011, the day before we returned. He doesn't remember leaving the bar and only remembers waking up in an alley with his money gone. Watch the Bartender pour your drink and always hold it when you visit Asia because it seems like this happens a lot. This method is a perfect way to disable somebody before taking them and cutting up their body to sell their organs on the black market, which I'll discuss later. Given the large amount of cash I had in the house, I'm sure it made it even worse, but I can see that scamming Americans is not only accepted by many but also encouraged. □Looking back to late June 2011, while I still lived in HCMC, I can see that when I kept escaping plot after plot, I noticed that the guys in my neighborhood that used to wave at me looked at me with blatant hatred. □□I now know it was because they knew I was a target the entire time and were only friendly because they were laughing at me as they waited for my demise. □But as my demise never came about, their true feelings showed. □

In early November 2011 in Mui Ne, when I realized Hong was involved, she exposed herself by angrily screaming at me as she asked who I was talking to on the Internet; I instantly got into a massive fight with her. She grabbed our son and held a knife to him as she said, "I'll kill him before I let you take him" ... I rushed her and grabbed the knife. Hong screamed something to her in Vietnamese, and Co Hai left the room as Hong told me that she told

Co Hai to call the police. I stepped into the hallway and watched as Co Hai went on the front porch, screamed something in Vietnamese, and then came back in without waiting for anyone to acknowledge her. I realized that she didn't call the police but screamed for reinforcements, so I decided to go to the hotel down the street but decided to come back ten minutes later and saw four motorcycles with two people on each bike in ages from 20 to 30 years old. There were seven guys and one girl, and they parked their motorcycles, one on each corner as illustrated in the map below, showing a satellite view of where they were. I decided too many people to risk getting into it with, so I returned to the hotel.

I wanted to get those guys on video, but they had already left. After sitting in the hotel room for 20 minutes, I couldn't help myself and decided to go back to the house, not caring about the danger. I had my phone video on as I drove up to the house, and after, I went inside to argue with Hong. I spoke broken English to her because she understood that better, so please excuse my obvious horrible grammar in the video I shot as I went back to the house that night.

We ended up leaving Mui Ne for good about a week later after Hong called a hit squad after she heard me talk with my mother when I stupidly thought Her friends might have framed Hong. I left for America with my son after being back in HCMC for a week once we got there from Mui Ne. I can't tell you how relieved I was the moment the airplane lifted into the air that night at 11:55 PM on December 2nd, 2011(also my son's one year birthday)

Mui Ne, Vietnam.

Mui Ne Fight. (Watch at bit.ly/dprefer14 or at "Section 1")

Time to meet the Devil Himself!

13 - Triad Godfather Luis Lui

I knew who Luis Lui was while I lived in Asia but didn't realize that he condoned and benefited from underworld attacks against Westerners that patron his saunas until a few months after returning to the United States for good. □I escaped Asia for good on December 2nd, 2011, but still noticed that my computers were being hacked. Since then, I have been spending 50 hours a week over the past year (it has been my full-time job) trying to get my computers secure, but the hackers I am up against are the best I've ever heard of. □They found ways to have their hack stay intact even after I did a low-level reformatting of my hard drive from another computer. □I now know that they used a program called TrueCrypt in addition to embedding rogue file systems that remapped the sectors of my hard disks that allowed their hack to live safely outside of the hard drive. My computer saw the drive as the entire drive, even though it only saw 95% of it at best. □They had hidden, encrypted operating systems running that would load the moment the hard drive received power, which is before the bios is even loaded, so their hack was controlling my computer before the bios even loaded and was undetectable. □I thought it was the Vietnamese hacking me the entire time, but little did I know it was the Triads that took over after I moved back to America. □I noticed the hacks were more complex and survived operating system reinstalls where the ones in Vietnam didn't. I also discovered random Chinese language files in directories that contained no other languages. □I could see that the hackers were ten times better than the ones I dealt with in Vietnam also so that, plus the fact that there were always random Chinese language remnants on my computer, made me realize that my nemesis was now the Triads, not the Vietnamese as I had suspected. □I suspected only the people in Vietnam since they were hacking me from April 2011 to December 2011. I was already blogging and talking negatively about them after returning to America. I rarely ever mentioned the Triads in that blog, so I assumed it was the criminals in Vietnam until I started to analyze it, at which point I set a few traps to try to figure out who it was. □

I try to only talk about technology when I think I can explain it so that most people will understand at least in concept what they used the technology for in their plots against me. If you are a techie and want to read more about their hacking tactics, go to http://bit.ly/triadhack □

I have since learned more about how they are doing it, but this contains the general framework of their hack. □Only read the hacking link above if you are a techie; otherwise, you won't understand what I'm talking about.

I also uploaded their hidden operating system that I discovered through pure chance to https://bit.ly/666-hack if you want to check it out (computer nerds only, I don't even understand it). □I named it 666hack because it is 666MB once extracted, which I think might be a message that these people are the Devil! Ha-ha. Another funny thing was that you couldn't burn the .iso file that is 666MB because it will error out and get stuck at 69%. □I thought that was funny too since sexual desires got me to move to Vietnam (the 69), and that led me to meet the Devil (the 666) :-) See the videos below. The first video shows how the Hidden Operating System was 666MB, and the second shows how it errored out during copying at 69%.

The 666MB Video is at https://bit.ly/666-hack2 or at "Section 1"
The 69% Video is at https://bit.ly/666-hack3 or at "Section 1"

But why did the Triads care to hack me when I already safeguarded my money, I thought. □It took me a few months to figure it out, but luck was with me. I decided to search for a business card I previously saved on my computer and my online "Evernote" cloud account for some unknown reason. When I searched for it, I realized that the business card picture wasn't on my computer or in my Evernote account. I knew with 100% certainty that I saved it there more than once. The image below is that business card, which is the business card of Luis Lui, whose company is G&L Group in

Macau. □I had a hard time locating it again on my computer even though I knew I saved it in several places.

The Public Face of Luis Lui

Everybody in Macau knows that the Saunas are all owned by the Triads. Still, most people don't know exactly who owns them within the Triads or what percentage they hold of the sauna market in Macau, but Luis Lui owns 95 to 100% of them even though his public company G&L Group makes no mention of Saunas.

As of 2013, if you search him on Google, you need to add "G&L Group" to his name, or you won't find him easily but instead will find another guy that owns Casinos who is a different person.

The next thing I will tell you is comical in the way it takes the word hypocrite to a whole new level. □Luis Lui is a long-time member of an organization called Skal International Macau. □On their website at https://bit.ly/skal-intl, they describe their organization with these exact words:

Skål is a professional organization of tourism leaders around the world, promoting global tourism and friendship. It is the only international group uniting all branches of the travel and tourism industry. Its members, the industry's managers and executives meet at local, national, regional and international levels to discuss and pursue topics of common interest. The first Club was founded in 1932 in Paris by travel managers, following an educational tour of Scandinavia. The idea of international goodwill and friendship grew and, in 1934, the “Association Internationale des Skål Clubs” was formed with Florimond Volckaert as its first President, who is considered the “Father of Skål”.

Skål International today has approximately 22,000 members in 500 Clubs throughout 87 nations. Most activities occur at local levels, moving up through National Committees, under the umbrella of Skål International, headquartered at the General Secretariat in Torremolinos, Spain.

After reading that, I had to laugh. □I was going to contact Skål and ask them if Luis Lui fits their member profile. □I don't think destroying people's lives, trying to steal all their money and sometimes killing them is a good way to promote "Global Tourism and Friendship." □My dealings with Luis made it 100% certain that I will never return to Macau, and I don't consider him my friend. □Can you believe this hypocrite? I also don't think human sex slave trafficking is a topic of common interest with other Skal members. Luis Lui is the Antichrist of International Goodwill and Friendship, but this is just one of many examples of the level of hypocrisy displayed by this man and his criminal organization. □The Triads in Macau will treat you like family and smile at you in a convincing manner and wait a very long time until your guard is completely down and also after they studied you for months from hacking you before they will attack. Still, once they attack, they will never stop; they will keep coming and coming no matter how many times you escape their grip. □They are like Herpes; you can't get rid of them once they latch on.

The Luis Lui he doesn't want you to know.

In early 2010, I originally discovered who Luis Lui was through pure chance when I was having drinks with a Westerner in Macau that had high-end business and political connections in Macau and lived there since before the Casinos were built. □He showed me the business card (which I took a picture of) and said, "Do you know who this is?" □I said no, and he proceeded to tell me that this guy owns more than 95% of the Saunas in Macau and is the most powerful guy in Macau but that he likes to fly completely under the radar, so you won't see him flashing around like the Notorious Triad Gangster Wan Kuok-Koi nicknamed "Broken Tooth" that was just released from prison. He told me that Broken Tooth answers to Luis Lui.

I sometimes wonder if Broken Tooth is there as a diversion to protect the anonymity of Luis Lui. □If you Google "Macau Triad Broken Tooth," you will see that he craves attention in a way that seems excessive for somebody that is supposedly a criminal trying to keep away from the grasp of the Chinese Government who exerts almost absolute power over Macau even though Macau is its own separate sovereignty. Maybe the whole personality and power are designed by Luis Lui as a diversion, but that is just a theory. I don't have evidence of that other than a very educated guess. □I think it's odd that a guy supposedly as powerful as broken tooth doesn't own even one Sauna and these saunas pull in hundreds of millions in revenue per year. Add to that the fact that he is always in the media and drives a purple Lamborghini makes it look like the whole thing is staged to keep Luis Lui and others hid from the public spotlight.

See https://bit.ly/dprefernyt where a N.Y. Times article from 15 years ago talks about how eager Broken Tooth was to jump at any opportunity to be in the spotlight. Here's a quote taken directly from that link:

"HONG KONG— When Henry Fong Ping first met the man who would become the subject of his latest film, he was so filled with fear he could not speak. Wan Kuok-koi, also known as "Broken Tooth"

Koi, is said to be the top triad boss in Macau, the tiny Portuguese colony neighboring Hong Kong. Last fall, Fong approached him about lending his life story to a Hong Kong gangster movie. Wan, who drives a purple Lamborghini, wears smart three-piece suits and a diamond bracelet, and has a distinct flair for self-promotion, did not hesitate. The answer was yes. "N.Y. Times June 11th, 1998

Back to my conversation with the Westerner: He said everybody that "really" knows Luis Lui is scared to death of him, and since he likes to keep a low profile, he isn't listed publicly as the owner of any Sauna. □Publicly he wants everybody to believe that he is entirely legitimate and only owns a Restaurant, a Travel Agency, and a couple of Beauty Salons. Still, I would be amazed if these admitted businesses he owns account for even 1% of what he makes from the businesses he doesn't want anyone to know about, which include:

- The Saunas (More than 50 in Macau alone)
- Illegal human trafficking all over the world.
- Illegal drugs
- Blackmail
- Corporate and High Net Worth Individual Espionage.
- Extortion in many forms.
- Body-part Trafficking

I heard this from several different reliable sources that would be in a position to know, plus the fact that the super-hackers only cared about purging Luis Lui's business card picture from my Terabytes of Hard Drives. This shows me that these criminals only cared about protecting Luis Lui, the secretive Triad Godfather, probably one of the most Powerful Mobsters in Asia. I'm sure he wouldn't be able to corner the entire sauna Market and keep the Hundreds of Millions of Dollars a year that these Saunas generate without Broken Tooth or some other Gangster muscling their way in unless he had the power to keep them out. □Luis Lui is the Triad equivalent of John Gotti.

Below is a picture of Luis Lui in 2011, where he was on the Committee for the Macau Moto Speedway Race. □Like I said, Luis Lui projects himself as though he is an honest, productive member of society but the crimes he commits behind the scenes rival those of a serial killer as to their evilness and lack of empathy whatsoever. He is a Narcissist with no conscious and anybody traveling to SE Asia needs to be aware of who these people are and how they operate to protect themselves.

I saw Luis Lui in person only one time from a distance back in 2010 in the Eighteen Sauna, and it was almost surreal to watch the workers as they scurried around very nervous the whole time. He was there but then relaxed and sat around a few minutes after he left. □Luis was the Boss all right; no customer would arouse such apparent fear in more than 30 workers as they strolled through. □I'm just amazed that he can keep who he is so private; I assume it is because victims are not lucky enough to know he was behind their demise (if they even lived), or they would be too scared to mention it even if they knew. □I'm very good with computers, and I almost didn't think I was being hacked. □I was a Lawyer before I started my own software company in California but needed to hire programmers for the coding part. Still, I know computers and have good computer common sense when trying to troubleshoot issues. □I was usually the one to steer the programmers in the right direction for every problem that arose. Still, their tactics are so stealth and hidden and never detected by any Virus Program, so discovering it was not easy, and the programmers I knew were at a loss for words when I tried to get them to help me solve it.

LUIS LUI

HOW TO PROTECT YOUR PHONE AND COMPUTER WHILE IN ASIA

All it takes is for one of them to plug a USB thumb drive into your computer for 5 seconds, and they will own you: □Computers, Smart Phones, Routers, and anything that connects to the Internet. □Never leave your laptop or phone unattended in Asia, and always use a locking briefcase to hold these items when you go to sleep, in addition to avoiding Wi-Fi. The safest route to take is to use your cellular connection for the Internet.□That will shut down about 95% of the ways they have to get you infected initially, at least. □If you already think you may be infected after visiting there, save yourself the hassle and sell everything you have on eBay that connects to the Internet, including any USB flash drives you either had over there or plugged into a device you used over there because they use these to spread the infection to take over other devices you didn't even take to Asia. Once you completely stop using the devices, or sold them, start fresh and buy all new computers, routers, smartphones, and USB storage devices and create a new email I.D., Apple ID, etc. They are also using your Apple ID and email address to access new devices you set up by hacking Apple or your email provider. □I know this sounds extreme, but I've spent over 2500 hours trying to get rid of these leeches, and I wish I would have done what I'm telling you a long time ago. □My Ex suggested that I buy all new devices and get a new Apple ID when I was in Vietnam when she was more loyal to me than them, but I didn't listen or understand why until now.

Macau's Criminal Underworld

Luis Lui's Triad Soldiers are Sworn to Silence as to who he is and will go to any length to keep it hidden. □Anybody that doesn't protect the identity of this Godfather will simply disappear, as I was told by a girl he enslaves.

I emailed John and "7" the business card of Luis Lui in early 2010 and said that this guy owns all the Saunas in Macau. □They didn't reply at all, which was strange because they were trying to kiss my ass the whole time to forward the scam up to that point and after, and would always reply to me within minutes. □Hong was loving me at the time and wasn't as loyal to the Triads like she usually was and told me that "7" and John would never admit who the Big Boss "Godfather" was, which I took as a tacit admission from her that he was the Boss. Since I told her "7" and John didn't answer me on the direct statement I made to "7" and John about him being the big Boss, her response "in my opinion" basically answered the question, but to be sure I asked her directly and she just smiled at me and walked away. Luis Lui obviously makes it clear that he doesn't want people knowing he is the Godfather because why else would everybody sidestep answering me. I asked 7 in person a month later when I was in Macau, and I watched as her face turned white, and she stuttered something and turned away and went and turned up the radio and started dancing right away to make sure I couldn't re-ask the question.

I know you are probably wondering why they got so nervous and fell apart or were silent rather than say no and lie as they do about everything else; the reason for that is that they knew I had a good source telling me he was the Godfather. Not many people know that, so they were scared to lose their credibility by saying something that I knew was not true. This also told me that Luis personally signed off on destroying my life since they would never have proceeded with the scam against me without making sure I wasn't off-limits since I had Luis Lui's business card.

They were clever and intelligent but not good under pressure; it was easy for me to turn the tables on their entire organization once I knew I was at war because they can't adjust quickly if their plan fails. They are cowards, so they need to spend a lot of time going over details before feeling comfortable to execute, so once I added a fast-paced "chaos theory" based fighting style to the game, they were always on their heels. I was able to fend off over 100 of them over eight months because I wasn't scared to fight back and quickly reacted to threats as they occurred in a loud & aggressive way during that insane eight months from April to December 2011 after the Airplane Scam. □I also taunted them the entire time to pull them out of their comfort zone. □I knew the Triads were listening to me through my computers because I could see a constant stream of Skype traffic being routed throughout my network. To taunt them, I did things like play "Chucky" by Bushwick Bill from the Geto Boys on repeat for three weeks straight since I knew they had to listen if they heard a noise to see what I was saying. It made their job 100 times harder, not to mention having to listen to that song on repeat the entire time, ha-ha. □I also put screensavers on my computers saying, "Get a job mafia loser," since I knew they had my computers hacked. □I did it both for pleasure and the mental warfare aspect of it. □I knew they had me in the computer area, so I had to even the tables in other ways to coax them out of the shadows to get a better idea of who my enemy was. □

Chucky – Watch at bit.ly/dprefer15 or at “Section 1”

Luis Lui doesn't want you to know that he owns the Saunas since a big part of their business is scamming the patrons. □Even though saunas are legal in Macau, Luis Lui hides that he is the owner because he preys upon his customers and tries to extract every dollar he can for his criminal organization. □The Saunas may be legal, but the way Luis Lui runs them is 100% illegal. □

Here are some more facts about Luis Lui that were told to me by one of the seven girls I talked about earlier:

Luis has many underage girls working there with fake passports saying they are 18 when some are as young as 15. □Hong used to run errands for her friend "7" and go pick up 4 to 6 passports at a time; now I know why she was doing it instead of these girls getting their passports. □The Passports Hong picked up were for the underage girls. □I didn't find this out until mid-2012, after I already moved back to America. Luis doesn't care if it is a Vietnamese Document that was forged since it's something that can't come back to him, like a document originating from Macau where he can more easily be implicated since that is where the business is located. □As you will learn about Luis Lui, he makes sure everybody but him takes the risk and will exact monumental punishment upon those in his organization that does not shelter him entirely from any involvement. □If they can get through customs with the fake documents, he feels safe and encourages these practices.

Luis Lui fully supports and advocates scamming the customers whenever the girls can. They are assigned "Scam Managers" (I BULLSHIT YOU NOT) like a sales manager that coordinates and motivates the girls to find ways to scam any customer they can. □ But since they are cowards, they pick and choose their victims very carefully and sometimes wait years to execute their scams if need be. □It's not only westerners, but she also told me that they scam Asians if the Asian lives more than 100 miles away due to the risk of rumors spreading if it was a local person. □The basic approach is always the same, although the ending varies. □The girls are taught how to get mainly Western Men to fall in love with them where they attempt to get the guy to fall in love so they can hack his computers, learn about him and patiently wait until they scam or kill him for his money. They usually blackmail the guy, who is too scared to report it due to embarrassment and fear of the Triads. Sometimes they plant drugs on the guy or even kill them if they think nobody will notice, at which point they sell his body parts. She told me that they started doing this on occasion, starting back in 2009. □The amazing part is that Luis Lui started investing in Surgery Centers throughout China and Vietnam in 2010, which I learned through the grapevine from a reliable source at the time. □I didn't think anything of the Surgery Centers until the girl told me that Luis is involved in Black-Market Organ Trafficking. □She didn't know if he was getting surgery centers for that reason. Still, it makes sense given the fact that he can have the premises used after hours to chop up bodies or have his hackers monitor who is in the surgery center and what blood type they are, etc. so they can send a hit squad to go shopping should the need for a $100,000 heart arise. □I'm just guessing on that part, but I believe the Body Part claim from her because Hong told me she was scared our son would get kidnapped and that they chop babies up for their organs. □This was around the time she was helping me in July 2011, so it makes sense that they made that threat to get her to go along with the scam on me. □Luis Lui is the Devil; I have never even seen a monster portrayed on Television that is eviler than this guy. □The girl either didn't know or wouldn't say if that was the original plan for either my son or me, but given Hong's outburst on the subject plus the fact that my money was in cash form that they had access to makes me think that their plans for me were to harvest my organs to make even more money from me. There was no need for an actual body to allow Hong to get my assets from being my Wife via my estate since everything I had was in a cash form in Vietnam in my house. I could have disappeared forever, and their scam would still have been a success since it was all in cash. Still, my ex resisted since I was the father of our son, so they appeased her and tried to frame me instead on the flight from Hong Kong to HCMC, but I escaped that only to have several murder attempts against me in the months that followed.

The girl told me that Luis runs the Saunas like a concentration camp and has the sauna girls beaten and sells them as lifelong sex slaves in Mongolia, Korea, or Indonesia if they refuse to scam the western guys when called upon to do so. □Other girls had simply disappeared when they did something wrong, leaving all the girls that work for Luis Lui in absolute fear of their lives.

The girl said it's common to delay "showtime" at the Saunas from 10 to 30 minutes from its regular 30 to 60-minute interval (depending on the Sauna). Luis Lui wants to make sure his top English-speaking girls are there when the western guys come back and watch "showtime" to maximize the girl's chances of landing him as a scam target since some guys only come once and leave forever. □They want to make sure they have the best girls on the floor to increase the fact that the guy will fall in love. They don't leave any money on the table; they want it all. □She told me that there is a better chance of the guy loving a girl he can communicate with. If the top English-speaking girls are busy, they will delay ShowTime or not let the English-speaking girl go out for ShowTime if the Western guy doesn't walk back there. They want to make sure they are available if he decides to come and see the next ShowTime in 30 minutes since the girl spends 60 minutes with the guy that picks her. □Luis Lui's organization is lying in wait like a pack of rabid dogs waiting for any opportunity to scam everything from his paying customers, and this guy is already a Billionaire. This was all said to me by the girl he enslaved—one of the girls who cared about me. Keep in mind that I heard similar warnings from people who lived there and were able to know. □This was not just a random claim from one girl. Since publishing this information on a now-retired blog, I have had one Asian guy, and two Western Guys contact me, giving me information about how they were scammed while in Macau.

She also told me that Luis Lui has Wireshark (a hacking program at https://bit.ly/dpreferwire) running in his Saunas on the free Wi-Fi network so his people can spy and gain access to a customer's computers. □She said they have a sauna worker signal when the guy goes online to determine which computer is his by connection time since sometimes more than 50 patrons are using the Wi-Fi connection at any time.

She told me that he has the girls beaten if they call off work for anything other than their menstrual cycle and forces them to have sex with up to 8 guys a day if they are popular enough to be picked that many times. The girls are beaten if they refuse. She said that if the Sauna suspects a girl is lying, they will force her to come into work, and a manager will physically put his finger in her and check that she is truly on her menstrual cycle. □She said that 25% or more of the girls always have black & blue marks from being beaten but that it is even worse than that since usually, the managers punch them in the head where their hair covers up the bruises. The beatings are so often that many managers get out of hand, throw them into walls, and cause visible marks on their bodies.

Every guy, not just westerners, is a potential mark when they enter the saunas. □Below is a pic of Kieu and an Asian Guy they scammed; notice how he has flowers for the girls. □This was inside 7's house; only scam targets (like me) get invited there! I was told by Guang Lin "AKA John Lam" that some guy gave Kieu $90.000 US just to give it to her and that Nhung had a guy give her $100,000 US just to give it to her and that the girls went back to Vietnam for a few months after getting the money. □The girl who recently told me everything told me that the money they got was the amount scammed from the victim; they do this all the time. □Aside from Blackmail & Extortion, which are their most popular scams, she said that they usually execute the "framing" scams that involve corrupt Police in Vietnam since there are so many willing participants. Luis would rather keep the "framing" scams away from Macau to assure he doesn't attract publicity. Still, she said "framing" scams are executed there too, as a last resort. □The Blackmail and Extortion scams are usually perpetrated against the men when they return to the United States if the Triads can get hidden video or information that would embarrass the victim. These scams do not require police involvement to pull off, plus they do not need the guy to live in Asia, so keep that in mind when you visit Asia. It happens to people that only "visit" the most; moving there is not a requirement for them to target you; it just makes it easier for them because they have more options if you live there.

Some of you are probably thinking, "Why Didn't You Just Leave?" Well, it wasn't that easy. □I had approximately $1.5 Million in Chinese cash total in my house that my ex stole my customs declaration form for, so I couldn't leave the country with the cash without giving most of it to the Vietnamese Government. I had my entire household moved there. I had my dogs, and most importantly, my son that I had with her after moving there. □The reason I had $1.5 Million in Chinese Yuan was that the Yuan was undervalued by 40% according to some reliable estimates at the time and, back then, the Bank of China wouldn't allow a non-citizen to keep Yuan in the bank, so I had to take the U.S. Dollars I had in the Bank of China account and exchange them for Chinese Yuan and keep the money in my house since Bank of China wouldn't let me keep Chinese Currency at that time. □It has changed since, but that's why I did it, to begin with. □There was nothing illegal about the money or that I had it in my house; it was an investment. □□I claimed the cash with Vietnam customs when I brought it from Macau to Saigon "HCMC" on December 17th, 2010. The law in Vietnam allows you to leave the country with money you claimed when you came into Vietnam, provided you had proof that you claimed it upon arrival. The Triads knew this, so they instructed my ex to find and steal my custom declaration.

KIEU WITH UNKNOWN VICTIM

The Money I Brought into Vietnam from Macau.

Watch at bit.ly/dprefer16 or at "Section 1"

The guy I circled below was a Triad Garbage bag that worked directly under Luis Lui. I was told that he would take out the sauna girls that they trafficked whenever one of them pulled off a big-money scam with the Triad's help and guidance, of course. He rewarded them with an expensive night out anytime they helped accomplish a significant scam on one of the clients that went to the Sauna. The girls only got about 20% of the take even though they did most of the work.

Shadow Enemies Everywhere

I had tons of derogatory evidence against them everywhere on my computers. Even though I blogged about only Hong and her friends from December 2011 to November 2012, none of the derogatory evidence I had on Hong and her friends in my Evernote account or on my computers was ever missing. Only Luis Lui's business card kept disappearing. □I decided to experiment and searched my 30 or so hard drives and was able to locate that business card in an encrypted hard drive. □I started saving it in different folders on my computer and would make a note to check those drives every few days. □I stored the business card with evidence I had on the Vietnamese and other random files and noted how many files I had in each directory. □I monitored and repopulated these folders over the next three months from March 2012 to July 2012 and even changed the file's name that was the image of Luis Lui's business card and noticed that only the business card kept disappearing but nothing else. □I even saved it with different dates, and no matter what date or name it was under, it would disappear. □I realized that the reason the Triads waited so long to hack me was that they didn't think I would ever escape Vietnam, so their Elite Hackers didn't get involved until I left Vietnam because it wasn't until then that they were scared as to what I knew about their Boss. They put the best hackers on the job to make sure I wasn't going to expose the guy who has somehow kept secret that he is the Triad Godfather who owns all of the saunas in Macau. □

The fact that I wrongly assumed that only Hong's criminal gang in Vietnam was scamming me while still in Vietnam saved my life. Suppose I was mumbling that Luis Lui was the Godfather behind the scam on me while still in Vietnam. In that case, I assure you that they would have made sure I died and not allowed the low-level criminals to do a job that the Triads didn't feel too strongly about at the time since it seemed Luis Lui's identity would be protected. □ They still wanted to kill me but didn't put too many people on the job since Luis Lui seemed protected. □My ex had a hit-squad come for me only one week before I returned to America. Still, I sensed the danger when she tried to lock me in the house to prevent me from going to a hotel and then even had the hotel give me a room off the property, saying that the main building was full when it wasn't even the busy season. □I kept protesting until they gave me a room in the main building at triple the going rate hoping I would say no, but I said yes. Even though I was in the main building of a 3-star Hotel in Mui Ne, Vietnam, the whole night people kept coming and knocking on the door, and my ex received a phone call from her sister at 2 AM that night even though I never saw her sister call her after 10 PM in the two years I knew her. □Below is my room card from that evening. □Even a 3-star hotel was easily talked into helping scam an American. The hotel was dead, but they tried to put me outside of the main building at the request of the people scamming me.

This is the 3-Star Hotel I stayed at in Mui Ne where the employee helped my enemies by attempting to put me in a bungalow on the edge of the property that wasn't in the main building even though it was the slow season and they had plenty of rooms.

novela muine

14 - The War Games in America

July 2012-Their Deception Has No Limit.

After being home for eight months, I used Match.com on the Internet and was contacted by an attractive Chinese Graduate Student. □I wasn't aware that they had me hacked as bad as they did, but they knew I was on Match.com in Pittsburgh even though they thought I lived in Florida (so I thought). □They had the girl pose as somebody interested in dating me. □I thought it was too easy to bring that girl home after we had dinner because it was her that suggested driving an hour back to my house after we finished our first date when I was saying goodbye, which was weird given how far it was and the fact that it was only the first date. □Her name was LeHong (so she said), her picture is below. □I went out with her one more time after that night when the following day, I caught her in my backyard taking pictures with her phone while returning from taking my dogs for a walk. □She was doing recon for the Triads. □I figured out what was going on and said to Hong on a Video call using Yahoo Messenger that I was thankful for the Chinese Girl they sent me a few weeks ago so that I could see her reaction. □Hong froze and went completely silent for 10 seconds and then acted like she didn't even hear me and tried to change the subject.

The Chinese girl in the picture below also wrote down my MAC ID on my Cable Modem when I was in the shower because, after that day, the hacking was so bad that every Windows or Apple update I downloaded was corrupted. □I called Comcast and spoke with Tier 2 support in the Security Department and brainstormed with the guy until he discovered a 2nd cable modem on their network with my same Mac ID that was a different model Cable Modem altogether. Still, when I had him send a refresh signal, it didn't work until he sent it the 2nd time because the Triads had the Cable modem clone between my house and Comcast main connection and spoofed Comcast's I.P. Address for the DNS. Hence, my router looked to their rogue servers for all web page requests, which they routed to fake Google, Apple, and Microsoft servers containing update files infected with their hack. □This caused the first refresh signal to knock their modem offline long enough for my connection to grab DNS from Comcast to be directly connected to Comcast, which explains why the second refresh signal worked on my modem the way it should have. □They were intercepting every bit of internet traffic coming to and from my house; the guy at Comcast was in awe as we pondered about how clever and impressive the hack was. □ He was in the security department and never heard of such a thing in his years at Comcast.

I went out with a girl a few times with a broken laptop that I fixed for her and updated at my house. They had my cable modem cloned during that time, but I haven't talked to her in months but recently said hello, and we started chatting. Within 24 hours of us conversing, she told me how her computer and iPhone were going crazy and took screenshots of what was occurring. It was the same stuff that was happening to me before I got it under control and replaced my cable modem. The Triads must have had a built-in alert set-up on her computer that looked for websites I frequented or had specific keywords or phone numbers entered with the keyboard, sending them a message alerting them that a computer was either being used by me or somebody that talks to me. We decided it was best not to speak anymore, and I instructed her on the steps she needed to do to eradicate the hack.

My love affair with the Triads on Match.com didn't stop with the Chinese Girl; they also had a Vietnamese girl contact me that I gave my phone number to about a week after I figured out that the Triads planted the Chinese girl but before I gave Hong a heads-up that I onto their games. I gave her my number to see how they would handle it because I assumed they sent her since I didn't call the Chinese girl back for about five days, and this girl contacted me out of nowhere. She called me three times a day for a couple of days until I finally answered, and she told me she was at the Airport, but can she call me later when she landed. I said yes, and she called me that night around 10 PM when I was out with my friend, and I didn't answer but waited until 2 AM and called her and just let the phone ring once and hung up. She immediately called me back four times, one after the other, since I wouldn't answer. I sent her a text message that said, "tell the Triads that I said.... Du Me ..." which means "Fuck your mother" in Vietnamese, and she didn't reply or call me ever again.

Here Comes Thunder Turd!

About a month later, a guy contacts me on Match.com and starts talking shit right away and said something that was meant for me to know who he was the messenger for since only the Triads knew what he told me regarding an iPhone I had over in Asia. Still, the guy was blonde-haired and had a complete profile talking about how he has two daughters with pictures of them too and is looking for the right girl. This goes to the level of deception they employ in their scams when they take the time to fill out a profile to make sure it's not apparent that it's coming from the Triads in Asia. Even the guy's screen name is related to the Triads because the Triad's code of conduct, "which you can Google," says that anybody violating their secret pledge will be struck down by 36 Thunderbolts or something along those lines. Still, the word Thunder is mentioned dozens of times, so this losers' choice of the screen name Thunder Buddy was no accident. I just referred to him as Thunder Turd because it popped in my head when I saw his screen name, and it stuck after that, so I called him by that name as we threw verbal blows back and forth for about a week before I lost interest. Remember, they are a secret society, and they play that role to the tee. The guy mentions in the message that he sent me "pictured below" that it's not too far to drive to Mountainview to let me know that they knew where I lived. It was right around that time I decided it was time to go to war with these assholes. Their attempts to scare me only empowered me and gave me the resolve to fight them. I don't scare easy, especially on my home turf. I told him to get ready for Phase 2, at which point I quietly took down my blog about Hong and her criminal conspirators in Vietnam and started to write the complete story that includes both the Triads and their partners globally.

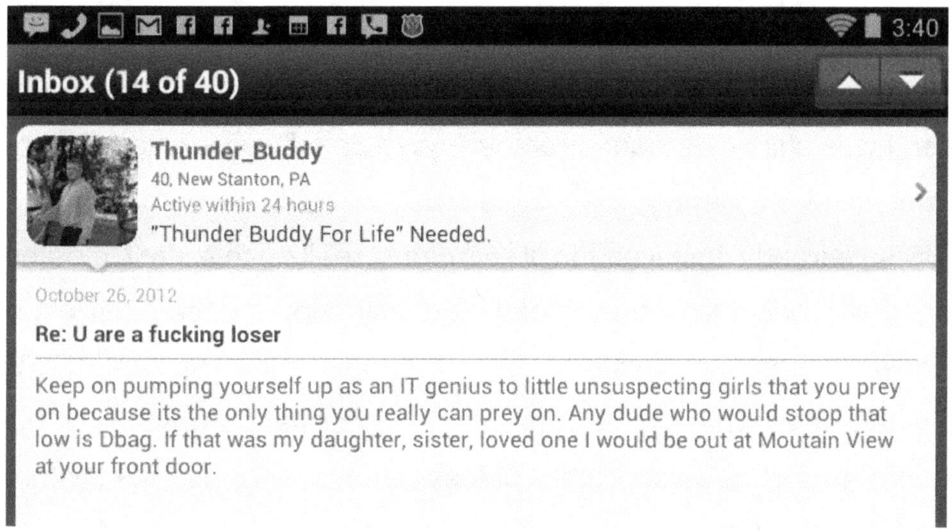

Getting Stalked on eBay!

A couple of months after they hacked my cable internet, I finally stopped being stubborn and decided it was time to get rid of everything I had over in Vietnam as far as electronics goes. I always had a sneaking suspicion that they implanted some kind of Nanodevice in something I had over there that would secretly send out Wi-Fi and Bluetooth malicious code. No matter what I did, every computer and phone I had were hacked within a day of having it. When I was still in Vietnam, there was an Apple Reseller store I went to that fixed my laptop and ended up giving it back to me with NTFS3G already installed on it. I didn't realize this until months later. Still, originally, they controlled my Apple Computers via Windows Operating System, but Windows runs on an NTFS formatted drive while Apple runs on HFS+ formatted drives. NTFS and HFS+ can't see each other unless you install a fuse file system that allows the two to interact with each other by sharing the same directories etc. There was no reason for that program NTFS3G to be on my computer because it is not included in Apple's Operating Systems and is aftermarket software. Like every other business I went to in Vietnam, the guy at that store helped the corrupt police and installed the hack before giving me the computer back. The guy at that store, out of nowhere, said that he heard they are hacking power supplies now. I realized later that he did that to see my reaction because that's how they were reinfecting me. They had a "Trasp Device" as I mentioned earlier with Hong's friend Hanh when she was searching for that word on Hong's computer that sent pulses throughout my electric grid in my house and somehow hacked into all my devices and radioed home to their rogue server so they could access it. They spliced my firewire port on my Apple Computers, and anytime I got a new Apple Computer, I would see a firewire connection become active out of nowhere. I ended up figuring out which device they planted it in but still sold everything just to play it safe.

The crazy part is that 75% of my items for sale on eBay were purchased by Asian names that just signed up for eBay that week. I thought it was more than a sheer coincidence that three different Asian people felt compelled to sign-up for eBay for the first time just to buy my used junk that was three years old or more. UPS called me after I shipped one of the items and said the address was wrong, so I called the guy for the correct address, and he stuttered and got very nervous. He said he would email it to me later and that he didn't know it. I emailed him the next day and said that UPS has his "Trasp Device." That's all I said, and he replied with the text message telling me that I still need to send the item even though the address was wrong. I laughed and responded by asking him why he thought I wouldn't send it? I didn't say anything that would have aroused suspicion with a non-guilty person because 99.99% of the population doesn't know what "Trasp" means, and even if they did, they would have asked what I meant by Trasp device if they were innocent. This guy was working for the Triads, and I easily set him up to clarify that fact. This guy had the nerve to say he wanted to return it because parts were missing. I told him that they are speakers that I unplugged from my computer with the cables still attached and put right in the box I shipped it in. I then told him how I know he is with the Triads, and he started to laugh nervously. I told him to fuck off, and he never asked to return it since, nor did he file a claim with eBay. Maybe they would put anthrax in the box, hoping I would open it; who knows. The picture below is the text he sent me. I saved his name as "Triad Loser." The phone is an old phone because I got tired of them hacking my iPhones, so I went to a 6-year-old non-smartphone that I knew they couldn't hack.

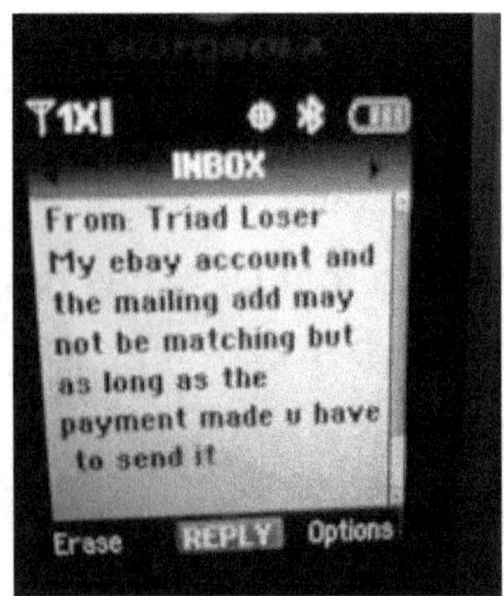

As of 2013, I had gotten the hacks somewhat under control, but they always seem to gain access to my computers, so I don't want to say I won yet. □I will tell you this though; one of the ways they gain access to your computer is by using USB Flash drives formatted as FAT16 with a boot flag that executes DOS code from 1998. I was shocked when I realized that the MBR on my hard drive was read-only. The only thing that could overwrite a read-only MBR is a DOS Based Floppy drive where you can overwrite the MBR on the infected hard drive by replacing it with the DOS-based MBR that is almost like modern MBR's. MBR stands for Master Boot Record and is the code that is initially referred to when a computer receives power.

NOVEMBER 6TH, 2012 - Time to Poke the Devil

On November 6th, 2012, I decided I would contact Luis Lui just before I released the blog about him. The email pictured on the left below was my first direct communication with Luis Lui, to which I got no response. I then waited for more than a month to contact him again, which I did after that girl told me everything, of which I already knew 80% of, but she confirmed the stuff I knew and told me things I didn't know, like how they initially planned on killing me and threatened to kill my son if Hong didn't play by their rules. She also confirmed that they did get the approval from Luis to scam me after they knew I had his business card, to which Luis said it's ok to scam me because he didn't know me or care who I was. So, after finding out this additional information and validating the things I already knew through undeniable circumstantial evidence, I thought about it for a few days and got extremely angry and sent the email pictured on the right below, on December 15th, 2012. I got no response to that email either.

EMAIL #1

EMAIL #2

You are a piece of shit Luis Inbox x

Edward 12/15/12
to Luis, bcc: me

You scam your own paying customers and terrorize little girls you fucking coward. But worst of all you are terrified of people knowing who you really are Turd Father. I know about your black market body part business too you fucking Monkey. One of your girls told me and the FBI everything. Hahaaaaa

Time mother fucker. Time

Ten days after the second email, I decided to start sending him text messages. I used Skype to send the text messages since they were international and not able to be sent by my cell carrier at the time. I know he got them because if Skype can't deliver the SMS, it will say "failed," but every message I sent to Luis went through within 15 seconds of me hitting the send button. The messages said the same type of stuff I said in the two emails. See a record of those messages below.

I never got a reply to the SMS messages I sent in December 2012 either. I sent Luis another SMS message on January 10th, 2013, and three more the very next day on January 11th. However, on the 11th, I decided to call Luis since he still didn't respond to me, so I called four times on the 11th, but you can't see the calls listed because the phone just rang and rang until I hung up after the 10th ring or so. Cell phone service in Macau doesn't have voicemail and will just ring 10 to 15 times before you get a recording from the cell phone provider that says the person is unavailable. I didn't wait to get that recording and waste paying for a call, so I hung up after 8 to 10 rings and just called back a few hours later on the 11th. The next day I called and was surprised to hear an answering service pick up the phone. Either it was sheer coincidence, or Luis got an answering service not to have to worry about answering the phone if I called. I'm sure he got a new phone and just gave that phone to the answering service to answer for him.

Luis never once replied to an email, a text message, or returned a phone call. If Luis wasn't the Godfather and didn't have a guilty conscience (not that he feels guilty about anything), why didn't he at least reply once, even by email or text message, and say, "Who are you? Don't you find that strange? I don't actually; these people are cowards that do evil things if the spotlight is not shining on them, but once you pull them out into the open, they are predictable and hide inside any crack they can find.

SKYPE CALL RECORD #1

https://secure.sk... Ident... Your Skype account overvie...
Search Norton Safe Web Share Vault Open Login Assistant
ert Select
ember 2012 December 2012 Janu

w All

time	Item	Type	Rate/min	Duration	A
30 00:54	+85366662266 , Macao - Mobile	SMS	$0.097	1	$
25 03:52	+85366662266 , Macao - Mobile	SMS	$0.097	1	$
25 03:51	+85366662266 , Macao - Mobile	SMS	$0.097	2	$
25 03:48	+85366662266 , Macao - Mobile	SMS	$0.097	2	$

SKYPE CALL RECORD #2

https://secure.sk... Skyp... Your Skype account overvie...
Search Norton Safe Web Share Vault Open Login Assistant
Convert Select

I called several times also on January 11th and the phone only rang and rang. The very next day Luis miraculously had an answering service active from day forward.

Date, time	Item		Rate/min	Duration	Amou
Jan 25 18:50	+85366662		$0.097	1	$0.0
Jan 25 05:21	+85366662266		$0.097	1	$0.0
Jan 12 04:59	+85366662266 , Macao - Mobile	Call	$0.095	03:15	$0.4
Jan 12 04:59	+85366662266 , Macao - Mobile	Call	$0.095	00:00	$0.0
Jan 11 15:06	+85366662266 , Macao - Mobile	SMS	$0.097	4	$0.3
Jan 11 15:01	+85366662266 , Macao - Mobile	SMS	$0.097	3	$0.2
Jan 11 14:55	+85366662266 , Macao - Mobile	SMS	$0.097	3	$0.2
Jan 10 04:45	+85366662266 , Macao - Mobile	SMS	$0.097	1	$0.0

I was able to hack these bastards myself back in 2012. I started to obtain tons of evidence on how these Triad scumbags operate, even though I didn't realize the significance of some of their communications at the time. As I said before, Hollywood's portrayal of Asian Gangsters is inaccurate. The gangsters at the top wear suits and don't look like criminals at all. Luis Lui was a complete shitbag with his hands in every illegal business under the sun (including organ trafficking). Luis Lui operated his illegal businesses in plain sight. Notice how his assistant "Erling" even had a Yahoo account. The part you do not see, though, is that Luis was a dirtbag Triad buying medical centers throughout Asia. Luis had no experience in the medical space but started buying up facilities and starting new facilities throughout Asia. According to my reliable sources, he bought these centers to expand his organ harvesting business. Hearts and Kidneys alone fetch over $100,000 U.S. each. While legitimate medical procedures may have happened during the day, this trash bag had disco-drugged, passed out people being brought in at night to take out their organs and sell them on the black market.

These scumbags even threatened my Ex once when she wasn't playing ball with them by setting me up by saying they would cut up and sell my son. The thought of these shitbags touching my son at all, let alone killing him, angered me to no end. My Ex told me in a roundabout way by saying she was scared for our son because they do this in Vietnam, and she saw it on the news, but her fear was evident. I knew someone must have threatened her for her to be panicked the way she was instantly. I have solid contacts in addition to the email proof to support this claim about organ harvesting. Pay attention to this lapdog Erling's wording in this email pictured in the image below. He even capitalizes the word "VERY," which is a wink-wink that means, "You know Luis is a powerful Triad piece of shit and can get anything approved." Remember that Luis only owned a small Chinese restaurant, a travel agency, and a hair salon on paper. This guy Erling is signaling that Luis is a powerhouse that can get anything done. The recipient of this email knew that too. Sole Chinese restaurant owners don't have that kind of clout; read between the lines.

Macao medical

Erling Pedersen <erlingip@hotmail.com> Mon, Oct 18, 2010, 8:40 PM
to Jeffery

Jeffery
I have talked to Luis about our idea and he would like to hear from you what you have in mind. He is definetely interested in doing a clinic project with your group. He mentioned that we could build a new facility to accomodate everything needed. It may be easier to do than to try to fit it into the LSL medical center.
I have been extremely busy in the clinic lately, creating quite a stir/interest around what I do. I will get back to Bobby with more material for him to read. The next step is really to define det scope of the new clinic complex - such as what will we treat there, how large a facility is needed, equipment, etc. A get together of the minds seems to be in order.
Let me know how you would like to proceed. The way Luis works is that he expects a proposal to be given to him in the form of a personal presentation of the project. Then he begins to act. A written proposal sent to him will take a long time for him to react on. He is so busy that he does not get to read all his e.mails very often. When I said what you had old me that you would make the project so Luis would not have to manage it but would be the door opener, and be part of it, he liked that. We will put the management team together and run it, and he would facilitate getting us positioned the right way here and in China. He is VERY good at that.
Erling

How I came up with the "turd" nickname for the triads

I made the video on the left in late 2012 and sent it to Triad Underling John Lam. Keep in mind that I went back to Asia 2 times after this video! If you don't understand why they hate me so much, this should convince you, lol.

Watch at bit.ly/dprefer17 or at “Section 1”

Part 2 – 2014-2021

15 – Hello Again Hong "2014"

I spent the remainder of 2013 and the first half of 2014 fighting Chinese hackers from my home in Pennsylvania, constantly being in a rage over what had happened to where I always fantasized about killing my ex and others involved in Asia. It was a very dark time for sure. Then, almost out of nowhere, in May 2014, I suddenly decided to forgive Hong and her family and wasn't angry anymore. It was almost as if God had flipped the hate switch off, and all thoughts of revenge just disappeared. I called Hong, and we started to talk again. In my mind, I somehow convinced myself that she was only evil due to pressure from the Triads and her family and that if I could just get her to America, it would be completely different. I had already written a book and had a blog detailing the information on the home page of this blog but decided I would stop selling the book and remove the blog also. I did that in June 2014 before making yet another mistake (going back to Vietnam)

Starting in May 2014, I began Face-timing Hong daily. I felt that my son needed to know who his mother is and that things would be "just perfect' if I could get her away from her evil family and the Triad scum controlling her over in Asia. After about a month of talking several times a day, I had the bright idea that if I was in Vietnam, I could move the process along with the State Department much faster. I bought a ticket for my son and me, and we flew to Vietnam on July 11th, 2014, with no set return date. I left my dogs at a kennel and set off to Vietnam with my son. Getting there was a nightmare. I missed the first flight and had to pay $1,000 extra to take a different flight, and worst of all, I wrongly assumed that I had a 5-year business visa for Vietnam when it was only a 3-year Visa, and the airline didn't notice that either whenever I checked in.

We made it to Vietnam only to be denied entry once we arrived. There was no internet in the HCMC Airport, nor did my sim card work there. I asked the guy seated next to me to locate Hong at the curb and tell her that we had a problem. Forty-five minutes later, I saw Hong walking towards us with a cop from the Airport. They wanted to send me back to Hong Kong until I could get a Visa, but Hong talked them into allowing us to stay at a government-owned and guarded hotel while we waited for the Visa to get approved. It cost me a $500 bribe, but that was much better than being forced to fly again to and from Hong Kong over 2 days. Two days later, I got my Visa and was allowed to leave the Government hotel and freely enter Vietnam.

The first five weeks there were uneventful and didn't include any drama whatsoever. We stayed at a hotel in District 6 near where her sister and husband lived and worked on getting Hong a Visa. On the 6th week, Hong said she wanted to get the drug "ice," and I said no. I told her it's not like 2011 when we had two nannies in a 7-BR house to care for our son. Still, she kept bugging me each day, telling me how her sister takes our son a few hours a day and we have plenty of time to do whatever while he isn't around, so after a few more days of her bugging me, I finally relented. I never did ice in the United States and never will, but Vietnam was so damn boring and miserable for me that it was easy to give in since I knew how fast time seemed to fly while doing ice. The picture below was taken around the time she started asking me to do ice with her.

About a week later, the bullshit started. I noticed I was being hacked, and the network settings I had manually set up on our devices kept changing (with the shadow help of Hong, of course). I ended up needing to buy a new laptop because I felt the one I had might have been firmware compromised. I randomly went to a big store and made sure to tell the guy I wanted the laptop I was pointing to on display. I figured it was safer to buy that than allow them to grab a pre-hacked one in the back. He sold it to me, but when I got it back to the hotel, I noticed the battery didn't work and that it needed to be always plugged in. Not good, since I already knew that they could access your computer through the power supply, so I unfortunately had to return it and be at their mercy as to whether they would give me a non-hacked computer. I played with the laptop for a few days but couldn't get it to run normally in a secure manner without strange processes running even when booted to a live Linux cd. So, I then decided not to use it but noticed that Hong kept plugging it in even though I had the lid closed and wasn't using it. Here we go again! Sleeping with the Enemy "Round 2".

Vietnam - July 2014

This picture was taken 3 weeks after I went back to Vietnam just before the bullshit games started again.

Surrounded on three sides

A couple of days after the store replaced the laptop, I started to hear random banging on the wall in the hotel from 1 to 2 AM. It wasn't just coming from one room either; it was sometimes coming from the room above, sometimes from the room to my right, and sometimes from the room to my left. It was becoming evident to me that the Triad trash was back. About a day or two later, I had an epiphany while fighting their hacks and changed the subnet on my device from 255.255.255.0 to 255.255.255.255. Don't ask me why; it just came to me as an idea even though I didn't understand its significance when I did it. I had five devices: 3 for me, 1 for my son, and 1 for Hong. As I changed this setting on each device, I heard a door slam or a chair get pushed from each of the three rooms within 2 seconds of me hitting "apply." I thought to myself, I don't know what that setting accomplished, but it seems to me that it cut them off from my computer, and they were reacting in anger as I "closed the door" for each device. I further knew this was significant because I kept checking my son's and Hong's machine and noticed the setting kept getting changed back to 255.255.255.0. Hong was changing it back to help these losers. I now know that this setting changed my device from accepting broadcast messages from 254 devices and reduced it to only my single device communicating with the router. They were somewhere on the network in one of the 254 addresses serving messages and commands to my devices but were cut off once I changed that setting.

The next night, at around 3 AM, they started to bang on all three walls for 5 minutes straight simultaneously. The following day, I saw that one of their doors was open while the maid was in their room and saw a girl waiting for the maid to finish. I started berating her and told her to send her pussy Triad boyfriend out to see me. He was hiding in the bathroom and didn't come out. Typical Triad, leave the woman to do the heavy lifting. Anyways, Hong's sister asked us to come to stay with them, so we moved out of the hotel the next day.

The first couple of weeks at her sisters seemed to be OK. I couldn't tell if I was hacked at first, but whenever I set up OpenDNS and linked it to the I.P. address I was connected to, I waited a few hours, checked the OpenDNS logs, and saw thousands of connections only to 1 domain, which was http://meterserver.vn. WTF! I grabbed Hong's phone and started going through the settings to see if I could find anything out of the ordinary. She had an Android phone, and I kept ending background processes while using her phone as a hotspot. One of the processes I ended caused her screen to freeze, but the hotspot was still working. Within 2 minutes, she came into the room demanding I give her the phone to play some games. I told her no and to use the iPad instead. She became increasingly angrier and wouldn't take no for an answer, at which point I knew for sure that I broke their hack and escaped their sandbox. They didn't know what I was doing and who I was contacting, so it was of the utmost importance that they regain control of the network in case I was transmitting a distress message or divulging information. I knew at that moment that it was time to leave.

I called United Airlines and asked when the next flight was leaving. They said in 2 days, so I told Hong we would move to a hotel in the morning that was closer to the airport since it was already 10 PM. I didn't want to leave the building until daylight due to the dire situation I just discovered plus the remote location of her sister's apartment. 2 hours later, Hong said that her cousin "Mi" was leaving to go back to the country where her family lived even though she had been staying at Hong's sisters for a month straight. This was the first I heard she was leaving. She asked if I could give her a ride to the bus stop for her bus ride at 1 AM. I said, "hell no." She was adamant and kept asking. I told her to call a taxi, but she kept asking until I became visibly angry. The next day we took a cab to the Park Royal Hotel near the airport, and I left with my son the following day and returned to America on November 28th, 2014, after being in Vietnam for almost five months.

Vietnam wasn't finished

I spent the remainder of 2014 arguing with Hong via facetime, trying to get her to admit to scamming me. True to form, she denied everything again and again. For reasons I can't explain yet (coming later in the story), I decided to go back "yet again" to Vietnam. Hong told me that we can stay in the ex-pat section in District 1 and that it is safe there since there are so many Westerners, etc. On February 12th, 2015, my son and I went back to Vietnam just in time for Valentine's Day for the final time.

The 2nd week we were there, we were on a motorcycle en route to eat at a restaurant when a Vietnamese guy was following us close behind. When I slowed down, he slowed down, etc. I finally just stopped and forced him to go around me. As he rode past, he kicked me, and I quickly told Hong to hold our son as I dropped the motorcycle and ran after him. The traffic was dense, so he jumped off his bike, ran into a restaurant and the kitchen area, and grabbed a large knife. I picked up a chair and attempted to move in on him like a circus trainer approaching a Lion. Several westerners came over and tried to diffuse the situation, so I decided to let the guy leave.

The hacking started soon after, and I was again erasing and reinstalling operating systems every day to escape the persistent hacks. A few days later, Hong asked if she and her cousin could take my son to visit her mom for the day since he may never see them again for years once we leave Vietnam. I said OK. Her father was at our hotel the day prior, supposedly en route to central Vietnam to visit family, and Hong asked if he could have my luggage lock to protect his suitcase. I said no; what the hell does he need it for? He only has clothes. I now know it was a ploy to plant drugs in my suitcase that I always kept locked. Hong left with my son and returned the following afternoon. The next day Hong said that she needed to go to the store but didn't return for 40 minutes. She was going to a convenience store next to the hotel, so I knew something was fishy. When she returned, I took her phone and ran a scan with a security program that I just ran 2 hours prior, only to see alarms go off saying that there were spoofed certificates installed that could perpetrate legitimate sites like Google, etc. I started screaming at her. She grabbed a knife and came at me to stab me. I grabbed her arm, and my son ran up to me and hugged me. Hong became insanely angry and screamed, "You chose him!".

I immediately called Delta and asked to be put on the next available flight. The lady from Delta said it would be eight days later and nothing was available until then. I said OK, but the call dropped before we could complete the reservation. I immediately called back, and a different lady got on the phone and told me that something was available the very next morning. Awesome, I thought. I was so grateful for the shitty Skype connection that dropped the previous call since it allowed me to leave a week sooner. Hong spent the rest of the day crying and begging me not to go, but I knew I had to get the hell out ASAP. I had to leave at 5 AM to get a Taxi. As I was waiting for a Taxi, Hong told me how she didn't have enough money to pay the bill at the hotel and needed money to live. I decided to give her $500 but as I walked up to the ATM, I changed my mind and told her to F' off.

The taxi ride was surreal. I was overcome with anger and just sat there thinking about how I needed to get the hell out of here for good. Once we got to the airport, my son ran onto the curb and didn't even say goodbye to his mother, nor did she attempt to say goodbye to him. It was very odd, but I just gave her a dirty look and proceeded into the airport and returned to the United States. Goodbye Vietnam, Goodbye.

Time for a change

After getting back to Pennsylvania, I decided to visit my friend Yanni in Vegas for a couple of days, and he and his wife kept telling me that I should move to Vegas and start my business again there. I decided to do just that and moved to Vegas on December 6th, 2015, with my son and two dogs. Get ready for a severe plot twist!

Once in Vegas, I went to find an office and signed a lease within two weeks of getting there. I was always good at making money, and it always seemed to come naturally to me, but something was different this time around. No matter what I did or whatever money I spent on marketing, everything seemed to produce nothing in return while trying to ramp up in Vegas. People didn't return phone calls, emails rarely were answered, I couldn't give away my services for free, it seemed. WTH is going on, I thought. I then created a new product that got great feedback from several people in the Auto Industry. I even closed a deal worth 1.5 million a year only to have the guy mysteriously cancel a few days later with no explanation for why. Nothing seemed to work; it didn't make sense.

FROM THIS POINT FORWARD, IF YOU DIDN'T ALREADY, I HIGHLY RECOMMEND THAT YOU OPEN THE LINK AT www.thedevilprefers.com/bookextra AND GO TO THE **SECTION 2** LABELED 2014-2021. THE AUDIO AND VIDEO FILES WILL OCCUR IN THE BOOK EVERY FEW PARAGRAPHS OR SO AND TYPING IN EACH LINK WILL BE LABORIOUS. I ORGANIZED THE PICS, AUDIO AND VIDEOS IN THE ORDER THEY APPEAR IN THE BOOK, SO PLEASE KEEP YOUR BROWSER OPEN AS YOU READ TO GET THE FULL IMPACT OF THE STORY. NOTHING IS MORE CONVINCING THAT THE ACTUAL AUDIO AND VIDEO RECORDINGS WHICH IS WHY THE BOOK PROVIDES THESE PIECES OF EVIDENCE FOR YOU TO GET THE FULL IMPACT

16 - $300 hr. Psychic? Why not

Towards the end of 2016, I received a phone call from an old friend I had fallen out with eight years prior and haven't spoken to. I was surprised to hear his voice, and we talked for quite some time. I said something to him that I never said to anyone before. I told him that I think my ex put a curse on me. The weird part was that I didn't believe in any of that stuff, so for me to say that was odd, even more bizarre was that I told it to him rather than saying it to any of the several friends I talk to regularly. When I told him that, he jumped into high gear with an animated story about how he has a friend that was married for ten years, but that she couldn't get pregnant and was constantly having health problems and that her husband used to make tons of money but was broke for the past decade, etc. He said the girl is doing great now and that she is healthy, her husband is making money, and they hope to have a baby soon. He told me that the girl was helped by a famous French psychic medium and a Muslim Witch that lived in Los Angeles, but that she was a good witch. Up until 2011, when the Vietnamese Psychic shocked me and gave me pause, I would have called b.s. immediately on anything regarding psychics and witches, but he had my full attention. He said that the French psychic helped her find out that her husband's ex-wife was putting curses on them and that the Muslim Witch cleaned her.

IMPORTANT TO NOTE: The French Psychic and the Muslim Witch didn't know each other at all, but this girl somehow found each of them to help her since they both had their skillset and she was into that kind of stuff. She had many connections that knew people in that realm. Once the French Psychic told this girl that she needed to be cleaned, she asked around and found the Muslim Witch later.

I asked him if he could connect me with the girl he was friends with, and he said yes. I called the girl immediately after hanging up with him and explained to her what my friend Eddie Swan had explained to me and if I could ask her a few questions. She said yes, and we proceeded to talk to the point where I was convinced enough and willing to risk $300 to see what this was all about and if it was legit. She gave me both the Psychic and the "Good" Witch's phone numbers, and I decided to call the Psychic first and set up a consultation.

At this point, I was willing to try anything because I was running out of money fast and wanted to understand why things were the way they were. Jasmine was the French Psychic's name, and she told me that we would meet on Skype Audio and that I needed to send her a photo of a deceased loved one that I was close to before our session. I sent her pictures of my dad, my grandmother, and my great-grandmother. Keep in mind that Jasmine knew nothing about me. She didn't know my full name, and I paid her with a PayPal account that didn't have my name on it either. All she had to go off were the pictures I sent and my deceased family member's first names. She also warned me that sometimes she can't reach loved ones on the first or second try, or ever even, but that she could do other things to provide value if she couldn't contact them in the spirit world. I was still very skeptical and didn't by any means think I would ever be able to talk to my dad, grandmother, or great-grandmother. I wasn't even convinced that our souls lived on after death but was open to it, given the amazing predictions made by the Vietnamese Psychic in Vietnam in 2011.

The day arrived for my session with Jasmine. It was early November 2016, and I called her on Skype "audio" at the agreed-upon time. I had already sent her the pictures the day prior. After saying hello, Jasmine immediately said that she has my grandmother with her and that my grandmother was sad when I was in Vietnam because it reminded her of when she lived in a different state when she was younger. I thought, whoa, how did she know I was in Vietnam, but that was counter-balanced by me telling her that she was incorrect because my grandmother only lived in Pennsylvania her entire life. She replied by saying, no, your grandmother lived in another state when she was younger. I said, no, she didn't; she replied, "yes, she did." After saying no, she didn't two more times and her saying "yes, she did," I remembered that my grandmother did run away with my grandfather to get married and that they lived in Detroit for a year back in 1942 before my dad was born. It hit me all at once, I indeed was talking to my grandmother, and I winced into tears with instant shame, thinking of the things I've done in life that she must have surely observed from her "Truman Show" POV in the spirit world. The Skype call was Skype audio, but the moment it hit me, and the tears came, Jasmine quickly blurted out, I'm sorry. It wasn't Jasmine; my grandmother felt terrible knowing how much emotion I was overcome with. Jasmine couldn't see me, and I didn't say anything when it hit me, nor did I make a noise, but my grandmother was there with me; she saw it and instantly channeled her response through Jasmine.

The way a legit psychic medium works is they have a special gift that works similar to a radio antenna. Powerful spirits can sometimes tune into that antenna and open direct communication with the psychic medium. Even though the first few minutes of the session was my grandmother talking to me through Jasmine, my great-grandmother took over after that and was the spirit I was speaking with 95% of the time going forward. Jasmine told me that my great-grandmother is very strong and was on her "channel" instantly along with my grandmother initially whenever she focused on her picture and called her name. My father, grandmother, grandfather, and friend "Jett" occasionally connected with her channel and spoke to me, but they couldn't do it as easily as my great-grandmother.

Even though I believed 100% now, my great-grandmother, that was now on her channel, wanted to make sure, so she told Jasmine to tell me something about my ex that I didn't tell anyone. She proceeded to tell me that my ex was raped by her father, her grandfather, and 3 of her uncles starting at the age of 5. I was floored! That is precisely what my ex told me one night in bed while she cried in Vietnam in 2011. When Hong loved me and wanted to protect me, she told me this story to warn me that her family was evil rather than come right out tell me that they were scamming me and trying to kill me. I wasn't prepared for this call since I didn't know if Jasmine was legit, so I failed to record this conversation. Still, starting with session number 2 going forward, I recorded 80% of them and will post highlights of these recordings and the context for each audio recording. I was amazed to learn the things I didn't know until I met Jasmine, and she filled in many gaps that were missing in the 2009 through 2015 section of the story.

At the end of the session, I thanked Jasmine and asked her to send me a time slot for next week to talk to her for 4 hours. I needed to prepare a long list of questions and knew it would take at least that long to get through it. In the meantime, I called the Muslim Witch Zulfiya to see what she could offer that was different from Jasmine. Jasmine, "channeling through my great-grandmother," told me that I needed to be cleaned and that I did have many evil curses and demons attached to me because of my ex and her family doing voodoo on me. Jasmine said that they were a devil family that did this all the time.

Zulfiya, the "good" Muslim Witch

I called Zulfiya the day after I spoke with Jasmine. Unlike Jasmine, Zulfiya needed to see me in person and was in Los Angeles, so I set up an appointment three days later and drove the 5-hour drive to L.A. to see her. Zulfiya's primary talent is that she is a good witch that can reverse spells and send the energy back to the person that put the curse on you in the first place. Zulfiya also can speak with spirits but can only speak to the ones that she uses regularly and not chosen ones like Jasmine can with my great-grandmother. When I met Zulfiya, she made me some coffee and sat with me while asking me to cut a deck of old tarot cards upon which she meditated after I cut them. She then proceeded to tell me about my ex and how her father and three uncles raped her as a child. Unlike Jasmine, she missed the grandfather part, but I was still thoroughly impressed, given that this was not supposed to be her core talent. She told me that Vietnam had very powerful women and that their voodoo is some of the world's worst and most potent.

Zulfiya told me that my ex did a massive job on me and that I had 88 evil spirits attached to me. Zulfiya said that Hong did several love spells and death curses on me. The evil she used included voodoo dolls mixed with rotten meat, my hair, my sperm that she saved, and that she spat on and stabbed the voodoo doll after and buried it in a cemetery. Zulfiya said the curse was a potent blood curse and that the only way to remove it was to sacrifice a black chicken. She didn't quote me a price but said to give her what I thought was fair and that she would contact me after she located a black chicken from the farmer she knows. I said OK and drove back to Vegas to await her call.

About a week went by, and I didn't hear anything from Zulfiya. I called her and asked her if she found a chicken. She said that the farmer doesn't have a black one right now and that she'd let me know. I asked her if I could try and locate one, and she said, "sure." I asked if gender mattered, and she said no, just make sure the chicken has black feathers. I was talking to her while at the gym and left the gym 5-minutes later to go home. I lived in N.W. Las Vegas, where there is some ranch-type land, but for the most part, it was residential housing. As though it was fate, I saw a guy riding a horse on the road as I was driving home.

I pulled over and asked the guy if he knew where I could buy a black chicken. He said, "I have one." I asked him if he'd sell it to me, he said sure. I asked how much; he said, whatever you want. I said, how's $40? He said yes and said I could come to get it tomorrow or whenever. I called Zulfiya right away and told her I found a black chicken. She thought I was joking at first but then realized I was serious. I asked her if I could come in 2 days, and she said yes. I could tell Zulfiya wasn't excited about making this sacrifice. I asked her when the last time was that she sacrificed a chicken, she said four years ago. I said, "why so long?" She replied, I haven't needed to, but your situation is very powerful and requires it.

Zulfiya then said I would need to pay her $1500 for the sacrifice ceremony. I wasn't happy to hear that, but I reluctantly agreed. I then called Jasmine and asked her to ask my great-grandmother if it was worth it. Jasmine told me that my great-grandmother said yes, do it. Keep in mind that Jasmine and Zulfiya don't know each other and that Jasmine telling me to spend $1500 with someone else is essentially taking money she could have gotten if she was a fraud. Jasmine then told me that Zulfiya is a bit scared because Zulfiya will receive the bad energy she releases from me the night of the sacrifice. Zulfiya knew she was in store for something brutal, which is why she was stalling me on finding a chicken. Click the button below to hear the audio snippet where Jasmine told me again that my grandmother and friend love Zulfiya and wanted me to spend the $1500.

Jasmine Speaking about Zulfiya

Listen at bit.ly/dprefer18 or at "**SECTION 2**" of the website at www.thedevilprefers.com/bookextra

It was the day before thanksgiving 2016, and I went in the morning to meet the guy with the chicken "Vic" and set off to L.A. with the chicken taped inside an empty case of beer. When I got to L.A., it was around 5 PM. Zulfiya said we needed to wait another hour until the sun went down. Zulfiya started reading verses from what may have been the Karan (not sure), but it was in a different language, so I couldn't understand what was being said. She had several candles lit, and when it came time to kill the poor chicken, she gently slit its throat without the chicken fighting or screaming out at all. It's as though the chicken knew he had to take one for the team. She then mixed the chicken's blood with some plant and different spices and then soaked candles wrapped in string with the blood before wiping the blood on several parts of my body, including my face. Then she poured candle wax over the chicken's lifeless body and wrapped the chicken up in a brown paper bag. She told me that I needed to take this bag at least 2 miles away and drop it on a side street somewhere and drive away from it without looking back. She then advised me not to clean the blood off until I lit and entirely burned one of 7 candles starting at midnight. She said that I should burn one candle each night at midnight for seven days. She also told me that my son was a very special, old soul and that he may see spirits in the house over the next several days. I said OK and started my journey back to Vegas, stopping 2 miles into the trip to drop off the chicken as instructed. The McDonald's drive-through girl looked at me like I was a psycho when I went through the drive-through with blood on my face, but like Zulfiya said, "do not wash off the blood until after the first candle is finished burning."

Vic - The guy that sold me the black chicken.

Best $40 I ever spent! I took this picture of him when I stopped to ask him if he knew where to find a black chicken. The video below was taken by me two days later when I bought the chicken from him

Watch at bit.ly/dprefer19 or at "**SECTION 2**" of the website at www.thedevilprefers.com/bookextra

17 - The Night that Changed it All

I arrived back in Vegas at 11:15 PM and told the babysitter, "Don't ask," as I paid her with the blood still on my face. My son fell asleep within 10 minutes of me getting home. I waited another 25 minutes until midnight and lit the candle as Zulfiya instructed. HOLY SHIT!!! Within 10 seconds of lighting the candle, I saw three transparent black smoked Asian-looking spirits that were around 5 feet tall floating through my living room, right past me and through the back door. I was dumbfounded and nearly in shock as I watched my first ever ghost sighting of my life. I wasn't drinking, I wasn't under the influence of anything, and I wasn't even tired yet, so I wasn't in a delusional state of any sort.

Within a minute of those three spirits floating out of the house, I saw what looked like a cloud of gnats forming in my living room. The black cloud grew and crept towards me. It was pure madness. I wasn't scared though; just standing there in awe. I turned towards the front door and saw a white spirit around 6 feet tall facing the door and moving its arms very fast, almost as if it was blocking something from entering. The black cloud of the gnat-looking energy was within inches of my face now. I stood there and stared at it, not quite knowing what to think about it. Was it evil? I didn't know, nor did I know what I was supposed to do. I remembered what my dad said to me when he visited me in my dream a week after he died. I forcefully said, "My relationship with Jesus Christ," as I simultaneously held my fingers up to form a cross-like you would see in a B-rated horror movie dealing with demons, lol. I shit you not, it worked! The black cloud instantly blew backward and splattered onto the ceiling and wall. For the next few minutes, it stayed there, almost as if it was breathing and regrouping. Then it started to form into a swirling cloud again and come towards me. I tried the cross thing again, but it had no effect. Then after about two more minutes, it exploded and disappeared, and out of it emerged a white spirit that was smiling at me for a second before disappearing also. I then took a shower and went to sleep.

View this single video at bit.ly/dprefer20 or at "**SECTION 2**" at www.thedevilprefers.com/bookextra

The video above was a video I came across on YouTube. The grey-colored spirit in this video is like the 3 Asian-looking spirits I saw in my house, except the 3 Asians were a black-tinted spirit and shorter than the one in this video, which is grayish. That night, the white-tinted spirit in my doorway looked like the spirit in this video, except it was taller and much whiter. From what I understand, the eviler the person while alive, the darker the color of the spirit once they die. Jasmine told me that Jesus' spirit is brilliant White. She said the same thing about my son. Please don't confuse the spirit's color with skin color on Earth; they are not the same. An evil white person on Earth has a dark-colored spirit in the spirit realm, while a good white person has a white-colored spirit after they die. The same applies to every race of people. Think of darkness as impurities that prevent a spirit from ascending higher in the sky, "Heaven." The less black energy one's soul contains, the more freedom they have in the sky. Pure spirits "white energy" can travel more places than evil ones "dark energy." Evil spirits are stuck on Earth and cannot freely travel the universe.

Watch video at bit.ly/dprefer21
or at "**SECTION 2**" at www.thedevilprefers.com/bookextra to see ALL videos and audio in one place

The video above is about Witches in Romania. The video at the 10-minute mark shows how the witch chooses a black chicken to clean a woman possessed by Satan. This was by design. Black chickens are very powerful when trying to reverse powerful curses.

The candles below are what the candles "drenched in the black chicken blood" looked like. These three candles don't have blood on them and were sent to me by Zulfiya later to help eliminate remnants of the spirits my Ex and her family had sent me once I had the operation on my leg.

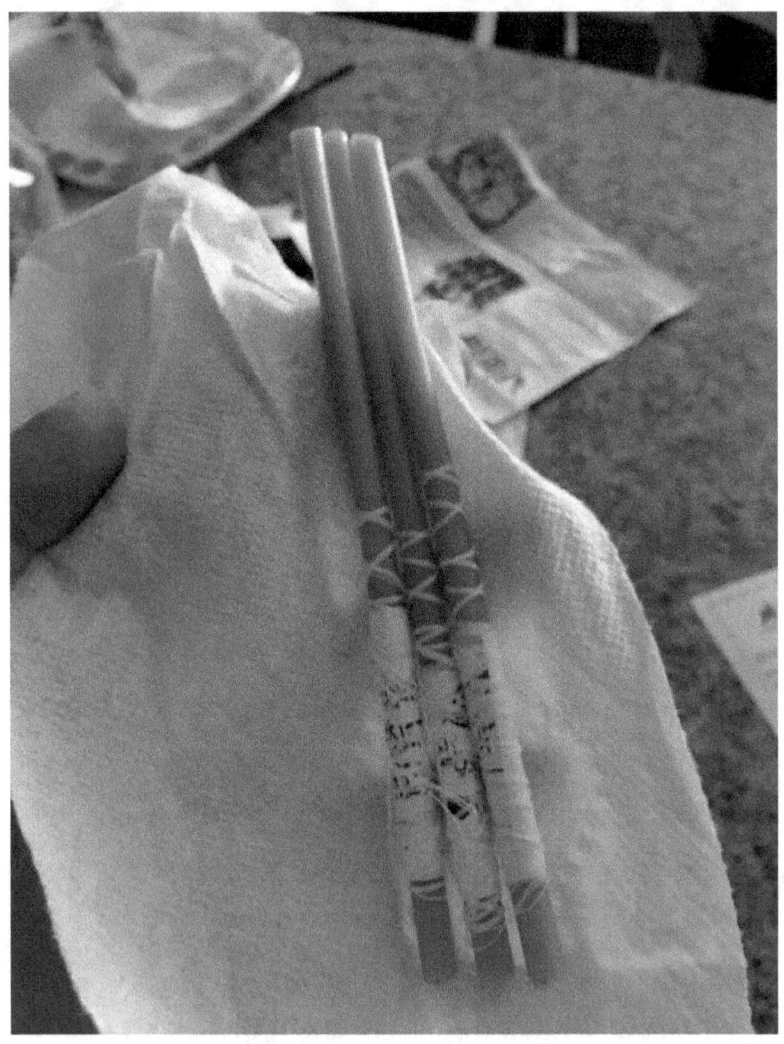

The next evening, I lit the 2nd candle at midnight. My son was awake this time, and we were lying in bed while the candle burned down for approximately 40 minutes in the kitchen. My son was only five at the time and knew nothing about the psychics or anything, but as we were lying there, he said, "Hey Dada, I see people." I asked him where and he pointed to the corner and the ceiling. I asked him how many, and he said 10. I asked him if they looked happy or angry, and he said "happy." Just as Zulfiya had predicted, my son would probably see things because he is a very old soul sensitive to these things. I was able to see grey clouds of smoke moving around the room for the next several days. Still, I didn't see anything as clearly as the first night when I saw the 3 Asian spirits, tall white spirit, black swirling gnat blob, and white spirit that emerged from the black swirl once it disappeared.

The next part of the story will detail the 40 hours I spent talking to Jasmine over the next three years. Now that you are fully aware that there is an accompanying website where I post all of the pictures, videos and audio in the order they are referenced in the book, I will no longer mention the link below. I will only mention the section. Whenever I mention Section 2, 3, 4 or 5 going forward, you should go to the link below and click the corresponding section to access the media files referenced, starting with “Section 2”. I suggest keeping the link below open on your device as you read so you can quickly watch or play the file as you are reading. I arranged the files to go from top to bottom on each section to make it easy to follow. Go to

www.thedevilprefers.com/bookextra

and click on "**Section 2**" to be taken to the page which lists all the audio and video clips in the order they appear in the book
and click on each of the audio and videos in the order they occur in this book from top to bottom from this point forward.

The individual links for each audio and video will not be posted with each separate video and audio link going forward, but instead will simply say See Section 2 or 3 etc. at thedevilprefers.com/bookextra to remind you where to find the files.

18 – Conversations with Jasmine

Conversations (via psychic medium Jasmine) with my great-grandmother from 2016-20, who died in 1997 at the age of 101

The audio recording snippets below were taken from one of the many phone sessions I had with Jasmine from 2016 to 2020. The conversations will reference my time in Asia and afterward here in America. In total, there were 30 plus hours of recordings out of the 50 or so total hours I had conversations with Jasmine. I spliced the highlights of those 30 hours to help tell the story. I recommend that you listen to these recordings from the perspective that Jasmine didn't know my story or anything about me. Jasmine knew more about me over time because we talked for hours, but if you view these conversations with an Orwellian Eye, you'll see that the things she tells me are not anything someone could guess. They aren't easy to predict things like, "you'll get a new job", or "you'll find love soon," but they are detailed events that happened to probably no one "except me." You'll notice that I am very animated and overly excited for most of the calls. Keep in mind that I knew I was talking directly to my great-grandmother that died almost 30-years prior that was also my guardian angel that had a front-row seat to everything. I had so many questions and couldn't get them out fast enough. You'd be amazed at how many details you miss about your life that someone with a Truman Show perspective can shed light upon. After about 10 hours of sessions with Jasmine, I knew with absolute certainty that the information was legit, so I began to give her leading questions to save time since she was $300 an hour after all. I needed to speed the sessions up to ensure I could ask all of the questions I prepared before each call. Still, I didn't ask leading questions until after she hit the bullseye on topic after topic, where she shed light on things only I knew or something that I assumed but wasn't sure about.

While most of the conversations dealt with what already had occurred, Jasmine also told me about future events. That was my great-grandmother telling her these events, but they were amazingly accurate. The only thing she was sometimes incorrect about were things that dealt with time.

I WILL POST THE AUDIO FOR EACH OF THESE BULLET POINTS BELOW, BUT I WANTED TO GIVE YOU A TEASER AS TO WHAT YOU'LL HEAR.

Some of the future predictions I was told by Jasmine that came true are:

In December 2016, she said my son's mother would die of cancer in 4 years, but in other recordings, she changed the prediction to say she would die in 1 year or even the next month when she still lived another whole year from the revised forecast. She ultimately did die two years and ten months after the original 4-year prediction on 9-11-2019, so her prediction was a little bit off but impressive nonetheless. Who predicts the death of a young woman as dying from cancer that is perfectly healthy when they make the prediction?

Even when she was not 100% correct, she was impressive because no one would assume a healthy, young woman will die from cancer in her early 30's. She also predicted several other deaths down to the day, which I'll discuss later in the Black Magic Battle section.

In late 2017, Jasmine said that someone would try and run me off the road soon and that I needed to be careful. (While living in Florida in early 2018, a friend and I were on our way to a sports event when a guy passed us at a high rate of speed, cut in front of us and slammed on his brakes, and played chicken with us for 10 miles on the Florida Turnpike. I didn't cut the guy off or anything; he appeared out of nowhere, targeting my vehicle. Jasmine said the Triads sent him to try and make me have an accident)

She also predicted that a friend of mine had a dishonest business partner trying to frame him and that his house would be raided by the FBI soon. He wasn't even aware that his business partner was trying to set him up at the time, but his house was raided by the Feds 2 weeks later, just as Jasmine had predicted. The dishonest business partner is currently in Federal Prison for a multi-million-dollar Ponzi scheme that will most likely be an episode of American Greed one day. My friend was never convicted of anything because he was also a victim of this guy and just made a mistake when he signed off on some papers he didn't read closely at the time.

Jasmine predicted that I would need a root canal on my rear molar (the #14 tooth). She said I would need it that year, and there wasn't anything I could do to stop it. I went to the Dentist, had a check-up, and even told him that I think the #14 tooth is having issues. I told him it hurt when the cold hit it rather than say a psychic told me, "Lol." He said the #14 tooth was fine; he even took x-rays. Six months later, I had intense tooth pain and went to the Dentist. He tried to fill the cavity that he could now see on the #14 tooth, but as he filled it, he said he is already into the root and that the tooth needed a root canal. This predicted event was all within one year, as Jasmine had predicted.

Jasmine predicted that someone would try and enter my house while I was sleeping and that I needed to be careful. A month later, at 5 AM, I woke up to hear keys jingling as if someone was trying different keys to open my door. I ran towards the door screaming WTF, and when I went outside, a girl was quickly walking away, saying she had the wrong apartment. The girl was close to 300 pounds, and I never saw her before. Jasmine said the Triads sent her to check if any of the several master-type keys they had would work and open my door to give them the ability to quickly enter during the day when I took my son to school.

The above examples are not nearly as convincing as the audio recordings themself. Still, I wanted to give you a few small examples (there are many more, which I'll show also) of the amazingly accurate information I was getting from Jasmine. I'm a Lawyer that is very analytical. I didn't just believe in God automatically, the same way I didn't believe in psychics and black magic. I honestly was that guy who would need to see undeniable proof to believe anything spiritually related. I believe in all three now after what I've seen, and I think most of you will feel the same after I'm done making the case. Go to the website to listen to each of the audio recordings. I will write about the context of each and detail the events that have happened to me from 2017 to the present in 2021.

The audio where Jasmine predicted a police raid on my friend by the Feds!

(See "**Section 2**" at **www.thedevilprefers.com/bookextra** to listen)

Tooth Audio #1 - This audio is where Jasmine not only predicts that my #14 tooth will need a root canal, but she also predicts that the Dentist won't find it during my next visit. She was 100% correct on both. I needed to get a root canal on that #14 tooth months later, even though I had zero problems with it during this audio recording.

(See "**Section 2**" at **www.thedevilprefers.com/bookextra** to listen)

Tooth Audio #2 - This audio was a few months after I got the root canal predicted in the above audio. Jasmine told me that the root canal wasn't done correctly and that I will have an infection soon. I didn't go to the Dentist right away as she suggested, but the tooth did become infected two months later, and the Dentist needed to redo the root canal on the #14 tooth (Just like Jasmine predicted in this recording)

(See "**Section 2**" at **www.thedevilprefers.com/bookextra** to listen)

Jasmine predicts in early 2017 that Hong will die in 4 years in this audio. The picture in the background was a picture of Hong a year after the prediction in 2018. Does this look like a girl that is going to die in a few years?

(See "**Section 2**" at **www.thedevilprefers.com/bookextra** to listen)

This audio clip was cool. I grew up in a housing complex in Clairton, PA called The Woodland Terrace that changed its name to Century Townhomes, which is now condemned, but my grandmother lived there from the late 1950s until 2002 while we moved out in 1984 when I was 12. The last ten years of her living there were unique because the demographics changed from what used to be 99% white to more than 80% black. This audio clip is significant because it was so random where Jasmine chimes in and says she sees many black people around my grandmother. Before she moved away in 2002, my grandmother fed the kids on the street, and it wasn't uncommon for her to have 6 to 8 black kids sitting at her table eating Pasta.

(See "**Section 2**" at **www.thedevilprefers.com/bookextra** to listen)

The Gay Uncle - This is one of the most convincing audio clips, in my opinion. In this clip, I discuss one of Hong's Aunts and her Husband that got very drunk and tried to smack me while he was drunk in 2014. Jasmine instantly went on a narrative where she explained to me how the guy was actually gay even though he was married with a kid. Notice how I immediately laugh and am astonished as Jasmine explains what happened as though she was there with a front-row seat. She was there with a front-row seat because it was my great-grandmother channeling through her, and my great-grandmother was my guardian angel the entire time and saw everything that happened. Not only that, but spirits in the sky understand all languages so she could hear everything they were saying. Please pay attention to how I agree with her in a heightened animated way because she told me things I already knew that I never talked about and told me something that I didn't know, but that made perfect sense to me after she said it. Jasmine filled in the blanks on so many things. I made the picture on the left to torment Hong's family when I posted it on a fake Facebook account in Vietnam in 2017 that I created to harass Hong and her family. The guy's face was her uncle, while the woman's face on the pig was his wife. The wife gave me poisoned food in 2014 in Vietnam and practiced black magic on me many times.

(See "**Section 2**" at **www.thedevilprefers.com/bookextra** to listen)

I circled the Gay Uncle and his wife in the picture above. The pic below was a picture I made to torment Hong's evil Aunt. I posted it on a Facebook account that I set up in Vietnam that Hong's family and entire village checked regularly. You'll learn more about this later in the Black Magic sub-section titled "Facebook Wars."

This audio recording was in 2018, where I told Jasmine I haven't felt financially secure in 9 years to where she corrects me and says, "10 years". She was correct. I knew the money party was coming to an end in 2008 but just said nine years to Jasmine since I was still making good money even though it was 65% less starting in 2008. She was correct; it was ten years, not nine years. One may dismiss this saying, "big deal, 9 or 10 years is basically the same", but this shows you the kind of precision information I was getting to where she corrected small details about my life that I lived. It was ten years to the month when I knew I would not retire from my current software company once the revenue dropped 65% over 30 days. She was more accurate than I was.

(See "**Section 2**" at **www.thedevilprefers.com/bookextra** to listen)

The Cursed Cologne, Shoes & Shirt

Whenever Jasmine and I did a facetime video call in late 2016, Jasmine told me that I had several items in my house that my ex Hong did voodoo rituals on that put severe curses on me whenever I wore them. I had 15 pairs of shoes in my closet, and Jasmine said that one of them was cursed. I turned the camera to the floor and asked her which pair she replied, the grey pair. The amazing part was that I left Vietnam "as far as moving out" 5 years prior, and the grey pair were the only pair I had left that was in Vietnam at that time. She then proceeded to tell me that I had a shirt with stitching on the front and that my ex wove a cursed thread into the stitching. Jasmine said that these curses on the shoes and the shirt were meant to get me killed by causing an accident. All my shirts were hung on hangers in the closet, and I had close to 100. I slowly walked my camera across the hanging shirts until Jasmine exclaimed, "that one, with the white sleeve." As I pulled out the shirt, I saw a logo on it like the Zoo York image below. The shirt is pictured below, along with the cologne and shoes, but the sleeve covers the logo in the picture. The Zoo York logo even looks like a Satanic emblem of sorts if you think about it. Here's another striking detail. The Zoo York shirt had stitching just like she said because the logo was sewn in, but the Zoo York shirt was also the only shirt of my 100 shirts that had any stitching on the front. You couldn't see the front of the shirt until I pulled it out from the shirts hanging there.

As I stood there in awe due to Jasmine (via my great-grandmother) picking the only pair of shoes I had in Vietnam and the only shirt that had stitching out of 100; I asked her was there anything else. She said yes, the perfume! Jasmine is French and calls cologne perfume. I said, "which one," she replied, "the big one." I then went to my bathroom, opened the cabinet, and saw three small bottles of cologne and one large bottle. I had just bought the three small bottles after moving back to the United States, but the big bottle was the only bottle I had over in Vietnam.

I was shocked for a couple of reasons, neither of which Jasmine knew, or that I even thought of until Jasmine said the big bottle was cursed:

1. I used to have close to 20 bottles of cologne in Vietnam before I moved back to America, but when the movers unpacked my items in Florida, there was only that one big bottle. I remember being furious, thinking that Hong stole the other bottles to give to some guy. Hong didn't steal the other 20 bottles to gift them; she just wanted to make sure that the only cologne I had to wear was the cursed bottle that they somehow removed the cap from and mixed in cursed ashes from an evil person that died.

2. From 2012 to 2016, I didn't even wear the cologne even once, even though I liked the smell. Jasmine told me that my great-grandmother prevented me from wearing it because it was cursed. I did wear it one time though, in Las Vegas on April 20th, 2016, which ended up being the night that a girl I was dating for three months told me she didn't want to see me anymore. The audio below is where Jasmine talks about the cologne and that night on April 20th, 2016.

The audio clip where Jasmine talks about the cologne pictured above.

(See "**Section 2**" at **www.thedevilprefers.com/bookextra** to listen)

The audio clip below discusses my grandmother's brown chair for the last 15 years of her life. My niece ended up with it but wanted to buy new furniture, so my sister asked me if I wanted it. I said yes since it was my grandmother's chair, and I wanted it as a keepsake. This was my grandmother's favorite chair. Notice how Jasmine says, "your grandmother keeps talking about some chair." I never mentioned this chair to Jasmine before her bringing it up.

(See "**Section 2**" at **www.thedevilprefers.com/bookextra** to listen)

Jasmine said that the lid that moves when I hold the water bottle on the left is being moved by my great-grandmother or friend Jett. There was flat water inside, and it doesn't always move. Jasmine said it only moves when my great-grandmother and my friend Jett are there with me.

(See "**Section 2**" at **www.thedevilprefers.com/bookextra** to watch)

The audio clip where Jasmine talks about the cologne pictured above.

(See “**Section 2**“ at **www.thedevilprefers.com/bookextra** to listen)

The audio clip below discusses my grandmother's brown chair for the last 15 years of her life. My niece ended up with it but wanted to buy new furniture, so my sister asked me if I wanted it. I said yes since it was my grandmother's chair, and I wanted it as a keepsake. This was my grandmother's favorite chair. Notice how Jasmine says, "your grandmother keeps talking about some chair." I never mentioned this chair to Jasmine before her bringing it up.

(See “**Section 2**“ at **www.thedevilprefers.com/bookextra** to listen)

Jasmine said that the lid that moves when I hold the water bottle on the left is being moved by my great-grandmother or friend Jett. There was flat water inside, and it doesn't always move. Jasmine said it only moves when my great-grandmother and my friend Jett are there with me.

(See “**Section 2**“ at **www.thedevilprefers.com/bookextra** to watch)

The remainder of the story will be separated into different categories and sub-categories. The first category I'll delve into is my battle with the Triads (mostly Macau Triads, but they are all connected). This battle started in 2009 when I first arrived in Macau and hasn't stopped to this day. This battle was already detailed earlier as far as the 2009 through 2015 period, but I still need to explain what's happened in the last 6-years and add the clarification Jasmine gave me for the 2009-2015 period. You'll be amazed at the different things they've done and how I escaped every plot, in addition to learning the extra details I wasn't aware of until meeting Jasmine. You will see how they have tried to kill me many times, how they follow me everywhere, and how they are constantly trying to hack my devices. Jasmine told me that they fear that I will make a movie and expose their enterprise of illegal activities. Jasmine also said that spirits heavily protect me in the sky and that it's nearly impossible for them to kill me, even though they have tried many times.

Part 3 – The Triads

19 - The Triads - Part 1

In ancient China, the Triad was one of three major secret societies. It established branches in Macau, Hong Kong, Taiwan, and overseas Chinese communities. Known as "mainland Chinese criminal organizations," they are of two major types: dark forces (loosely organized groups) and black societies (more mature criminal organizations). Two features that distinguish a black society from a dark force are the ability to achieve illegal control over local markets and receiving police protection. The Hong Kong triad refers to traditional criminal organizations operating in (or originating from) Hong Kong, Macau, Taiwan, and south-east Asian countries and regions, while organized-crime groups in mainland China are known as "mainland Chinese criminal groups." ~Wikipedia

My battles have always been with the Macau-based Black Society Triads that have connections globally. They have people on the inside at all major corporations and telecoms in addition to having blackmail on people in politics throughout the world. They can pretty much do whatever they want, but like most scumbag organizations, their Achilles heel is that they fear being exposed. They would love nothing more than to see me dead, but I've been lucky to date and don't think God will allow them to kill me anyway, so my level of concern is low even though I do proceed through life with caution. My war with them continues to this day and will probably continue for the rest of my life. As you'll learn later, I signed up for this and have no regrets.

By now, you should have already read the numerous battles I've had with the Macau Triads from 2009 to 2015. I wish I could say that it ended in 2015, but "true to form," the Triads are like Herpes and don't ever go away no matter how many times you deliver a solid "L" to them. That said, let me continue detailing the many other battles I've had with them from 2016 to the present, in addition to straying from time to time to add context to the 2009-2015 period using the additional information gathered from Jasmine.

Jasmine warned me that the Triads were having people follow me, especially when I was at the gym since I didn't go anywhere but the gym or pick up my son from school. Sometimes I went out, but for the most part, I was a hermit that stayed home from 2015 to now. Whenever I thought someone was possibly following me, I didn't just take Jasmine's word for it, but I made sure I randomized the times I went to the gym, and if I saw the same person arrive after me, I was able to put two and two together and knew that they were tailing me.

The guys below were at the gym at least 90% of the times that I went, even if I went at 9 AM on some days, 11:30 AM others, and 2 PM on others. I went at different times constantly and knew who was following me. Not only were they following me, I knew the Triads sent them, but I also knew by the way they behaved. They would change the guys every few months but always had 1 or 2 guys at the gym whenever I was there that would always arrive a few minutes after me. Jasmine told me many times that the Triads feared I would expose them, so they also wanted to scare me in hopes I'd shy away in fear. They would have these different goons follow me around the gym and get on a treadmill two treadmills away from me, and their timing could not be ignored. They always seemed to get on the treadmill at the 10-minute mark of me getting on. They did this to send a message. They didn't confront me or do anything like that; they always did subtle things that made it obvious who they were sent by. Below are pictures of guys the Triads sent that passed the 90% or more test I used above and people that got on a treadmill or elliptical two machines away from me at the same 10-minute mark every single time. Jasmine also confirmed each of the people below as being sent by the Triads.

This guy pictured below also passed the 90% test and randomized times I mentioned above, but the way that I discovered him was unique. If you pay attention, you'd be amazed at how much guidance you receive from your guardian angels. I was pulling into the gym and saw a spot, but I missed it by 5 feet to the point where I needed to back up to pull into the spot. For some strange reason, I instead chose to drive all the way down the parking section and come back down the other side to where I parked in a much worse spot but felt drawn to the guy in this car. This guy was waiting for me to arrive, and it was my friend Jett's spirit that somehow pushed me toward him to see the enemy.

This guy here nearly shit himself when he saw that I knew he was filming me while he was on a back rowing machine as I was on the treadmill. I saw him aim his camera towards me while I stared at him as he looked up. He instantly got nervous and stopped facing his camera towards me.

Above are only 6 of the people. There were many more than that, but I didn't take pictures of them all because I grew tired of it after a while.

MURDER FAIL

CLOSE CALL - In 2019, I went to watch a football game with relatives. The route I took home was desolate and only had a vehicle go past every 5 minutes or so, but it was the fastest route according to Google Maps, and the Triads knew that and plotted accordingly. About 10 yards before a sharp left bend, I felt my wheel give way, and I had to hard-pull the steering and overcorrect as I went into the curve. I barely missed hitting the telephone pole that was located very close to the road. The Triads had someone put a spring-loaded device on the road that punctured the sidewall instantly. I didn't see anything on the road as I was driving. It was the perfect place to do it too. This was the 2nd time they tried to make me have an accident. Tire sidewalls don't just bust like this, and I couldn't see, nor did I feel myself run anything over.

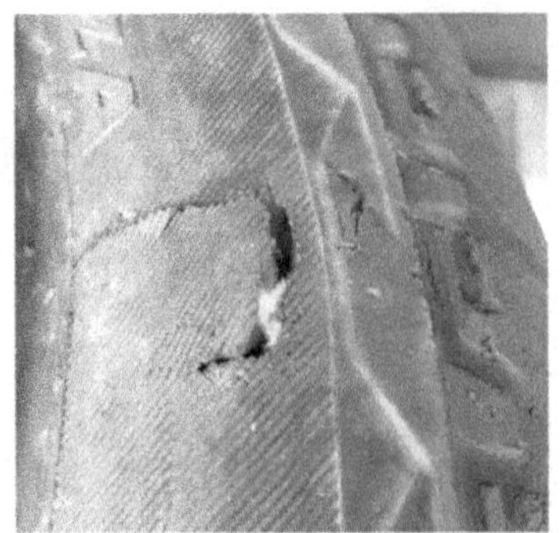

LOCAL TRIAD SHITHOLE

This strip mall has a Chinese Restaurant on the far right and a laundromat on the left down a ways. This is not a busy strip mall, and there is always plenty of parking for every business. After I sent Jasmine this video, she (via my great-grandmother) told me that the Chinese Restaurant is a local business in my area where the Triads meet (probably owned by a Triad, but I forgot to ask Jasmine). Jasmine said that the reason these guys parked next to me and went to the Restaurant, only to come back a minute later and wait there the entire time I was there (1-hour 10 minutes total), was that they feared I discovered their secret meeting place. They stupidly panicked and sent these goons to watch me, which gave it away in addition to the Fat Mexican guy I explain in the next section. The Chinese Restaurant was the first business when you entered the strip mall also, so they needed to pass it and drive an additional 100 yards to park next to me only to walk back 100 yards to go to it, and then return 100 yards to their car and wait over an hour until I left.

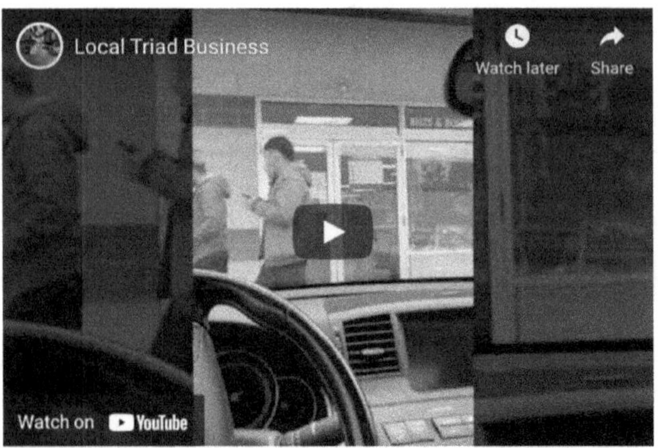

(See "**Section 3**" at **www.thedevilprefers.com/bookextra** to watch)

PLEASE NOTE: I tend to label people and give them "rude" nicknames. I also tend to use colorful, crass language against those that I know are my enemy. You won't see political correctness in this story because I am talking about men and women that tried to kill me. I give the absolute least amount of respect I can to these people when I describe them in the story. Please keep that in mind and excuse the language I use for these cretins because they all deserve the least amount of respect possible!

The Fat Mexican - AKA "El Gordo" - God works in mysterious ways. The place I currently live has a school bus stop at the end of the development, and my son was the only kid in our development, so he was the only one waiting for the bus to go to school at that bus stop the first year we lived there. I always drove to the bus stop and stayed with my son until the bus arrived. A year later, a new kid started showing up at the bus stop. I didn't think anything of it at first. Still, the same day I saw the Asian guys at the laundromat in the above video, I also saw that same kid's father walk into the Chinese Restaurant alone. He didn't leave for 15 minutes but left without food and didn't return either the remaining hour I was parked at the strip mall. This guy was hard to miss. He was as big as a house, and he was Mexican. Not a lot of 400-pound Mexicans where I live, so it was hard not to notice him. He worked for the Triads, and they moved him into my housing plan in hopes that he could befriend me and have me possibly invite his wife and kid to wait in my car on the cold days as we waited for the bus since 75% of the time, they walked to the bus stop and stood there in the cold. Jasmine confirmed this and said they would stuff drugs under my seat and have someone call the police to frame me as a drug dealer. Typical triad bullshit. The amazing part is that this laundromat wasn't the closest to my place. Whenever I needed to use a laundromat, I would go to one only 1/2 mile away. The only reason I went to this one was that I told my mother that I needed to wash my comforter and her husband suggested that I go to a new laundromat that I never heard of before. The very fact that he suggested this place was divine intervention, in my opinion, meant to shed light on where my enemies operated and even who my enemies were since I just happened to go at the perfect time and pull up as "El Gordo" was entering the Chinese Restaurant.

Meet "C.C." (short for "Cambodian Cunt")

Above is a picture of a woman I labeled CC. My Thai girlfriend said she thinks the lady is Cambodian from hearing her yapping on her cell phone when she came home one day. CC always seems to be walking outside the very moment my girlfriend or I come home. In the winter, she always seems to be walking out to her car to get something the very moment we are pulling up. We can leave the house four times in one day, and three of those four times we come back, CC is just walking outside. The timing couldn't be more obvious. She lives in the front of my building but could not get outside that fast whenever we come home just by watching from her window because you can't see a car coming until it is 50 yards away from the apartment. I knew the Triads sent her to live there in hopes she could cause me to argue with her, upon which she would press charges to get me in trouble. The Triads know that I have a bit of a temper, and they try to exploit that to their benefit. Jasmine confirmed this even though I instinctively knew what they were up to, given my vast experience fighting the Triads and understanding how they operate. CC has two cars, one with PA plates, another with CA plates. CC doesn't have a job that she goes to and is home 99% of the time. These garbage bags fund her entire life. They pay her to live there to have a set of eyes nearby in addition to a hacking center nearby.

How did CC know that my girlfriend or I were coming home? See below for that explanation. But keep in mind that she was never outside whenever we randomly left the apartment, but only when we were returning or during easy to predict times like when I had to take my son to the bus stop or go pick him up since those times were predictable. They knew that schedule, and CC was there, being the annoying eyesore she is nearly every time. They also use CC's apartment as a hacking base where they attempt to hack me wirelessly by remotely connecting to the devices in CC's house and using them as a launch point to try and break into my wireless network.

CELL TOWERS AND HOW CLEVER HACKERS CAN TRACK YOUR EVERY MOVE JUST BY KNOWING YOUR CELL PHONE NUMBER - Most people don't realize that whenever you are driving anywhere, your cell phone connects to a cell tower that is closest to your location, and depending on how far you go, your phone may connect and disconnect from dozens of different cell towers along the way. The Triads know my phone number in addition to my girlfriends, so it's easy for them to have a general idea of when we are coming home since we connect to our local cell tower, and they can monitor when we are pinging off that tower. Once we ping off that tower, they send "CC" an automated message using some app that lets her know that we just pinged the local cell tower and will most likely be pulling up in 5 minutes. That's why she can always be walking out the door the very moment we arrive, even though the view of us approaching is only 50 yards away and impossible for her to even be watching and exiting the front of the building that fast. My son and my girlfriend noticed it; we laugh every time we see her walking out just as we are pulling up. It happens more than 75% of the time we come home but 0% of the time when we are leaving unless we are leaving at an easy to predict time, like when I have to drop off or pick my son up from the bus stop.

20 - The Triads - Part 2

Time for Jasmine to shed light on my battle with the Triads for the period 2009-2015

KILL ATTEMPT #1

Many of you may remember earlier in the story that I went to Vietnam for seven weeks in 2009 to decide if I would move there but mostly to find a place and move there since I wanted to be with Hong. These two recordings on the left are jaw-dropping in my opinion because I remembered after Jasmine jogged my memory that I became deathly ill when I was at 7's wedding when she married the Triad, where I was supposedly the best man. Jasmine is explaining exactly what they did at that wedding. The picture below shows Hong with Nhung only moments before Nhung offered me a sip of a drink that had poison in it. I seriously thought I was going to die that night but chalked it up as Jungle Fever. Jasmine said that they didn't believe in me because I gave them the impression that I still might change my mind and not move there. Jasmine was 100% correct. I didn't realize what had happened until she told me, but it makes 100% sense now that I relive the events that took place while I was there at that wedding.

(See "**Section 3**" at **www.thedevilprefers.com/bookextra** to listen)

HONG & NHUNG

I took this picture in November 2009 in Can Tho, Vietnam, just moments before Nhung gave me poison. I became deathly ill, and Hong didn't even accompany me back to the hotel because she thought I was going to die and made the excuse that she needed to stay at 7's house all night to help prepare the wedding. Pure bullshit. They thought I would die that night, and I almost did. You can practically see in Hong's eyes that she thought she would never see me again. Fuck these conniving bitches.

Ho Chi Minh Wannabe

This scumbag on the left that looks like Ho Chi Minh was the guy that Jasmine said wanted to have my passport and gave the order to poison me that night. He is triad scum and is now dead, according to Jasmine. The guy on the right was his driver. Enemies in Asia always come with a smile; keep that in mind. Jasmine said he wanted to take a picture with me because he was impressed that I didn't die from the poison they gave me the night before. They tried to poison me again right after this pic was taken by my ex because I became deathly ill again but recovered within 30 minutes this time.

KILL ATTEMPT #2

I bought Hong's family nine motorcycles in January 2011. This is where Jasmine explains how they tried to poison me a month after that. I remember getting extremely ill around that time too. Jasmine jogged my memory about things that I almost forgot but remembered once she brought up the subject. It was truly amazing how the information she gave me caused me to remember things I almost forgot.

(See "**Section 3**" at **www.thedevilprefers.com/bookextra** to listen)

The Chinese Ogre - Jasmine explains how the Triads had guns at a nightclub in Macau where I almost got into a fight with a tall Chinese Guy and that I was lucky not to get killed this night.

(See "**Section 3**" at **www.thedevilprefers.com/bookextra** to listen)

Smuggling $350,000 US worth of Chinese Yuan to Singapore

Remember the 1.5 million Chinese Yuan above that I had to smuggle out of Vietnam after my ex and her friend Nhan acted as though they were cleaning my office but were only doing it to search for and steal my custom's declaration for when I brought that money into Vietnam? Jasmine explains what went down there while I was at the airport in the audio on the above right.

(See "**Section 3**" at **www.thedevilprefers.com/bookextra** to listen)

HCMC Airport Scam on 4-14-2011 (Jasmine clarifies below and adds to what really happened)

This audio mentioned above is where Jasmine confirms that Zulfiya was correct when she said that the necklace her friend gave me was cursed and would have gotten me killed had I not flushed it down the toilet on the airplane. I thought it was a drug set-up, but it was a set-up for smuggling a stolen necklace from a museum that had serious black magic added to it to give me serious bad luck in addition to it being a stolen necklace. Notice how Jasmine reminds me of what I forgot because it was my great-grandmother talking through her. I also discuss with Jasmine how I destroyed my home security hard drive because I feared that they hacked it and made it look like I was a drug dealer. The truth of what they had planned was much more sinister. They wanted to set me up as though I was having sex with kids (I wasn't, but they were going to make it look like young girls were coming into my room even though they weren't).

I took this video only minutes after Hong realized that I just microwaved the surveillance hard drive containing the fake video that they doctored to make it look like I had young girls entering my room in Vietnam.

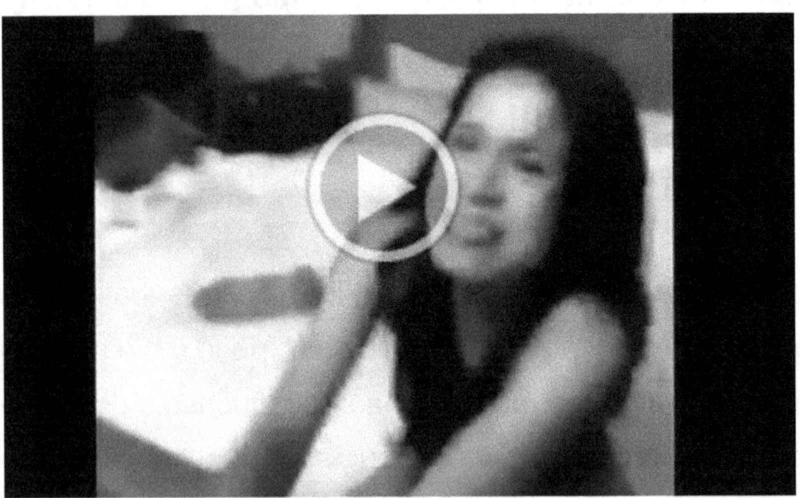

(See "**Section 3**" at **www.thedevilprefers.com/bookextra** to watch)

The audio explains how Hong lied to the Black Magic Guy and explains exactly why Hong was so furious in the video above. Jasmine didn't see the video above at all but notice how everything fits and gets pulled together as far as what their sinister plot for me was.

(See "**Section 3**" at **www.thedevilprefers.com/bookextra** to listen)

This audio is where Jasmine explains why they chose the necklace that they chose. It was ancient and had ancient stones, making it easier to infuse black magic into the necklace.

(See "**Section 3**" at **www.thedevilprefers.com/bookextra** to listen)

These audio clips are where Jasmine explains to me about the cop that walked me outside and even tried to take my passport at the airport on 4-14-2011 but relented after I wouldn't release my grip on my passport. The cop was in on the scam but now supposedly views me as a folk hero since I was able to get away that day. The mentioning of Facebook in this audio was Jasmine referencing a fake Facebook account I had where I exposed Hong, and her family and friend requested all of Hong's friends in addition to their friends to the point where I had 5,000 friends. Everyone involved in the plot to take me down from Vietnam watched that Facebook account when I pushed it in 2016. The account has since been removed for community violations, lol.

(See "**Section 3**" at **www.thedevilprefers.com/bookextra** to listen)

Poison, Poison & more Poison - The many attempts to kill me with poison

This audio below is also the point where I realized that Jasmine meant my "Great-Grandmother," not my grandmother that she was talking to 99% of the time.

(See "**Section 3**" at **www.thedevilprefers.com/bookextra** to listen)

Once I was back in the United States, I noticed flyers that were left on my door from time to time. I walked around the neighborhood and saw that the flyer was not on any other door, even not on the door of the upstairs apartment that I knew was vacant. I surmised that the flyer was left for me in hopes I would order and that they would send me poisoned food. It was always a Chinese place a few miles away but not close to my home either. It didn't make sense, and Jasmine confirmed that it was a plot to send me poisoned food.

(See "**Section 3**" at **www.thedevilprefers.com/bookextra** to listen)

May & June 2011 - Two Months in True Hell

After escaping the airplane plot detailed above, my enemies became bolder and bolder and started to do things like smash bricks off the wall where I spent 90% of my time in the house. There wasn't a window on the side where they smashed the bricks, so I had no way of knowing who was doing it. This was also when Hong brought Giang into the house and made up the story that he wanted to complain to her about his wife, but he was there to kill me in reality.

As detailed earlier in the story, Giang brought me a gift of Japanese Swords (below) but held the swords tightly after my ex left the room, which I now know was supposed to be the moment for him to kill me with the sword. God made me very naive at that time because if I caught on to what was happening, I would have killed that piece of shit and ended up in jail with my money confiscated. I will never forget how Giang stood there breathing hard but didn't try to swing the sword. I now realize that it was God blocking him and that I was protected from being killed. The naive cluelessness I had subsided two days later after a second kill attempt when he brought four guys to my house, but they all just sat there arguing before two of the guys got up and left. That too was a block move by God that prevented me from being killed. Only about an hour after all four guys left did the fog clear, and I realized what just happened over the past two days, and I went into a rage against Hong by accusing her of helping them try to kill me. As luck would have it, the interpreter that I hired from California just so happened to be in Vietnam at the time and came over after I requested that he moderate an argument between Hong and me since Hong did still speak broken English. It wasn't easy to explain details to her. Below is the audio where Jasmine explains that he was a good guy and knew Hong was scamming me but didn't know how to come out and tell me.

(See "**Section 3**" at **www.thedevilprefers.com/bookextra** to listen)

21 - The Triads - Part 3

The Cattle Prod- This audio is where I tell Jasmine how I tormented my pursuers that were constantly harassing me by smashing bricks off my house

(See "**Section 3**" at **www.thedevilprefers.com/bookextra** to listen)

The Motorcycle Chase - This audio is where Jasmine details what happened the day I was chased by three motorcycles across town as I tried to get the remaining $100,000 US out of my house. This chase occurred only days before I left Vietnam with my dogs when my friend came to help me hire movers and get the hell out of the country.

(See "**Section 3**" at **www.thedevilprefers.com/bookextra** to listen)

December 2nd, 2011- I escaped Vietnam with my son.

December 2nd, 2011- These three audio clips bring chills to my spine to this day. I left Vietnam with my son on his 1-year birthday with the full consent of his mother. I got to Pennsylvania to my mother's house 24 hours later and called Hong immediately on Skype. I thought it was extremely odd that she was panicked and going crazy when she answered the phone. She was screaming and saying, "where are you? Where is my son?" to which I replied by telling her that she knew it would take 24 hours for me to get back. Jasmine blew my mind when she shed light on this in the three audio recordings on the left. I remembered after these recordings the thing Jasmine kept saying my grandmother wanted me to remember about an envelope. Hong gave me a big manilla envelope with Vietnamese food inside it and told me to give it to my mother as a gift. I remember thinking it would spoil by the time I got to America, so I threw it in the trash before going through security at the airport in Vietnam. Hong supposedly had a cop working on the inside at the airport that was supposed to check my luggage and find the drugs she had hidden inside the food. The plan was to arrest me and bring my son back outside to Hong, but since I threw the food away, there were no drugs to find when I went through security, so they had to let me pass. That explains why Hong was so crazy when I called her on Skype once I got to Pennsylvania. What a Bitch!

(See "**Section 3**" at **www.thedevilprefers.com/bookextra** to listen)

Surrounded in 2014 on three sides

Jasmine explains the real reason behind why they had three people banging on my hotel walls in 2014 in Vietnam. They wanted me to move somewhere else to more easily be able to kill me since the hotel was on a busy, well-lit road.

(See "**Section 3**" at **www.thedevilprefers.com/bookextra** to listen)

Jasmine told me what I already suspected. Jasmine is not a computer geek; this was my great-grandmother explaining what happened and how isolated they had me to be able to kill me without messages for help reaching anyone. The Triads' completely controlled Internet had my entire internet environment isolated and running on their own servers. They even had English-speaking customer service reps answering local Vietnamese numbers for Google Suite support. They had vast parts of the internet cloned that they use to push their targets onto just before they go in for the kill. The purpose of this is to intercept all emails and messages because you are not connecting with the actual website; you are using a fake clone that they host. They spoof SSL certificates and trick your devices into thinking they are at google.com or facebook.com when you aren't.

(See "**Section 3**" at **www.thedevilprefers.com/bookextra** to listen)

Airport Escape 2015 - Only God could have pulled this one off

This audio clip details how Hong was trying to lie to the police and have me arrested in Vietnam in 2015. Listen to the absolute level of detail Jasmine gives. It's insane.

(See "**Section 3**" at **www.thedevilprefers.com/bookextra** to listen)

Jasmine explains how impossible it was for me to get on the airplane. When I first called the airline, they said they had a ticket in 8 days, but the call disconnected. When I called back right away, they said they had a flight leaving early the following day. Jasmine said it was a miracle because the airplane was full. I remember confusion at the ticket counter once I arrived, but they still issued the ticket, and I left. Even the aircraft took off 10 minutes early. Everything was working in my favor, even the impossible!

(See "**Section 3**" at **www.thedevilprefers.com/bookextra** to listen)

These two audios below do a deeper dive into the amazing escape in 2015 at the HCMC Airport. Unbeknownst to me, Hong was waiting for the police from her hometown to show up at the airport with arrest papers to stop me. The amazing part is that Jasmine said I didn't even have another 5 minutes to spare, and my flight just happened to take off 10 minutes early. She said that my guardian angels were busy at work, causing people not to notice things or make keystroke mistakes when checking me in. She even said that my Great-Grandmother and friend Jett caused an accident on the freeway to slow down the cop delivering the arrest papers. My ex didn't say goodbye to my son because she knew he wouldn't be leaving the country (or so she thought). Hong's sister was calling me non-stop once I got back to the States. I now realize that she did that to see if I made it back to the U.S. Notice how Jasmine also says that Hong was mad because I didn't give her money as I pretended. Before we got in the taxi, I remember walking up to the A.T.M. machine but then stopped and thought, "Fuck Her," and turned around without giving her a dime. Jasmine knew thls; she knew every detail. My family in the sky was there the entire time and saw it all.

Time for Jasmine to shed light on my battle with the Triads for the period 2016-2021

CATCH ME IF YOU CAN - In this audio, Jasmine guides me through what the Triads know about me and the different ways they try to kill me. The first audio was recorded a month before the one below it. Notice how she even knew that I canceled my Sprint service. She explains that they will never kill me because I am protected, and my karma doesn't allow me to die at their hands.

(See "**Section 3**" at **www.thedevilprefers.com/bookextra** to listen)

HATERADE - In this audio, Jasmine explains how badly the Triads and my ex's family in Vietnam hate me.

(See "**Section 3**" at **www.thedevilprefers.com/bookextra** to listen)

Hacked Firmware- In this audio, Jasmine explains how the Triads still had my computer hacked even after I did a complete reinstall of the operating system. I surmised in this audio that they had my computer chip hacked but later discovered that it was the hard-drive firmware that they had hacked. Once I replaced the hard drive, the computer ran as expected without strange processes running in the background or unexplained firewall logs. Jasmine was right again, as usual.

(See "**Section 3**" at **www.thedevilprefers.com/bookextra** to listen)

In the next audio, Jasmine discusses and explains who this guy is that I posted about earlier.

(See "**Section 3**" at **www.thedevilprefers.com/bookextra** to listen)

AMATEUR LOCKSMITH (Me) SAVES THE DAY - In this audio, Jasmine explains how the fat white girl tried to enter my house again when I was visiting my mom in Pennsylvania.

(See "**Section 3**" at **www.thedevilprefers.com/bookextra** to listen)

<u>The Triads Are Coming!</u> - This audio explains the calm before the storm where Jasmine said I would be hacked. She was correct; I made a mistake a week later and went to a local MetroPCS where the girl working there was paid to give me a cloned sim card. It was a nightmare. I ended up erasing my iPhone and driving an hour away to buy a new sim card.

(See "**Section 3**" at **www.thedevilprefers.com/bookextra** to listen)

This audio shows Jasmine telling me how I changed everything on my computer and escaped the Triads (a.k.a "The Chinese"). I didn't even tell Jasmine about the big moves I made, but she obviously knew without me telling her because my great-grandmother talked through Jasmine. What I did was monumental because I not only changed my iTunes account, but I enabled restrictions on the iPhone that prevented account changes once I had the account set up. This crushed their hack because it was impossible to enable game-center while that restriction was turned on, and they were tracking me using game-center. I knew I had a breakthrough once I figured that out, but Jasmine knew without me telling her a thing.

(See "**Section 3**" at **www.thedevilprefers.com/bookextra** to listen)

Below are three different links (click each box to view) to a blog I wrote in 2012 detailing the different ways the Triads were hacking me back then, which still work to this day, so be careful. I replaced all my devices in 2015 at one time and essentially defeated those hacks, but it shows you how screwed you'll be if they can get physical control over even one of your devices. Scary Stuff!

https://bit.ly/dpreferhack1
https://bit.ly/dpreferhack2
https://bit.ly/dpreferhack3

<u>The Turd Father</u> - This audio discusses Macau's #4 most powerful Triad Luis Lui. I used to think he was the most powerful in Macau but discovered later that he was only #4 in Macau. This guy looks like a Monkey and is a prime example of how pathetic the typical Triad is. Below are pictures of him where he tries to act as a productive member of society. In reality, he is a criminal piece of shit that hides in the shadows while masquerading as a legitimate businessman.

(See "**Section 3**" at **www.thedevilprefers.com/bookextra** to listen)

The funny part is that the middle pic below (Luis' business card) is a business that doesn't even exist anymore. I harassed this piece of shit so much that he changed the name of his company, changed his phone number, and took down his website, lol. (try to visit the website on the business card or call the number; you'll see). The Triads are trash; they will buckle if you know how to isolate and identify the top guys. I mastered fighting these dirtbags over the past decade. They are very predictable at this point.

G&L
GROUP
9th Floor, Edificio Nam Kwong,
Avenida do Dr. Rodrigo Rodrigues, MACAO
www.glgroup.com.mo
G&L
GROUP
Luis LUI
chairman

THESE 2 AUDIOS ARE UNREAL - In the first audio, you'll hear where Jasmine warns me that Thanksgiving will be a dangerous time and that I'll be hacked around Thanksgiving. The 2nd audio was on 12-8-2017, where I tell Jasmine that I discovered the hack on Thanksgiving

Day. They somehow added a malicious A.D.S. file "alternative data stream" to my Windows folder in the root directory of my computer. This was an amazing prediction by Jasmine. I discovered this A.D.S. "alternative data stream" hack on Thanksgiving Day.

(See "**Section 3**" at **www.thedevilprefers.com/bookextra** to listen)

THIS BITCH HERE!!!!!!!!! - Jasmine nailed this 100%. After this recording, I remember that when I took this girl home, I needed to stop on the turnpike and use the restroom due to a huge stomachache and diarrhea. The Triads sent this P.O.S. Woman to try and poison me. I met her on Match.com, and the rest is explained in the audio.

(See "**Section 3**" at **www.thedevilprefers.com/bookextra** to listen)

This girl approached me at a bar in Vegas and sent me this picture of herself the next day when I asked for a photo. She took 10 minutes to send the pic because she didn't want me to have proof of who she was since she was hired to scam me.

JASMINE HELPED ME FIND A TRACKING DEVICE ON MY CAR- In this audio, you'll hear me on a facetime video call with Jasmine where she is telling me where the Triads implanted a tracking device on my car. After I got off the call with her, I jacked up my vehicle for a better view and was able to find the device in the general area she referenced on the call.

(See "**Section 3**" at **www.thedevilprefers.com/bookextra** to listen)

AUGUST 2021

I made this website live around July 10th, 2021 but didn't advertise it or even list it with any search engines. Below are statistics for the domain www.thedevilpreferslivestock.com that points to this site. Notice how the traffic exploded on Monday, July 19th, 2021, in the 1st image below. Also, see how Hong Kong and China have the 2nd and 3rd most visitors in the image on the right below. The Triads obviously got news about this site. Not that I'm surprised, but about a week later, starting July 26th, 2021, I didn't see any more Asian guys at the gym when I was there. Not even one. The Triads saw this site, instantly shit themselves when they realized that I've been gathering evidence all along, and then decided they better crawl entirely back into the shadows since they know I'll post every move they make. The same happened with that "beauty" I called "CC." CC hasn't been outside at all when I came home for over a week now since July 26th, 2021. This was about the same time the Chinese guys disappeared from the gym.

thedevilpreferslivestock.com ▾ Add site Support ▾ Engli

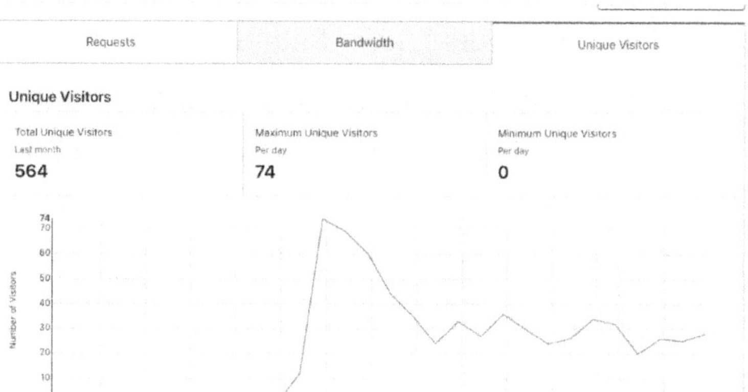

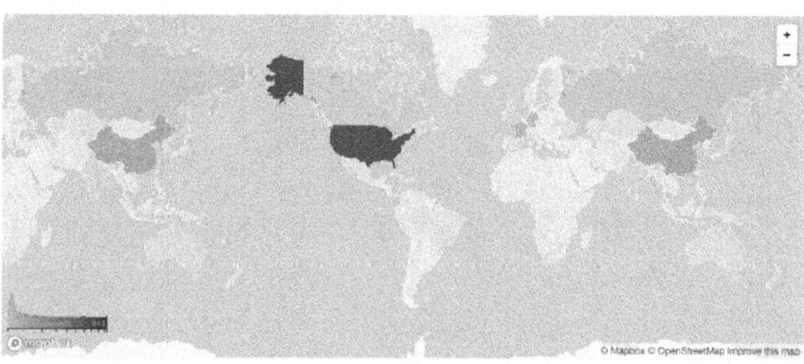

Top Traffic Countries / Regions

Last month

Country / Region	Traffic
United States	843
Hong Kong	495

The screenshots below are typical of how the Triads try to instill fear in me (except it never works, lol). I have a family member that lives near Uniontown Hospital. The Triads are trying to send me a threat meant to say they will put this person in the hospital if I don't back off. In the image on the bottom right, I answered it. I cheerfully said hello, knowing already that it was them, and got the same loser response as usual when they spoof phone numbers to try and send me subtle threats. They just by saying nothing and hanging up after a few seconds. These clowns are so easy to predict.

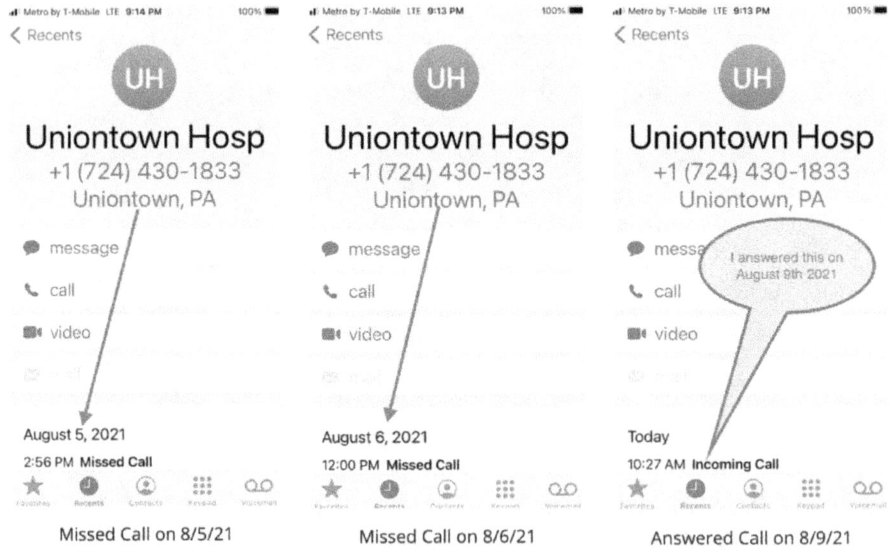

Missed Call on 8/5/21 Missed Call on 8/6/21 Answered Call on 8/9/21

The image below is a cable bill I received that stated I ordered a movie called "Murder." I didn't order it; my girlfriend didn't order it, and my son didn't order it. The Triads somehow hacked into Comcast and added that movie to my bill to try and send a message and scare me.

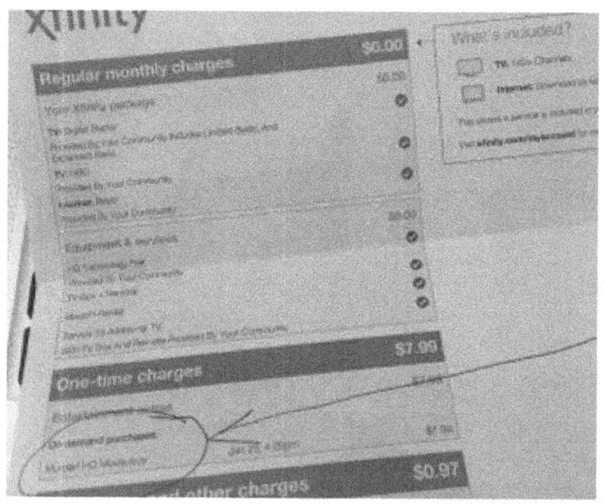

Today is August 10th, 2021. My war with the Triads continues to this day. Jasmine informed me that the Triads would attempt to make me have a car accident soon by either sabotaging my car or running me off the road. They seem to think that if they can at least injure me, it will give them a chance to kill me with black magic. I will update this section once I have more stories to write about, but now it's time to read about a much stronger opponent than the Triads "Evil Spirits summoned by Evil People." Click the button below to proceed to the "Black Magic Battle," which is still happening at this very moment!

Part 4 - BLACK MAGIC BATTLE

22 - Jett & My Dogs

My friend Matt "Jett" that died in 2009

The guy above and below was a good friend of mine that died in January 2009. His name is Matt, but we all called him "Jett" because he was a pilot in addition to being an actor and a model. Jasmine told me that without him, I would be dead. She said it was his spirit that fought the hardest to save me in the many near-death experiences I had. Jasmine said that since he died an angry death that he could have prevented, his spirit was stuck in the Earth realm for a few years, "Hell for spirits," and that he was a spirit that my enemies couldn't see in their card readings since they were always looking up to see what my great-grandmother was doing. Jett was my brother two times in a past life, and Jasmine said he gave every ounce of his soul to help save me. I owe the most credit for my survival to him. Jasmine said he fought demons constantly to protect me and even brought me back to life when I died for a few minutes due to the harmful drugs they gave me to kill me. Jett's website before he died was www.gqpilot.com. I keep that site up in his honor but also made a memorial site for him at www.forjett.com

The BLACK MAGIC BATTLE explained...

Some of you reading this believe in Black Magic, some are open to the idea, and some don't believe at all. Hopefully, I'll be able to convince even those that don't believe at all, but black magic is not just Voodoo Dolls and evil spells, there are many ways to fight a war with black magic, but you need to understand how it works before you can strategize.

Everything comes down to positive "good" ... & negative "bad" energy. Jesus and Buddha were examples of perfect spirits that are the epitome of positive, white "good" energy, while Satan and people like Hitler are examples of negative, black "bad" energy. In between Satan and Jesus are spirits of different levels of good and bad mixed energy "everyone else." The Dali Lama is very close to the level of Jesus and Buddha, while Hitler is very close to the level of Satan. People who murder people, commit suicide, or die from drugs are very low vibrating spirits when they pass onto the spirit world. This means that they are pretty much stuck in the Earth realm and cannot freely travel throughout the solar system or the universe as a spirit. The higher the level of spirit you are, the more freedom you have once you die. Jesus and Buddha are free to travel pretty much anywhere throughout the universe. At the same time, people like Pol Pot are stuck in the Earth realm (or below) until they can work out their base-level desires and pay back their karma, which may take dozens of reincarnations to work out "If ever." The Earth realm is considered hell to spirits that are in between incarnations. There is no such thing as burning in hell because spirits don't feel physical pain, but those stuck at the earth realm do suffer mentally from misery of many forms.

The more negative energy your soul is hampered with, the more easily you are tempted by things like the seven deadly sins. Until you can resist these sinful urges, at least, for the most part, you are stuck in the wheel of reincarnation. Think of sin and these base urges like doing drugs, infidelity, and committing crimes as magnets holding you at the earth realm. Once you can resist these urges plus overcome ignorance, you can ascend and escape the endless cycle of reincarnation like Jesus and Buddha. If you want to learn more about spirits and God's rules, check out a book called "The Spirit's Book" by Allan Kardec. You can read the eBook for free at the link below. This book was written 170 years ago and is unique in explaining how things work and our purpose on Earth. You'll also notice how the book references Jesus many times because the Bible is legitimate the same as most religious texts are, but misinterpretation and incorrect translations make things confusing. The Spirit's Book is unique because it is written in clear English. It was written over four years in the 1850s when a man asked over 1,000 excellent questions to 2 mediums connected with near Jesus-level spirits that answered them. If you are both intelligent and flush with common sense, you'll instantly understand that these questions are being answered by a higher power and make 100% sense as coming from what God really wants. You need to have common sense and intelligence to appreciate this book, but once you do, it will change your life and answer tons of questions you want answers to, in addition to solutions you didn't even realize you needed until reading them.

Spirit's Book https://bit.ly/dpreferssspiritsbook

If you like to listen to audio, another gem of a person is a guy that died in 1973 named Alan Watts. He is very popular on YouTube, and people had uploaded hundreds of hours of his recordings that he made in the '60s and early '70s before he died. Learn more about who Alan Watts was at:

https://bit.ly/dprefersalanwatts

Jett as an Angel

Two of the three videos below were taken on 11-27-2017, while I took the 3rd in January 2017. I have a water bottle that says "Always & Forever"... Jasmine told me that Jett and my Great Grandmother make the lid move on the water bottle. They chose this particular bottle due to the wording on it to let me know they are there. After about six months of this bottle lid moving, they started making other bottles move that I have.

Jett "in death" as a spirit saved my life in Vietnam in 2010, 2011, 2014, and 2015. I met my Ex Hong in Macau in 2009 and fell in love with her only eight months after Jett died. Jasmine said that Jett was constantly battling evil spirits and directing me to keep me alive when I moved there in 2010. Jett is my hero; according to my psychic, he saved me many times.

Bottle Video #1 #2 and #3 are located in Section 4.

(See "**Section 4**" to watch)

The Water Bottle above was empty and contained flat water in it before I drank it. There was no carbonation, and it doesn't move every time. It moves 75% of the time when I hold it and only about 25% of the time when I don't hold it. Sometimes it moves after sitting idle for 3 hours. Jasmine said it moves whenever Jett and my Grandma are present; sometimes, they are busy and aren't there. It moves more when I hold it due to my energy exciting theirs more and allowing it to happen. According to Jasmine, it's not easy for them to move it.

I saw Jett once in my house in 2016 as I was almost asleep. I felt energy sweep through the room and looked up and saw him waving at me. Jett is still among us, and he's a formidable angel, a true warrior that has helped me and many others since he died. Jasmine told me that Jett and I were brothers two times in a past life.

This clip is where Jasmine explains how Jett was the #1 factor I survived.

(See "**Section 4**" at **www.thedevilprefers.com/bookextra** to listen)

This audio clip is where my psychic explains how my ex and her family were doing tons of black magic on me and how Jett protected me. PAY CLOSE ATTENTION to the

50-second mark and the 1:12 mark where you can hear Jett. She never met Jett, but you can hear that it's him talking. That's exactly how Jett talks if you knew him well. It gives me chills every time I listen to it.

(See "**Section 4**" at **www.thedevilprefers.com/bookextra** to listen)

The audio clip below is where my Psychic confirms it was Jett that visited me in late 2016

(See "**Section 4**" at **www.thedevilprefers.com/bookextra** to listen)

How Jett helped me in Vietnam

Below are several examples of what happened to me in Vietnam that I escaped and survived. My Psychic Medium told me that I had several relatives helping me from heaven but that Jett was by far the X-Factor. Jett's unexpected passing caused him to be caught in between Earth and Heaven, where he could foil and prevent many things they did to me without them being able to see him in the tarot cards. To say it was a spiritual war of epic proportions is an understatement.

1. After I knew I was under attack by the Vietnamese where I lived, I was in my home office at 2 AM and had the strangest feeling that I needed to go to the garage for some reason. As I stood there in the garage confused, within 30 seconds, I heard the window open a few stories up and heard keys drop onto the street. Seconds later, a motorcycle pulled up, grabbed the keys, and took off. My ex-wife was giving someone the keys to come in and kill me. I stayed awake all night fighting with her before taking refuge at a hotel the next day for a few days. MY PSYCHIC TOLD ME THAT JETT PLANTED THAT SEED IN MY HEAD TO GO DOWN THERE AND THAT THEY WERE GOING TO ENTER THROUGH A

PAD-LOCKED WINDOW AND KILL ME ONCE I FELL ASLEEP.

2. I was doing drugs in Vietnam, smoking ice, which my Ex claimed was designer ephedra at first. I wouldn't say I liked it over there, and the drug allowed me to have time pass quickly. My psychic told me that my Ex was trying to kill me with poison and that the drugs and the food I was eating were poisoned many times. Still, I was very resistant and didn't die "obviously" except for one time where I actually did die for a moment, but my psychic said Jett did something to wake me up and bring me back to life. The amazing part is that she told me it was the time I was in a hotel and that when I woke up, people were going through my wallet looking at my credit cards. I never told anyone that, not even my friends and family, but she was right. She said Jett brought me back to life that night.
3. After barely escaping Vietnam in July 2011, I went back in August 2011 because I had to try to get my son out of there. I hired a Vietnamese Lawyer that ended up secretly helping my ex when she "the Lawyer" told me that I could more easily get a Visa for my ex if I were to give her $20,000 US in an account of her own. This would show that she has money to return to and is less likely to overstay her Visa. It made sense to me, so I had my lawyer friend in America wire her $20,000,

but it was sent back because the account number was wrong. I ended up not sending it again because I got in a fight with my ex where she said she was going to take that money and disappear with my son, never to be found again. My Psychic told me that Jett made the banker screw up when entering the wiring information. If not for that, my ex would either disappear while I was sleeping or would have me ambushed and killed. Jett saved me there again.

4. I touched upon the video below in the "Triads Part 2 section," where Jasmine explains in more detail the entirety of the police scam my ex was attempting to do against me. I had a 4-camera security system with a hard drive that recorded several days of video. A little voice in my head told me to destroy it. I didn't know why I was destroying this system that I paid $1,000 for, but I decided to put it in the microwave for 5 minutes to make sure I ruined the hard drive. After I finished, my ex came downstairs and went ballistic on me. She never lost her composure like that before, but for some reason was beside herself because I destroyed that security hard drive that I bought with my money. It didn't make sense. I later rationalized that she must have had her Triad losers in the shadows hack it and possibly splice frames into it where it looked like I was perhaps selling drugs or something. MY PSYCHIC SAID IT WAS MUCH MORE SINISTER THAN

THAT. She told me that young girls were coming into my house that were underage and doctored the video to show them walking out of my room naked. I wasn't in the room at the time, but they edited the video to look like I was. They were trying to set me up as a pedophile, and the edited video would have shown me going into my room with them following and walking out naked. I didn't do any of this; it was all cleverly edited. My psychic said that the police would raid my house in 4 hours when Jett and my great-grandmother planted the intuition in my head to destroy that hard drive. That's why my ex went insane. They were planning it for a whole month, but I foiled it without even realizing what I was doing when I did it. Look at the video below that I recorded minutes after I destroyed the hard drive. She went insane. Jett, with the help of my great-grandmother, saved me yet again.

(See "**Section 4**" at **www.thedevilprefers.com/bookextra** to watch)

23 - The Drugs Saved my Life

The pictures below were taken by me in Vietnam (left pic) and Macau (right pic) on one of my many drug binges with Hong and her friends. Jasmine told me that being on drugs saved my life since my ex and her family were practicing so much black magic on me to kill me and that if I weren't on drugs, I would have died. She said that the drugs took me to a different dimension and gave my soul a much-needed break from the constant spiritual battles that were taking place, even though I may not have been consciously aware of them at the time. Jasmine said my body was very strong and able to handle the drugs but that my soul at the time, while strong, was not strong enough to fight the onslaught of spiritual attacks. Jasmine said my soul is much stronger now, "almost three times stronger," and that I could easily defeat those attacks without being on drugs. Drugs are not the answer 999 times out of 1,000, but in my unique case, they saved me, and I believe it.

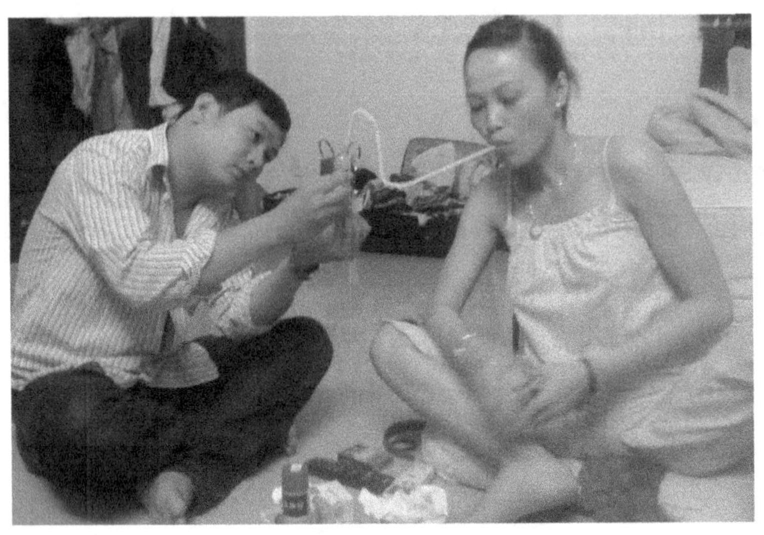

2010/07/30

Here's where Jasmine explains how the drugs saved me!

(See "**Section 4**" at **www.thedevilprefers.com/bookextra** to listen)

The fact that evil spirits were constantly attacking me from 2009 to 2016 manifested differently back then than it currently does. As detailed in the 2016 section, I wasn't aware of black magic or that I was under attack in any way until after Zulfiya cleaned me. God blessed me by ensuring I had a "spiritual" firewall up that prevented me from seeing the truth "and the demons" until Zulfiya cleaned me in 2016. After I was cleaned, I instantly started to have vivid dreams and battles in those dreams and was finally ready to fight the fight that was there the entire time since 2009, even though I was blocked from seeing the truth until late 2016. I currently don't have this "firewall" and can fight them without it, but back then, I was constantly miserable and angry but didn't know why. The attacks resulted in severe depression, but I didn't have the scary dreams and spiritual battles in my dreams until after I was cleaned.

POST 2016 - WHAT I NOTICED WHILE AWAKE

Black Magic battles mainly occur while you are just drifting off to sleep or when you are asleep, but the effects of these attacks are 24/7. If someone puts a curse on you to have an accident, the black magic will affect you by causing you not to pay attention at a critical moment. If the curse is a death curse other than accident-related, it will usually manifest as a horrible dream that seems like it's real, and you'll be so scared that you'll have a heart attack. Another attack is for you to get sick and die from cancer or something, in which case you'll feel tired and drained of energy while the evil spirits do their thing over months or years until you get cancer. There are thousands of ways to die from evil spirits; I'm just giving you a few examples to open your mind to the possibilities.

While I was fully awake but lying in bed at night, I would hear the wall creak in succession many times in a few seconds. Jasmine told me that this was the evil spirits showing up or was an actual attack while I was awake even though I wasn't aware of it. God blessed me again in the fact that he gave me my dog "Louie." Louie just passed away on January 18th, 2021, at the age of 15 years nine months. According to the UK Kennel Club, he would be the oldest Boston Terrier ever since the oldest they have on record was 15 years, eight months. Anyways, Louie was a special dog, according to Jasmine, and was a gift from God. Louie had this uncanny ability to snort three times in quick succession whenever black energy was a second or two away from arriving. Whenever I heard Louie snort, it caused me to pay attention, and I would notice the creaks in the wall, etc. This alarm helped me a ton in understanding how the spiritual world worked pertaining to energy. EVERYTHING IS ENERGY, including us.

Jasmine explains the frustration of my Ex and the people she hired to kill me with Black Magic. She also describes how spiritual attacks are much easier at night and easier to do on someone if they drink alcohol or do drugs. Spiritual Attacks are like hacking into a computer network. The demons want inside and can't hurt you until they are inside your body (your network)

(See "**Section 4**" at **www.thedevilprefers.com/bookextra** to listen)

This audio is where Jasmine explains my dog Louie and my female American Bulldog "Ginger", and how it works with animal spirits.

(See "**Section 4**" at **www.thedevilprefers.com/bookextra** to listen)

LOUIE & GINGER IN 2009

24 - Tiger

The girl on the below was a true sweetheart. She was only 16 when I met her in 2009. She was a girl from my Ex's village who always hung around my Ex's house. I nicknamed her "Tiger" because she snapped at someone in Hong's family one time, and I was impressed at how such a young girl could hold her own like that. Tiger was fond of me and always smiled when I saw her. She seemed to follow me whenever we visited Hong's parents. One time my ex's family was bringing a pig to slaughter, and I observed the men as they carried the pig upside down while it was tied to a bamboo stick. There were two guys on the front and 2 in the back, but the pig was a good 160 pounds and fighting for its life, so the two guys in the front were struggling as they carried it since they were older than the guys in the back. Tiger was there, and she gave me this look like W.T.F.! I didn't want to show off or anything, which is why I didn't jump in and grab the bamboo from the guys in the front that were older, but after Tiger gave me that look, I felt like I had to do something, so I reached in and grabbed the front from the two guys and lifted it to where they had to let go. I easily held up the front of the bamboo and even refrained from resting it on my shoulder, which my ex told me made me the talk of the village as though I was superman. OK, I'll take what I can get, lol. I was informed by my Ex 2 months after I moved back to the U.S. in

January 2012 that Tiger died of cancer. I cried when she told me that. Tiger was such a sweet girl and always made me happy when I saw her even though I couldn't speak to her. It wasn't until five years later that I learned what really happened to Tiger with the 3 Asian Demons.

This video was the pig I helped carry. I didn't kill this one, I just helped carry it. You'll see "Tiger" walking out of the house carrying a large pan at the 42-second mark. She was such a sweet girl; I still can't believe my Ex killed her.

(See "**Section 4**" at **www.thedevilprefers.com/bookextra** to watch)

The 3 Asian Demons

As I wrote in the 2016 section, I saw the 3 Asian-looking demons walking "floating" out of my house after I lit the first candle of 7 at midnight after Zulfiya killed the black chicken and cleaned me. Jasmine told me that the same three black demons my Ex used to try and kill me were the same three demons that my Ex sent to kill Tiger. Jasmine said that my Ex was jealous of Tiger and gave her a cursed drink containing the same three black Asian demons that she cursed me with. Unfortunately, Tiger wasn't as strong as me, and the 3 Asian demons killed her within a year of her drinking this cursed drink. Once I was cleaned in 2016, these same three demons returned to attack Hong and eventually killed her three years later. See the four audio clips below that explain this.

(See "**Section 4**" at **www.thedevilprefers.com/bookextra** to listen)

The Black Monster in 2011 in my house in Vietnam- This audio is impressive. Jasmine talks about a black monster "evil spirit" that my Ex, her cousin, and the Nanny saw on the ceiling in 2011. After talking about this in the audio on the left, I remembered when this happened. I didn't believe my Ex when she came to tell me about it. My Ex told me that there was a huge demon on the ceiling and that my big dog was barking at it, but my small dog was terrified. Even though I didn't believe her, my little dog never walked down the stairs again after that night and needed to be carried downstairs from that day forward. Jasmine also said that my ex was scared when we made love. I remember that right around that time, we had sex, and she kept gasping out in fear. It was the oddest thing. I guess she thought I was going to kill her. Jasmine said that my family in the sky sent the monster to scare her in hopes she would stop trying to have me killed. In a different recording, Jasmine said that the monster showed my image to my Ex with a fire ring around it and shook its head in disapproval.

(See "**Section 4**" at **www.thedevilprefers.com/bookextra** to listen)

88 Devils - To understand how evil works, you must first realize that almost everyone in the world has demons attached to them or come whenever the person drinks alcohol or gets angry. Evil spirits aid in emotions like anger and fear and amplify them. This explains how some people become violent whenever they drink. Those kinds of evil spirits come and go, but the worst spirits of all are the ones that come but don't go. These spirits are usually the spirits someone sends to you as a curse using black magic. A black magic spell may or may not expire after a certain period, but the way to get rid of the spell is that you need to be "spiritually" cleaned. You all have seen movies like the Exorcist, where a Priest does an Exorcism to expel

demons attached to a person. Britannica defines "exorcism" as: an adjuration addressed to evil spirits to force them to abandon an object, place, or person; technically, a ceremony used in both Jewish and Christian traditions to expel demons from persons who have come under their power.

In my case, a regular ol' exorcism wasn't enough due to the gravity of the curses my Ex, her family, and the two black magic shamans she hired put on me throughout the years, starting in 2009 until I was cleaned in 2016 (talk about 7-years bad luck, oy vey!) Zulfiya said she didn't need to sacrifice a chicken in over four years because the usual prayers and candles were enough to clean 99.9% of the people she saw. Jasmine said the job they did on me was huge and complex and required a sacrifice to counter it.

In this audio, Jasmine explains how I had close to 100 demons on me "88 to be exact, which also happened to be my Ex's birth year".

(See “**Section 4**“ at **www.thedevilprefers.com/bookextra** to listen)

LET THE VOODOO BEGIN!

Jasmine told me that the first time I went to Macau, Hong put a love spell on me the 2nd time I saw her that first trip. She said that Hong saved my sperm and used it to put a powerful love spell on me, making her irresistible. This made sense; even though I was very spontaneous, it was odd that I decided to go back to Macau only three weeks after the first trip. I had a business to run in addition to the fact that I was still casually dating other girls in Los Angeles. I also loathed flying.

The second time I was in Macau, only three weeks later, Hong sealed my fate and made sure I would do anything she wanted. According to Jasmine, make no mistakes about it; my Ex was a very powerful witch, more powerful than everyone in her entire family. Most of them were evil witches, murderers, and rapists, as I learned in 2016 after hiring Jasmine. Jasmine said she became physically sick when she watched the video from my wedding because the evil that was present was off the charts. She said it was a party of devils like she never saw before.

The picture from 2009 below was taken the morning after we woke up from a party at her friend's house. I remember waking up and feeling as though a truck ran over my leg but didn't give it another thought at that time. It wasn't until Jasmine explained what happened to me that night that it all started to come together. Shortly after returning to America from that 2nd Macau trip, I began to get a small growth on my right knee that I thought was a wart. I never paid much attention to it after that because it didn't grow more, nor did it hurt, but Jasmine explained how her friends drugged me that fateful night in Macau, and once I was out, Hong injected cursed ashes into my leg (which is why my leg hurt in the morning). Jasmine said that Hong used my knee as a spiritual portal to easily send demons to control me from that point forward. I know this sounds crazy, but Jasmine was dead on as far as the timing. I remember how her friend told me to take off my jeans and to get comfortable just before I passed out the night before. They wanted to assure my leg was exposed to inject their evil cocktail into my leg. The pic below from 2014 shows what it looked like, the 2016 pic was the day of the operation, and the 2018 pic is what it looks like today. I remember how the nurse blurted out that it looked like an eyeball when they cut it out. Talk about a real "evil eye" I didn't even look. For an entire week after the operation, my entire body tingled as though my body fell asleep like how your leg becomes when you sit in an airplane seat too long. Even more strange, my orgasms for the past several years were watery and clear, but they "instantly" became white again after that operation. Sorry for the visual, but this is important to understand. Jasmine said my ex had a powerful curse on my sex that prevented me from having regular sex or loving anyone but her. Everything went back to normal once that growth "eyeball" was removed from my leg. Jasmine said I needed both the chicken sacrifice and needed the operation to be fully clean from the seven years of constant Voodoo they did to me. She said my power began to grow at an amazing rate from that point forward, which was needed, given that only three months after the operation on my leg, Hong hired a black magic guy to kill me that Jasmine said dwarfed the people before him and was the #4 most powerful black magic guy in Vietnam, and #1 in South Vietnam. The next section is mainly about this evil "now dead" guy, and all that took place during my 6-month long battle with him until he eventually died.

2009

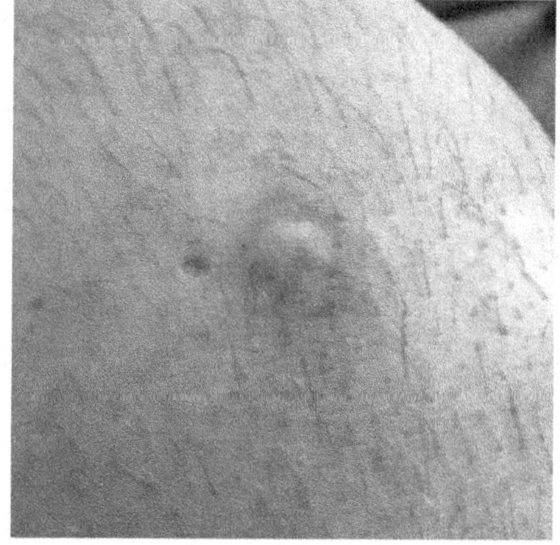

2014

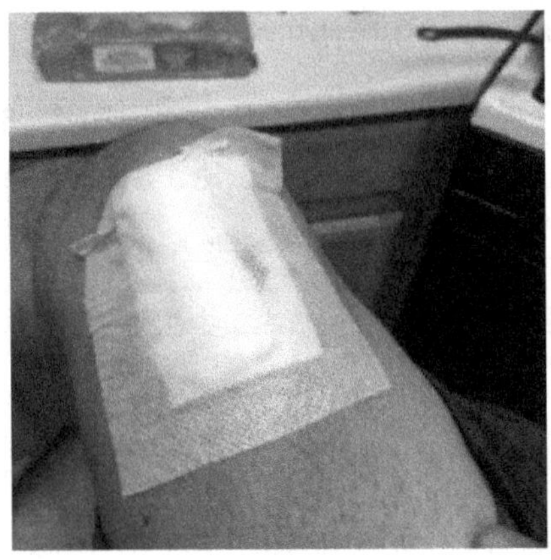

2016

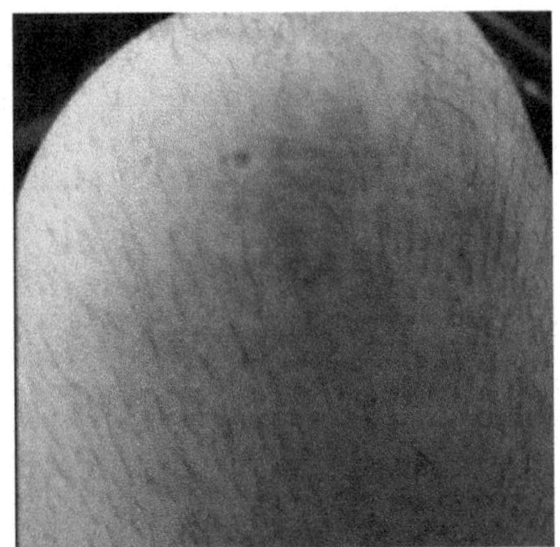

2018

Jasmine explains the effects of my leg being operated on and how good it is for me.

(See "**Section 4**" at **www.thedevilprefers.com/bookextra** to listen)

In this audio, Jasmine explains how the black chicken was needed and how much Zulfiya helped me.

(See "**Section 4**" at **www.thedevilprefers.com/bookextra** to listen)

In this audio, Jasmine explains how I'll never need a black chicken again now that my power has grown. She said my anger alone could easily send bad energy towards my enemies.

(See "**Section 4**" at **www.thedevilprefers.com/bookextra** to listen)

25 - Vietnamese Black Magic Guys 1 & 2

In early 2011, Hong hired a powerful black magic guy in HCMC to help her since everything the Triads she and her family did was not getting the job done. The first guy they hired was the same guy who put several curses on the stolen necklace I had in my possession during the airplane scam on April 14th, 2011. This garbage bag was behind the scenes working on me from 2011 to 2017 until he died due to me sending everything he did back to him when Zulfiya cleaned me. In late 2016, Hong hired a 2nd guy that lived near her village in the deep south of Vietnam near Vi Thanh, Vietnam. This guy only worked on me for about a year before dying, and the most powerful guy of the 3, "the 3rd guy Hong hired in March 2017," ended up only working on me for six months before he died.

In this audio, Jasmine explains details about the 1st two black magic guys and some of my ex's problems because of me sending everything back to them.

(See "**Section 4**" at **www.thedevilprefers.com/bookextra** to listen)

In this audio, Jasmine explains how the 1st black magic guy knows death is coming.

(See "**Section 4**" at **www.thedevilprefers.com/bookextra** to listen)

In this 1st audio, Jasmine explains how she thinks one of the first two black magic guys died and how the 3rd guy wrongfully assumed I died since I moved, and he couldn't find me with his spirits in Vegas anymore.

(See "**Section 4**" at **www.thedevilprefers.com/bookextra** to listen)

In this audio, Jasmine explains how the 1st black magic guy is dead for sure. She also tells me that Hong's Aunt is very sick. I found a picture below a week after this recording when I was snooping on Hong's cousin's Facebook account. The lady in the picture is Hong's Aunt that Jasmine said was very sick and dying just the week before during this recording. She took the picture at a hospital near Hong's village in Vi Thanh, Vietnam.

(See "**Section 4**" at **www.thedevilprefers.com/bookextra** to listen)

I met the first black magic guy in 2011, even though I didn't know it at the time.

(See "**Section 4**" at **www.thedevilprefers.com/bookextra** to listen)

Below is Hong's Aunt mentioned in the audio recording above. She helped take care of my son in addition to the Nanny when my son was born on 12-2-2010. Hong told me that we needed her also since the Nanny was never a mother before. Jasmine told me this woman was evil even though she seemed sweet and that she was staying at my house to help Hong practice black magic on me. Jasmine said she also helped care for two other kids Hong had before she met me and that Hong killed the fathers with poison. Jasmine said one father was from Australia and the other was from the United States and that both were love scams like mine where the dogshit triads helped in every way and profited the most. Jasmine said that Hong gave the kids up for adoption before she met me. Hong indeed was a black widow, unbeknownst to me at the time.

There were two other guys that Hong didn't kill but instead framed them for serious crimes. Jasmine said that these two guys are both in the prison next to her village to this day and that their family sends extra money to them for better living quarters, half of which goes to the Triads.

The picture of the dead guy below is Hong's uncle and was taken at his funeral. This guy is the husband of Hong's Aunt above and was the guy that the Vietnamese Psychic predicted "in April 2011" would die in 2011. He did die "as predicted" in November 2011.

In this audio, Jasmine explains how all of them are constantly sick and vomiting. The devils they send to me go back to them within a couple of weeks now without needing to get cleaned anymore. My power is now stronger than every devil they send, so it automatically goes back to the sender once it fails to attack me.

(See “**Section 4**“ at **www.thedevilprefers.com/bookextra** to listen)

The Black Magic #2 Guy Hong hired in 2016 throws his "Hail Mary."

One night in February 2017, while lying awake in bed listening to YouTube on my iPad, my iPad crashed and rebooted the very moment my neck made a bone creaking sound like when a chiropractor adjusts you. I was admittedly concerned and called Jasmine. In this audio, she explains how they killed a tiny pig in Vietnam and severed its spine that very moment to send a kill shot vibration to me in Las Vegas. This was the most potent attack I noticed up to that time because the 3rd guy was two weeks away from being hired. The 2nd Black Magic guy knew he would die soon, and this was his last significant attempt to kill me.

(See "**Section 4**" at **www.thedevilprefers.com/bookextra** to listen)

BLACK MAGIC ATTACK SYMPTOMS

This audio is where I discuss with Jasmine the different things that happen during my dreams where the dreams I was having went from my Ex being naked to my dead dog biting a severed crocodile head while a childhood friend of mine ripped my dead dog's skin off her skull. Crazy shit, but it's all part of evil's strategy when they cause you to have different dreams, hoping it will open a portal into your soul. Fear and other strong emotions can open a portal into your soul that evil spirits can enter through.

(See "**Section 4**" at **www.thedevilprefers.com/bookextra** to listen)

This audio is where Jasmine and I discuss how my ears are popping at night while I'm in bed. It was the result of bad energy "evil spirits" trying to enter my body.

(See "**Section 4**" at **www.thedevilprefers.com/bookextra** to listen)

Jasmine explains how I fought a fire devil while in Vegas in 2017. Demons don't like to lose and will even recruit other demons to help them if you defeat them. She also explains how incarnated humans have more power than spirits since they benefit from "matter."

(See "**Section 4**" at **www.thedevilprefers.com/bookextra** to listen)

In this audio, Jasmine and I discuss Hong's dead father and how his spirit is constantly trying to attack me. We also discuss how I defeated their family and how angry they are as a result.

(See "**Section 4**" at **www.thedevilprefers.com/bookextra** to listen)

In this audio, I discuss with Jasmine the only time I got sick from the black magic attacks, which she said resulted from the 3rd black magic guy in Vietnam.

(See "**Section 4**" at **www.thedevilprefers.com/bookextra** to listen)

Jasmine explains how my son absorbed the black energy until I was strong enough to fight it myself.

(See "**Section 4**" at **www.thedevilprefers.com/bookextra** to listen)

Jasmine explains the spiritual knock-out blows the black magic guys were sending me that only manifested as loud sounds in my house since my power was strong enough to defeat what they sent.

(See "**Section 4**" at **www.thedevilprefers.com/bookextra** to listen)

Farting Devils!

(See "**Section 4**" at **www.thedevilprefers.com/bookextra** to listen)

In this audio, Jasmine tells me that the black magic guy #3 is coming in 2 weeks and also touches on the state of my Ex's family and how they are fed up with the first two black magic guys

(See "**Section 4**" at **www.thedevilprefers.com/bookextra** to listen)

26 - Vietnamese Black Magic Guy #3

Time to fight the 4th most powerful Black Magic Guy in Vietnam (#1 in South Vietnam)

AKA "Vietnamese Black Magic Guy #3 " ... AKA "The Young, Stupid Guy"

Once the first two black magic guys gave up and resided to their fate that they'd be dead soon, Hong found another guy whom I referred to earlier as "Vietnamese Black Magic Guy #3". This guy was mixed, according to Jasmine, and was in his mid-twenties. Jasmine said she thinks his grandfather was French. This guy had a strong reputation throughout the deep south of Vietnam as a very powerful voodoo guy and was about a 2-hour car drive from Hong's village deep in the mountains. Jasmine warned me that he was very powerful and that the attacks would be much stronger than what I was used to. She said I didn't need to worry too much, but that my great-grandmother didn't want me to drink alcohol during the full moon for the first few months, he was attacking me. As usual, Jasmine was right; the first attack from this guy was off the charts. It was during the full moon in March 2017, and as I was lying in bed, I heard a loud sound of banging on what seemed like my front door. I jumped up to check, but no one was there, nor did my Ring Doorbell catch any movement. I thought, damn, W.T.F. was that? I would find out soon enough because 20 minutes later, as I drifted off to sleep, it's as though a theatre curtain ripped open over my eyelids. Everything became bright, vivid, and insane as I found myself in a different dimension of sorts. Several human-looking evil people were in my face looking either angry or laughing as weird energy swirled all around me. It was pure chaos. I remember a western-looking guy within inches of my face as I choked him while screaming, "Do you think you're going to kill me mother-fucker"? After a few minutes of this, I woke up with my heart beating a mile a minute as I heard a fast-crackling sound coming from my nose. The rest of the night, I kept hearing the banging sound "4 knocks" every few minutes, but nothing happened once I fell asleep. The audio clips below are discussions regarding my battle with this guy from the start until his death six months later.

This audio was recorded two days after the first attack by the young black magic guy mentioned above.

(See “**Section 4**“ at **www.thedevilprefers.com/bookextra** to listen)

The Audio Clips below all deal with and discuss this same "Vietnamese Black Magic Guy #3" and were recorded

within a few months of the audio clip above. Listen to each row at a time before going to the next row. The oldest audio is on the top and chronologically proceeds along the timeline as you advance to each row.

(See "**Section 4**" at **www.thedevilprefers.com/bookextra** to listen)

The audio above was the brunt of the fight with the Vietnamese Black Magic Guy #3. The audio below was recorded after the audio above and shows how this guy isn't a threat anymore.

(See "**Section 4**" at **www.thedevilprefers.com/bookextra** to listen)

The Vietnamese Black Magic Guy #3 is now Dead! The audio below was recorded after the audio above. It shows how this guy is dead in addition to the #1 and #2 black magic guy.

(See "**Section 4**" at **www.thedevilprefers.com/bookextra** to listen)

The Ghost Pigeons

(See “**Section 4**“ at **www.thedevilprefers.com/bookextra** to listen)

The audio above talks about the masses of spirits I had in my house in Vegas in 2017. It was a real-life haunted house. The pigeons on the left were on the neighbor's house behind my backyard (They were facing my bedroom window and stayed there all day, even into the night sometimes). Jasmine said that both good and evil spirits controlled these pigeons and used their bodies to park their energy near my house. Spirits just can't float around forever; they need a living organism to take shelter in. It can even be an insect or a plant, but it makes it much easier for them to remain near someone if they can take over a living creature as a shelter of sorts. The amazing part is that there were no pigeons to be seen in my entire neighborhood except for the house next to mine. My friend Yanni heard the neighbor chasing the pigeons away and struck up a conversation with the guy when the guy said that these pigeons just arrived a couple of months ago and haven't left since.

27 - The Facebook Wars

Some of you may be thinking, "what the hell does Facebook have to do with Black Magic?" Everything (in my case, at least). My God-given skillsets include the ability to drive people crazy when I want to. I am very adept at mind games and always have been. I didn't do black magic on anyone; the only thing I did was get spiritually cleaned, which essentially caused all their attacks to return and attack the person(s) that sent it. Once Zulfiya cleaned me though, my power grew at an accelerated rate, and from that point on, I didn't need to be cleaned anymore. My power alone was now high enough to almost instantly send back all of the attacks. I had more power than the demons they sent to attack me. Once those demons were sent back, the best way to assure the demons succeeded in attacking them was to make them scared and to make them less confident.

I used Facebook as a weapon to accomplish both of those tasks. I started by friend requesting everyone in Hong and her family's Facebook friends list; then I requested their friend's friends. Within a month, I had 5,000 friends, with at most 2 degrees of separation from Hong and her family. Over time, I had three fake Facebook accounts created only to harass my Ex and her family in retaliation to what they did to me and the black magic they continued to practice on me. All three accounts have since been banned, but I caused absolute hell for my Ex and her family while they were up. I exposed all of their secrets, from how her father and uncles raped many children in the village, to the scams they ran against people in the village, to the young girl they killed in the village that everybody loved.

The posts were a true shitshow "mash-up" meant to get people talking and sharing, with the ultimate goal being to expose who this evil family was. I posted taunting videos to intimidate them plus show how their attacks using black magic were ineffective. The mocking nature of many of these posts was meant to be entertaining for those who knew Hong and to drive her family nuts. My goal was to get everyone talking and sharing. The benefit of this was that it made it much easier for the demons attacking them to penetrate their souls. A fearful or angry person has many more attack angles, "open doors" that a demon can take advantage of to wear that person down.

Below are just a few examples of what I did on Facebook to drive my Ex and her family insane! The audio clips below are sorted by time. The Facebook War lasted over a year. The audio clips towards the top were towards the beginning of the Facebook War, while the ones towards the bottom of the page were recorded near the end of the Facebook War.

This video was taken the day after the first attack by the Vietnamese Black Magic Guy #3, supposedly the strongest voodoo guy in all of South Vietnam. Please forgive my broken English in the video; my Ex spoke very broken English and understood broken English better when talking to her. I posted this on my fake Facebook account in 2017 that her whole village followed to drive her nuts and show the guy attacking me that he had minimal effect on me.

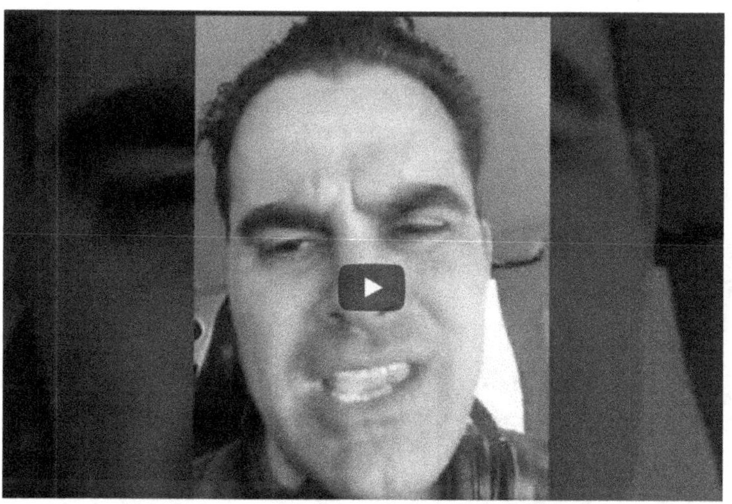

(See "**Section 5**" at **www.thedevilprefers.com/bookextra** to watch)

Don't ask me why I hated this disgusting woman the most. Maybe it's because she hand-fed me a poisoned spring roll "twice," perhaps it's because she nicked my son with a razor blade several times when he was four months old, saying it helps expel the sickness, who knows... Jasmine also said she was the strongest next to my Ex, so I wanted to wear her ass down mentally. This video was one of many posts I did to strike the fear of God in these devils.

(See “**Section 5**“ at **www.thedevilprefers.com/bookextra** to watch)

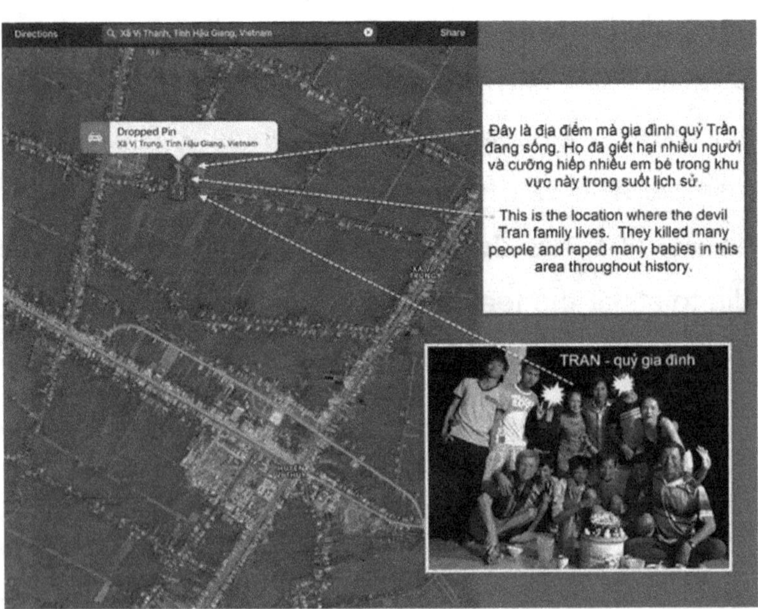

Người đàn ông dưới đây là chồng cũ của anh Tuấn Cường Trần. Tuoi gửi năng lượng màu đen cho anh ta và anh ta không cảm thấy tốt. Anh đã đến đền thờ nhiều lần để được giúp đỡ nhưng anh vẫn còn nhiều ma quỷ từ những gì em gái Hồng của chị Mười đã làm với anh. Nếu ai đó biết anh ta, nói với anh ta rằng anh ta cần phải làm sạch để loại bỏ các quỷ Tuổi gửi cho anh ta.

Tuổi bây giờ đã kết hôn với một anh chàng Úc biết rằng gia đình cô ấy là ác. Người đàn ông chuyển đến Thái Lan với Tuoi để trốn khỏi Việt Nam vì anh ta sợ rằng gia đình của Tuoi sẽ giết anh ta vì tiền như họ đã làm với nhiều người trong quá khứ. Anh ấy muốn ly dị cô ấy. Anh vẫn ở bên cô nhưng anh đang gặp nguy hiểm.

The Guy above is Tuoi's ex-husband Cuong Tran. Tuoi sent black energy to him and he doesn't feel good. He has been to the temple many times for help but he still has many devils from what Hong's sister Tuoi did to him. If anybody knows him, tell him that he needs to get cleaned to eliminate the devils Tuoi sent to him.

Tuoi is now married to an Australian guy that knows her family is evil. The guy moved to Thailand with Tuoi to escape Vietnam because he is scared that Tuoi's family will kill him for money like they did to many guys in the past. He is also in danger.

This audio discusses the Facebook account and this picture below.

(See "**Section 5**" at **www.thedevilprefers.com/bookextra** to listen)

The Videos below speak for themselves, lol. Pure Madness, but each got over 10,000 views and accomplished the job I set out to do: get people talking in her village.

(See "**Section 5**" at **www.thedevilprefers.com/bookextra** to watch)

I sent Jasmine this picture below after receiving it from Hong's friend that was involved in the scam against me. As you can see, she was petrified. Don't feel sorry for this girl; they are ruthless "Sirens" that help the Triads kill people.

The Audio Clips below all deal with Facebook and how it affected my Ex and their family.

(See "**Section 5**" at **www.thedevilprefers.com/bookextra** to listen)

Jasmine explains how Tiger's family now believes that Hong killed Tiger with Black Magic in the audio above. The image on the left was another image I pushed on Facebook in Vietnam to expose my Ex and her evil family. I referred to Tiger as "the sweet girl" because I didn't know her name and didn't trust Google Translate to explain with clarity why I called her Tiger.

(See "**Section 5**" at **www.thedevilprefers.com/bookextra** to listen)

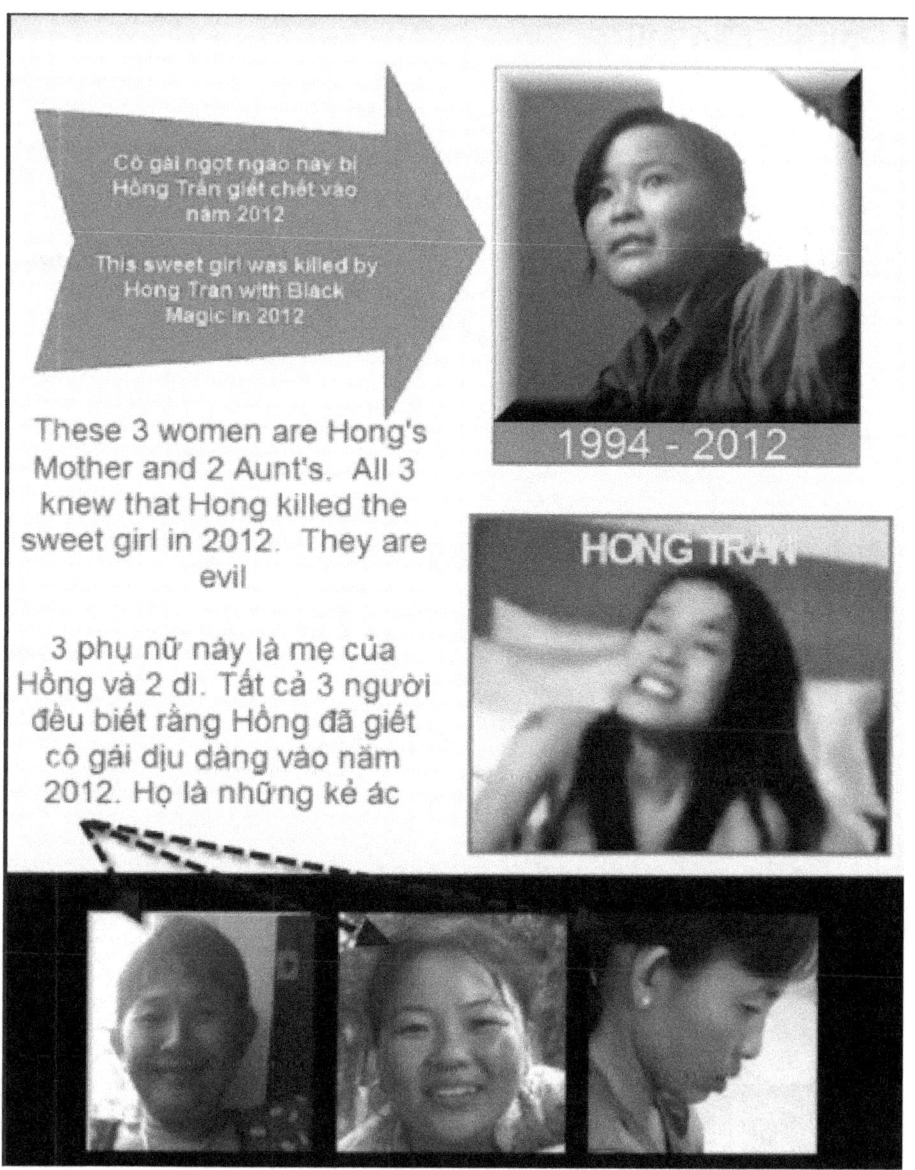

(See "**Section 5**" at **www.thedevilprefers.com/bookextra** to listen)

Mind Games can kill!

(See "**Section 5**" at **www.thedevilprefers.com/bookextra** to listen)

The next section goes into what happened after the 3 Vietnamese Black Magic Guys died. The Black Magic Battle was far from over; it was just getting warmed up.

28 - My Little Buddha

Phật nhỏ của tôi

My Ex's friends, my Ex, and My Ex's family all "supposedly" belonged to a militant sect of Buddhism in Vietnam called the "Phat Giao Hoa Hao." Phat Giao Hoa Hao Buddhism is like all religions in the sense that they have a few bad apples that are hypocrites that do anything but follow the founder's principles. After studying Phat Giao Hoa Hao Buddhism in 2018, I now believe 100% that my Ex, her family, and her friends were hypocrites that did not abide by the doctrines set up by the Hoa Hao founder Huynh Phu So. That said, when I initially moved back to the United States in late 2011, I noticed the book below (on the left) was in my belongings when I unpacked and must have gotten packed by accident since it was Hong's and not mine. The strange part was that it was the only thing of Hong's that got packed in my belongings. I did a quick Google search in early 2012 on the book's title because I was curious about the book, and I read about the founder Huỳnh Phú Sổ (on the right) and what it was about on Wikipedia but didn't give it any thought after that day in 2012.

This video details the Phat Giao Hoa Hao founding by Huynh Phu So in 1939 and its explosive growth and impact on Vietnam

While living in Florida in 2018, I was on the treadmill at the gym when a powerful thought entered my head and would not go away. I guess you could call it a voice. Still, whatever it was, it kept saying, "your son is Huynh Phu So." I tried to dismiss it as random daydreaming, but it persisted the rest of the day and the next day until I finally messaged Jasmine with this LINK and said, "Is this my son reincarnated?" Jasmine replied after a few minutes and said, "YES, how did you find out?" Keep in mind that it was my great-grandmother there giving her the answer, but the only question I presented Jasmine with was if it was my son or not. My great-grandmother only answers questions asked "BY ME" and can't give a narrative.

Jasmine called me a minute later because Jasmine was as curious as I was at this point. As we talked, Jasmine was able to get more information from my Great-Grandmother and find out that it was a gift from the sky, "an information download," where unnamed spirits in the sky felt that it was time for me to know who my son was. Once I knew who he was, it made complete sense because both Jasmine and Zulfiya kept telling me that my son was very special "even referred to him as a little Buddha before I knew who he was" and that he was pure, white energy. This also coincided with my uncanny luck that allowed me to escape unscathed from every imminent disaster I faced my entire life, let alone the past decade. My son's spirit and his nearly unlimited guardian angels helped my guardian angels make sure I survived to complete this mission I had with him.

Millions of people still follow Huynh Phu So to this day. Many still believe he is alive somewhere even though he disappeared in 1947. The article below was written in January 2021. Huynh Phu So would be 101 if he were still alive. Although most people believe he died in 1947 when the Viet Minh abducted him, many hold out hope that he is still living and have not accepted the idea that he died. Those people are not happy with me since not only am I saying he died in 1947, but I'm also claiming he lives again as my son in America.

101st birthday of Hoa Hao founder marked in An Giang

Sat, 09 Jan 2021 18:14:00 | Print | Email Share:

The Central Executive Board of the Hoa Hao Buddhist Sangha held a ceremony in the Mekong Delta province of An Giang on January 7 to mark the 101st birthday of the founder of Hoa Hao Buddhism, Huynh Phu So.

Vice President of the provincial Vietnam Fatherland Front Committee Truong Hoang Trong hailed the Hoa Hao Buddhist Sangha for standing united and staying side-by-side with the nation.

Through five congresses, Hoa Hao Buddhist followers have actively responded to the national target programme on building new-style rural areas and civilised urban areas as well as spread charity models, contributing to local socio-economic development.

Amid the COVID-19 pandemic, the organising board prepared body screeners, hand sanitiser, and thousands of masks to participants.

There are more than 2 million Hoa Hao Buddhist followers in Vietnam at present, with An Giang being home to the largest number.

By: VNA/VOV

Source: https://vov.vn/en/society/101st-birthday-of-hoa-hao-founder-marked-in-an-giang-829438.vov

For this reason, several of his followers hired black magic people to kill me, in addition to the dozens hired by the Triads. The three images below are recent images posted by people on Facebook that belong to the Phat Giao Hoa Hao religion. They celebrate and honor Huynh Phu So in a big way to this day.

I know, I get it 100%, everyone thinks their kid is special, but in this section, I will prove to you why this wasn't just some typical "unconditional love" B.S... You be the judge after I finish making the case below.

This picture below was taken only minutes after my son was born and before my Ex allowed me in to see him. Is it me, or is he saying, "Who the Hell is this evil bitch?"... lol. He knew right out of the womb whose side he was on and who he had to protect. He was looking at his mother when this picture was taken. The nurse took the picture from what I was told, and the hands you see are Hong's Mother's hands. At the time this picture was taken, Hong's evil cousin Kiwi was guiding me on a goose chase around HCMC, waiting for Hong's call to say if I was the father or if it was Hong's Vietnamese Husband Cuong Nguyen. If I wasn't the father, the order was for Kiwi to take me to a waiting hit squad that would kill me. Fucking BITCH!!!

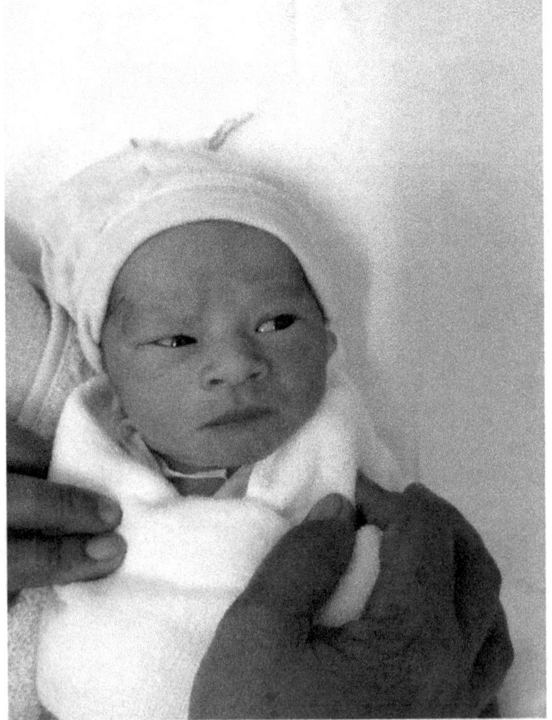

P.S. I guess Pink "not blue" was the only hat they had available, lol... I only paid around $2,000 U.S. to the hospital for the entire birth, so no complaints here.

P.P.S. I later found out from Jasmine that Hong was never married to a Vietnamese guy. I found passport photos with Hong's first name and his last name on them because Hong was trying to change her name in hopes she could escape her police record.

The audio clips below were recorded **BEFORE** Jasmine and I knew my son was Huynh Phu So. As you'll see, all we knew was that he was a very old soul, was very religious in past lives, and was a Singer, a Writer, a Monk, and a Priest in several past lives, and that I met him while in the Army in a past life.

(See "**Section 5**" at **www.thedevilprefers.com/bookextra** to listen)

CLARIFICATION: Jasmine refers to my son both as a Priest and as a Monk. In later conversations, she clarified that he was a Priest a few hundred years ago but was a Monk when I met him in the 1940s and a Monk before that. Those were all different incarnations.

(See "**Section 5**" at **www.thedevilprefers.com/bookextra** to listen)

Jasmine explains how my son's mother is attacking my son with Black Magic (See the video of this below also)

(See "**Section 5**" at **www.thedevilprefers.com/bookextra** to listen)

In the audio below, Jasmine and I again touch on how my son screamed for me when he was only five months old and wouldn't let go of my neck as he hugged me when my Ex tried to get him out of the house to allow people to come inside and kill me. I didn't let her sister leave the house with him after that incident. He saved my life that day.

(See "**Section 5**" at **www.thedevilprefers.com/bookextra** to listen)

In the audio below, Jasmine explains how my Ex's family knew that my son was very special, and she describes how desperate her entire family was to get him back to Vietnam. (See "**Section 5**" to listen)

I shot the video and the picture below and sent it to Jasmine in 2018. My son was waking up at precisely 3 AM on the dot every single night for almost two weeks. He would start dry heaving and acting like he would vomit but rarely did anything ever come out. Jasmine confirmed my worst fear: my son's mother was trying to kill him with Black Magic. I wanted to fly to Vietnam and rip out her throat. Jasmine said that my Ex knew that we were never returning to Vietnam, so she figured it was better that my son died if she couldn't have him. I asked Jasmine how his mother, who was much weaker than my son, could hit him so hard with an attack since my son had double her power. Jasmine said that it's because she is his mother and has a special connection that can also, unfortunately, be abused.

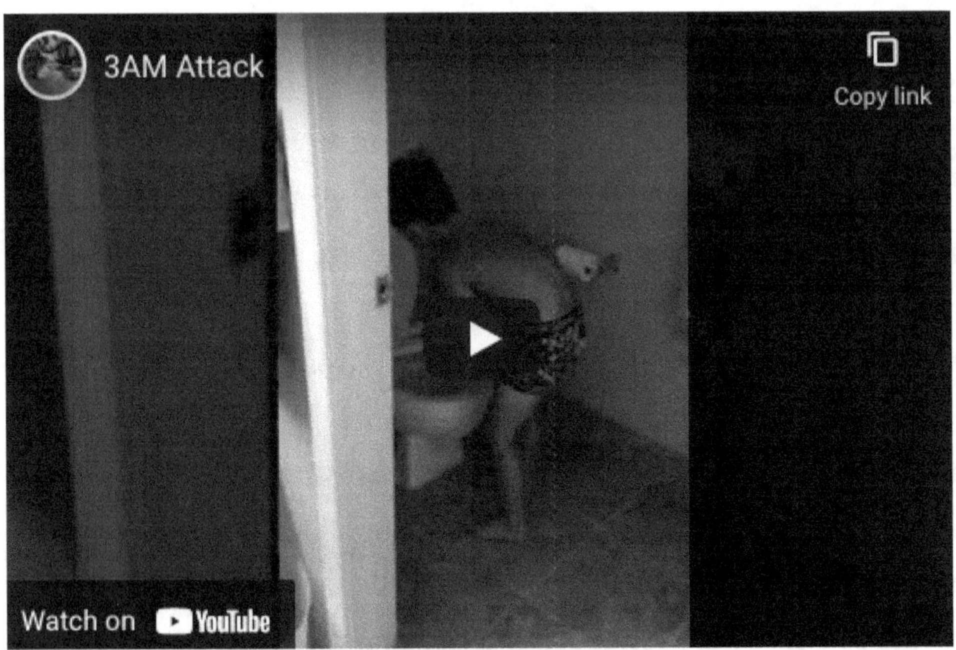

(See "**Section 5**" at **www.thedevilprefers.com/bookextra** to watch)

In these 3 Audio Clips, Jasmine goes into detail about how my Ex is attacking my son.

(See "**Section 5**" at **www.thedevilprefers.com/bookextra** to listen)

In one of the three audio clips above, you'll see where Jasmine said that my great-grandmother was crying when my son was being attacked. This audio is very significant because it was when I drove from Florida to Pennsylvania to visit my mom for Christmas in 2017. Jasmine also said that my power moved from 8 to 12 instantly during that trip, making me equal to my son. I now believe (and Jasmine recently confirmed when I posed the question) that the reason God gave me that instant boost "4 levels" that 99.999999% of the population doesn't get their entire life was because my great-grandmother saw something where I was going to die. Still, the fact that God gave me that blessing in the gift of power that trip, I was able to escape death. The crazy part was, the night before I left, the moment I closed my eyes, Hong instantly appeared in my consciousness and was talking to me while I was wide awake. She was still alive, and Jasmine later said it was a demon pretending to be her. The people attacking me with black magic found a demon that could enter my consciousness. My great grandmother saw them entering my consciousness while driving back to Florida and causing me to drive into a wall, killing both me and my son. The four levels of power boost I got made my spirit that much stronger to the point that the demon couldn't pull that trick on me, and I lived because of that huge blessing from God. I went to sleep at my mom's a few minutes later at 10 PM, but for some odd reason, I woke up at 12:30 AM full of energy and felt it was time to go. I remember that it was only 8 degrees when I started to drive back to Florida. Jasmine said that the Triads had people waiting for me that started driving past my mother's house at 6 AM. They never thought I would leave before 6 AM. I needed both the power boost and to leave early to avoid the asshole Triads.

This audio is where Jasmine explains how my son's mother is attacking him, but Jasmine also says that there is music I can play at night to help fight the attacks. The image on the right is a message I got from a Vietnamese guy only days later that believes my son is Huynh Phu So. Notice how he recommends I play a song when the evil comes. The sky helps us in so many ways that we don't even realize. Jasmine says I need to play music, and only days later, a guy recommends I play this song. This is divine intervention

(See "**Section 5**" at **www.thedevilprefers.com/bookextra** to listen)

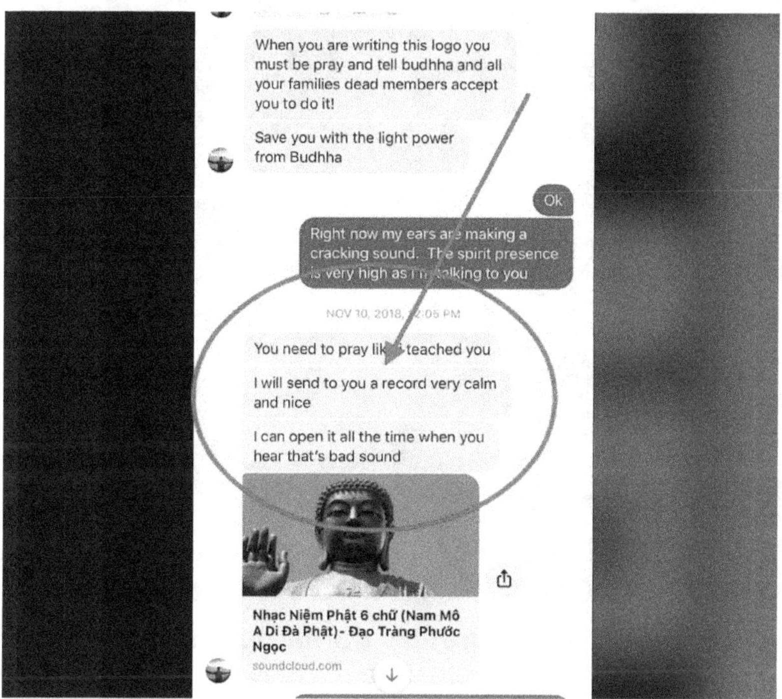

I still find it hard to believe that a girl that looked so sweet could be so evil as to attempt to kill her child with black magic over a period of weeks. This wasn't just a momentary lapse in sanity; this was a considerable effort done every day for weeks.

I later found out that once she failed to kill him, she found a way to plug into his energy to extend her life.

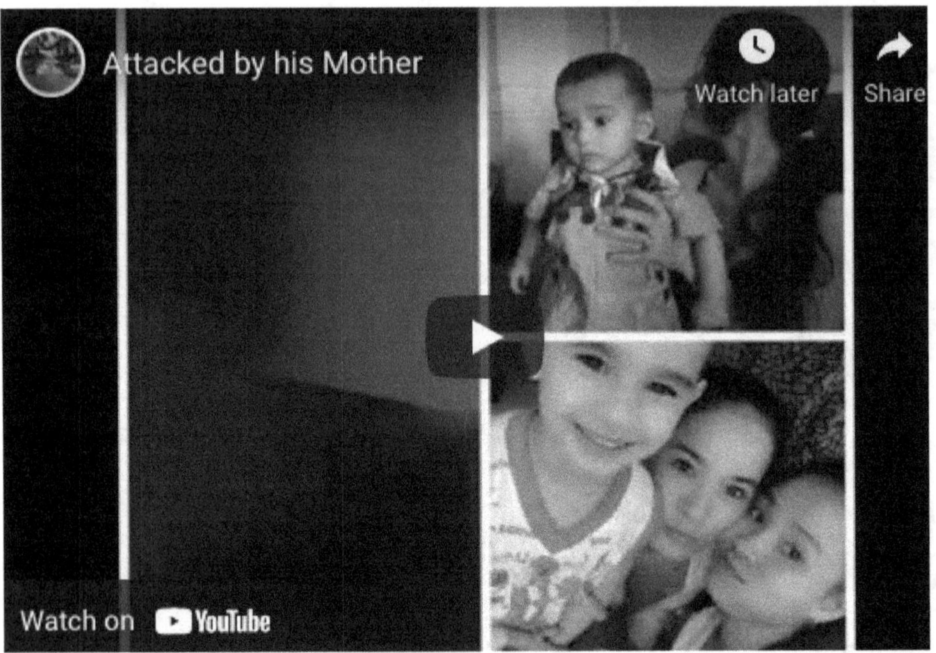

(See “**Section 5**“ at **www.thedevilprefers.com/bookextra** to watch)

This audio discusses how everyone thought my Ex would die that week, but since she was able to plug into my son, she was able to extend her life. She indeed was a talented Voodoo Princess.

(See “**Section 5**“ at **www.thedevilprefers.com/bookextra** to listen)

Jasmine explains how my son was perfect at the airport during our escape from Vietnam. His spirit knew it was time to go, and he assured everything went smoothly. She was right about everything;

it's as though my son wasn't even there the way he didn't make a sound or go to the bathroom either in Vietnam, during the flight to Tokyo, Japan, at the airport in Tokyo, and even well into the flight from Tokyo to Chicago. Notice my voice and how amazed I was because as she told me this, I remembered how he didn't ask for anything. He quietly tagged along and didn't bring any attention to us the entire way back. The guy sitting in front of my son even commented that he never saw a kid travel like that where his seat wasn't kicked once and not a sound was made. The guy felt the urge to tell me that as we got off the airplane in Chicago, which is why I so quickly remembered as Jasmine told me.

(See "**Section 5**" at **www.thedevilprefers.com/bookextra** to listen)

This audio is where Jasmine explains how my friend Jett and my great grandmother didn't know my son was special right away until he was a few months old.

(See "**Section 5**" at **www.thedevilprefers.com/bookextra** to listen)

In these three audio clips, Jasmine explains how my son acted as a sponge to absorb a large portion of the black magic they were sending me while I was in Vietnam and the States until 2017, when I became strong enough to handle it all by myself. Jasmine also said that my little black dog was special and also helped until the day he died.

(See "**Section 5**" at **www.thedevilprefers.com/bookextra** to listen)

In this audio, I tell Jasmine how she predicted that my son would have an I.Q. over 132. Only 2% of the country has an I.Q. over 132, and Jasmine said he would have that and be in the gifted class. I post this because it shows how Jasmine was again correct about something that only happens in 2% of cases.

(See "**Section 5**" at **www.thedevilprefers.com/bookextra** to listen)

Here's where Jasmine tells me that my Ex was told my son would be one of the most powerful spirits on the planet. Jasmine also says something I already knew: my Ex wasn't even sure my son would be mine until after he was born because she had sex with her Ex that same week before I arrived in Vietnam on February 24th, 2010.

(See "**Section 5**" at **www.thedevilprefers.com/bookextra** to listen)

In this audio, Jasmine explains how my son is unique, and it's like having a little Buddha. REMEMBER, this is all before I had the treadmill epiphany that my son was Huynh Phu So. After the epiphany, I researched Huynh Phu So and found that he is considered a Buddha by millions in Vietnam. All the signs were there and support the fact that my epiphany was accurate once you factor in Jasmine and Zulfiya both agreeing my son is Huynh Phu So. Many Vietnamese people believe it also; I'll discuss that evidence later.

(See "**Section 5**" at **www.thedevilprefers.com/bookextra** to listen)

FACEBOOK "Take 2" – NO WAR INTENTIONS THIS TIME

All the audio clips below were recorded after discovering that my son was Huynh Phu So reincarnated. A couple of months after I found this out, I decided to start a new Facebook account where I friend requested only people that were followers of Phat Giao Hoa Hao

"PGHH" currently. At first, most people were pissed and angrily reacting to my posts. Still, after the initial shock of someone claiming that their leader was reincarnated as half white, many started to believe once they had the chance to check with Shamans and other spiritually gifted people that they trusted to be able to find out the truth through meditation or mediums that could find out the answer. Over time, the Facebook account I set up went from regular likes and angry face reactions to regular likes and "love" reactions. Below are a few examples of these posts and how the mood changed over time.

This post was on November 16th, 2018. As you can see in the reactions, the angry reactions outnumbered the love reactions with even a couple of laugh reactions.

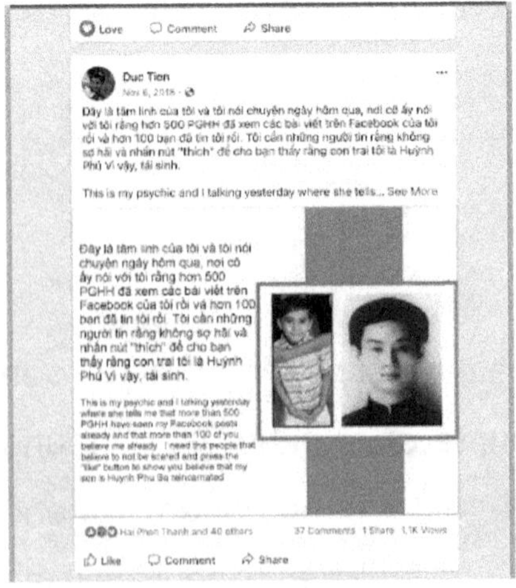

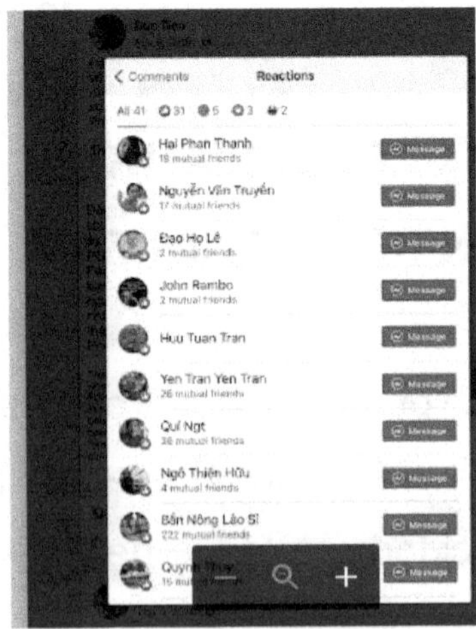

This post was two months later, on January 14th, 2019. As you can see, the likes and loves are way up while only a single angry reaction happened. The 99 in the picture was meant to symbolize that it's been 99 years since Huynh Phu So was born in that reincarnation when he founded the PGHH religion.

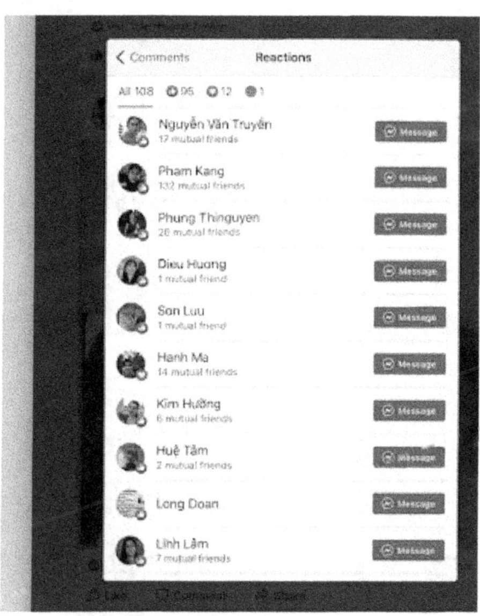

In this audio, Jasmine explains how some people believe me on Facebook while others don't. She also discusses my Ex.

(See "**Section 5**" at **www.thedevilprefers.com/bookextra** to listen)

In this audio, Jasmine tells me how my Ex's family knows who my son was in his past life and how angry they are because they think I have the "Gold".

(See "**Section 5**" at **www.thedevilprefers.com/bookextra** to listen)

REGARDING THE DEATH OF HUYNH PHU SO IN 1947 (taken directly from Wikipedia)

See https://bit.ly/dpreferPGHH1 (case sensitive link)

According to Vietnamese police documents, Huỳnh Phú Sổ was arrested and executed on December 22nd, 1947, by the Viet Minh in Long Xuyen. The southern Việt Minh leader, Nguyễn Bình, realizing that Sổ would not subordinate himself to the Việt Minh, set up a trap. Sổ was caught and executed in April 1947. His body was dissected into many small pieces and scattered so that his followers could not gather them and turn it into an object of veneration or as a shrine.

After Huynh Phu So was executed in 1947, he reincarnated again right around the time I was born in

1972. Jasmine said that he died though as a teenager around 1984. This audio discusses that.

(See "**Section 5**" at **www.thedevilprefers.com/bookextra** to listen)

In these audios, Jasmine explains how I was always in the Army in my past lives. She says that I died in 1946 in Vietnam after meeting my son. According to Jasmine, I was a spy for the United States Government that was sent to spy on the French and what they were up to in Vietnam at the time. I somehow got killed in Vietnam a year before Huynh Phu So was murdered in 1947. In later conversations, Jasmine said that I reincarnated again around 1950 and went to Vietnam again as an American Soldier but died around 1970 or so before being born in this current life in 1972.

(See "**Section 5**" at **www.thedevilprefers.com/bookextra** to listen)

In the video, Jasmine explains how Huynh Phu So died at the hands of the Viet Minh in 1947.

(See "**Section 5**" at **www.thedevilprefers.com/bookextra** to watch)

The audio clips below talk about how many people believe that my son is Huynh Phu So.

(See "**Section 5**" at **www.thedevilprefers.com/bookextra** to listen)

The guy in the 2nd pic below sent me the message pictured below (which I translated with Google). He believes 100% that my son is Huynh Phu So. Keep in mind that my son truly was born into a devil's house. Hong and her family were evil; I was doing drugs and devil shit at the time, while the only decent person was my son's Nanny, a 55-year-old virgin (3rd pic). Hong's cousin Oanh was good too, but it was pretty much a devil house with those two exceptions. Even though the Nanny and her cousin Oanh were good, they still knew that I was being scammed and sort of went along with it even though they both tried to help me at times.

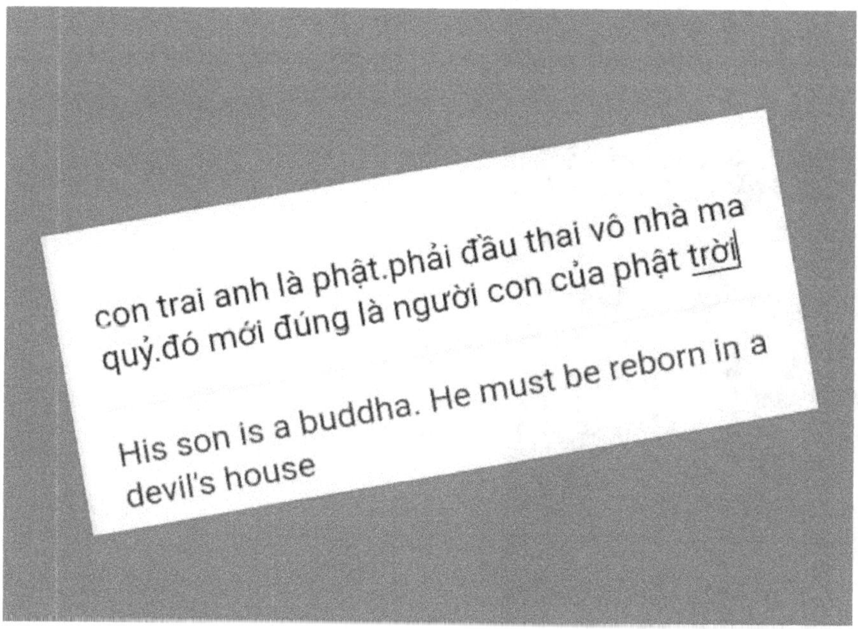

Just when I thought I finished my Black Magic Battles, it then heated up worse than ever. Click the "Voodoo Army" link below to see how

29 - Voodoo Army

I also pissed off a few people from Vietnam that weren't with the Triads but tried to kill me with Black Magic nonetheless. Once the Triads failed in killing me again, they decided the best way to attack me was to pour hundreds of thousands into hiring Black Magicians from throughout Asia. The latter part of 2017 through 2020 was unreal; the events discussed below focus on that.

About a month after the #4 most powerful evil guy in all of Vietnam died, I had two months of pure bliss. I was able to sleep through the night every night, and I didn't hear sounds, nor did I have any dreams. Then out of nowhere, just before Christmas 2017, things started to heat up big-time.

Just before Christmas of 2017, I started feeling powerful energy on me as I laid in bed in addition to having insane dreams. I also started to hear my nose making those cracking sounds as I woke up from an intense dream. I knew I was under attack again, but unlike before, the attacks were every day, not just during the full and the new moon. I called Jasmine to ask what was going on. She told me that the Triads hired close to 20 Black Magic Guys throughout Asia to kill me but that none of the 20 were nearly as powerful as the young guy that just died "Vietnamese Black Magic Guy #3" (see audio below) ...

Given that there were 20 though, Jasmine said they all have different styles and that not all attack during the full moon, etc. OK, here we go again.

When I say "powerful energy," I mean that I almost feel as though I am in a low-energy microwave oven where some kind of force or radiation is penetrating me. My palms would always get very warm, and my stomach would constantly groan and make noises during these times. These were the black magic attacks playing out. Jasmine said that I was too strong for them to really hurt me but that I would still feel some effect from the attacks, which was this energy and stomach grumbling I was constantly having.

(See “**Section 5**“ at **www.thedevilprefers.com/bookextra** to listen)

Jasmine told me that not only did I have 20 Triad hired Black Magic Guys working on me, but I also had several Vietnamese hired black magic guys hired by people who were angry that I said my son was Huynh Phu So reincarnated. The audio on the left discusses this.

(See “**Section 5**“ at **www.thedevilprefers.com/bookextra** to listen)

This audio makes complete sense. Earlier in the story, I told you how Giang froze whenever he was holding the sword. My Ex came after me with a knife and was in motion to stab me, but her arm stopped just before connecting. I didn't even try to stop her that time, but I did try to stop her on a different occasion when my son was there. Please pay attention to how Jasmine said that they are not allowed to kill me. This was destiny and part of the life path I have. Jasmine said I am on a critical mission and have a spiritual wall up that they can't cross when it comes to killing me.

(See "**Section 5**" at **www.thedevilprefers.com/bookextra** to listen)

The Triads hire the 2nd strongest Voodoo guy in all of Asia to kill me!

After almost a year of fighting every night with the onslaught of evil people the Triads hired, in addition to the several sent by the Vietnamese I angered, I had a few months of calmness and thought everyone was either dead or gave up. Then I started to get attacked like never before. Unlike the other attacks that dealt with intense dreams and sounds while awake, these new attacks were different. I felt something that I can only describe as an invisible blanket of energy laid upon me all night as I tried to sleep. I would wake up feeling not only the radiation type of energy but was just exhausted in addition to that. I started to have to take a 2-hour nap every day just to function. I called Jasmine and asked her what the deal was. Jasmine said that the Triads found a terrible old guy in Cambodia who looked like a Monster, that was stronger than everybody in Vietnam, and the 2nd strongest in all of Asia, with maybe 1 or 2 people from Africa being stronger also. According to Jasmine, I had the 3rd or 4th strongest Voodoo guy in the world trying to kill me with black magic. I even had to stop drinking altogether and eat very healthily just to feel good during the day. Thankfully, I adjusted and got used to the attacks. Jasmine said the guy would be dead in about six months, but I just had to see it through. I played my usual head games on Facebook and posted things that mocked the guy attacking me by telling him that he's weak and needs to send me more energy. (SEE VIDEO BELOW)

This video below was a video I posted in the comment section of a Facebook post that I knew the Triads monitored. About a month after I posted this video, I knew the very moment the Evil Cambodian Guy died because my entire room was swirling with energy, and I would start dreaming while I was still awake and kept drifting off and coming to all night with a non-stop intense dream that I could see happening while I knew I was still awake but just had my eyes closed. Jasmine said that this was due to all this guy's demons releasing from his body the moment he died and that they all came to me since his focus was only on me for over six months. This was in November 2020. Jasmine said the guy would never have dreamed that his death would come at the hands of a white guy. He killed hundreds of people throughout his life. He was plucked straight from Satan's ass-crack

(See "**Section 5**" at **www.thedevilprefers.com/bookextra** to watch)

The next and final section for the Black Magic Battle deals with Hong (My Ex and Son's Mother) and her family. Jasmine told me that her family is the evilest in ALL of Vietnam. She said that her family has done nothing but kill, steal and rape for many generations. They rape all of their children starting at age five, and Hong even told me that her father killed an American guy in Cambodia once and shared his liver with three other people. This was when I could tell she loved me and was trying to warn me that her father was dangerous.

30 - Hong & Her Family

Jasmine told me that Hong's family is the evilest in ALL of Vietnam. She said that her family has done nothing but kill, steal and rape for many generations. They rape all their children in addition to other people's children starting at age five, and Hong even told me that her father killed an American guy in Cambodia once and then cooked and shared his liver with three other people "Cannibalism." This was when I could tell she loved me and was trying to warn me that her father was dangerous. The entire family was dangerous, but they all smiled and used deception to the fullest. Below are several examples of how evil this family is (was, since many have died in the past five years)

Listen to Jasmine "Once Again" tell me something I already knew but wasn't thinking of until she told me.

(See “**Section 5**“ at **www.thedevilprefers.com/bookextra** to listen)

This audio explains how Hong put 2 of her western Ex's in prison near her father's house in Vi Thanh, Vietnam. Hong was only 22 when I met her, but she managed to kill two guys with poison and imprison two more before meeting me. Hong also had two kids that she sold before having my son. Her body was perfect though, and she didn't have any noticeable scars or stretch marks. She knew how to take care of herself since that was needed to make money. She was the ultimate "Siren"...

(See "**Section 5**" at **www.thedevilprefers.com/bookextra** to listen)

In this audio, Jasmine explains how my Ex was a devil even as a child, and was the strongest in her entire family.

(Whenever I say "Strong," I mean that the spirit is strong and that the person is very hard to kill, the stronger they are. A strong spirit is different than a strong human. A strong human may have a weak spirit and can be easily killed with black magic, while a small woman can be very hard to kill with black magic if she has a strong spirit. The character we play in life does not always mirror our spirit as far as strength)

(See "**Section 5**" at **www.thedevilprefers.com/bookextra** to listen)

Jasmine explains the obvious here when she said all the men in Hong's family were lazy and women have the power. I noticed that right away after I moved there.

(See "**Section 5**" at **www.thedevilprefers.com/bookextra** to listen)

This audio explains the lady and the baby I circled in this photo. It's incredible how much Jasmine, "actually my great-grandmother," knew. These were details I noticed but never spoke about because they were petty, in my opinion. My great-grandmother indeed was there every single minute, studying everything to protect me. My friend Jett was the same. They were my top 2 guardian angels.

Hong's Sister Tuoi

Zulfiya and Jasmine confirmed that Hong's sister Tuoi was in jail in 2018 and would return again.

(See "**Section 5**" at **www.thedevilprefers.com/bookextra** to listen)

This audio discusses Hong's sister's Australian Husband and her Ex-husband, that was Vietnamese. The Vietnamese Husband died in late 2017 because of Hong's family doing black magic on him. In Vietnam, her sister and their criminal connections isolated their email accounts to prevent emails from going out that they didn't want to be delivered.

(See "**Section 5**" at **www.thedevilprefers.com/bookextra** to listen)

This audio was recorded six months after the one above that talked about Tuoi living in Vietnam with the Australian husband while still being near the Vietnamese ex-husband. As you'll hear, the Australian husband went back to Australia, and the Vietnamese ex-husband is now dying.

(See "**Section 5**" at **www.thedevilprefers.com/bookextra** to listen)

The guy named Cuong below (pictured with Tuoi) was Tuoi's Vietnamese Ex-husband that is now dead. Tuoi doesn't look like a killer at all, but just like her sister and Father, they were ruthless and had no issues killing people. Tuoi wasn't this evil when I first went to

Vietnam because I saw her upset with Hong once whenever she knew Hong tried to kill me (I did spoil her too, though). Still, the demons in this family take over eventually, and Tuoi blossomed into a ruthless black widow, just like her sister.

The End of an Evil Dynasty

(See "**Section 5**" at **www.thedevilprefers.com/bookextra** to listen)

The audio on the right was recorded in late 2017. In this audio, Jasmine discusses Hong's fate and what her life will be like for decades in the spirit world once she dies.

(See "**Section 5**" at **www.thedevilprefers.com/bookextra** to listen)

This audio discusses the image below.

(See "**Section 5**" at **www.thedevilprefers.com/bookextra** to listen)

The audio below discusses Hong's Mother, who is pictured in red on the left. This audio was recorded at the beginning of 2018, and Jasmine predicted that Hong's Aunt would die 1st, Hong's Uncle 2nd, Hong's Mother 3rd, and Hong 4th. I posted this picture on Facebook in early 2018 before anyone died. In the end, Jasmine correctly predicted 1st, 2nd, and 3rd but was off on Hong passing that year since Hong didn't die until September 13th, 2019. Remember how I told you that Hong somehow plugged into my son's soul and energy and was able to prolong her life.

(See "**Section 5**" at **www.thedevilprefers.com/bookextra** to listen)

The audio below discusses the uncle listed above the subtitle "2ND - 2018" above.

(See "**Section 5**" at **www.thedevilprefers.com/bookextra** to listen)

The audio below discusses how Hong missed the funeral on the Aunt above because she was too sick to attend. The audio below that one on the right outlines how Hong is sending me spirits, hoping that I'll stop sending everything back to her and her family.

(See "**Section 5**" at **www.thedevilprefers.com/bookextra** to listen)

THE GOOD BROTHER

This audio is so sad. I remember how Hong's young brother wasn't at the father's house when I was in Vietnam in 2015. Hong's piece of shit father threatened to kill him because he wanted to help me.

(See "**Section 5**" at **www.thedevilprefers.com/bookextra** to listen)

In this audio, Jasmine explains how Hong only ever loved me and will die with my memory.

(See "**Section 5**" at **www.thedevilprefers.com/bookextra** to listen)

In this audio, Jasmine explains how my Ex hired a Lawyer to get my son back to Vietnam.

(See "**Section 5**" at **www.thedevilprefers.com/bookextra** to listen)

In this audio, Jasmine discusses how the Chinese "Triads" are trying to steal my money and how they are trying to purport me as an "unfit parent" to help my Ex... I didn't realize what would come about six months later, but as usual, Jasmine "via my Great-Grandmother" was prophetic.

(See "**Section 5**" at **www.thedevilprefers.com/bookextra** to listen)

HONG DIED ON THE FULL MOON ON 9/13/2019 "FRIDAY THE 13th" AT THE AGE OF 31. A FULL MOON OCCURRING ON FRIDAY THE 13th IS VERY RARE AND WON'T HAPPEN AGAIN UNTIL 2049. THE DAY OF HER DEATH COULDN'T HAVE BEEN MORE FITTING

After everything that happened, part of me still loved her until the end. Jasmine said she was dying in September for sure, even though some of her prior predictions regarding Hong's death were

off since Hong somehow spiritually plugged into my son for power to stay alive by doing some ritual in addition to non-stop meditating on him. I knew she died the moment it happened. I felt a jolt of energy, and the walls creaked from corner to corner. As I was falling asleep, I started to dream a minute before falling asleep; it was like being in the twilight zone. The dreams were intense and non-stop all night. In my dream, I saw an ugly witch that wouldn't come closer than 20 feet but kept trying to spit on me as she scowled. The dream's setting was in my apartment complex, and I was walking down the street at dusk and saw red eyes peering from all the apartment windows. It was crazy. I called Jasmine the following day and asked if she died, and Jasmine said yes. Jasmine said that the witch I saw in my dream was a witch that lived inside Hong and that when Hong died, the witch was expelled from her body and came to attack me out of anger since I essentially evicted her, lol. It was ten years, one month, two weeks & 3 days after I first laid eyes on her that she died.

Goodbye, my little "em yeu." I truly wish things could have been different. I waited a day before telling my son that his mother had died, but he was OK. He didn't cry; he didn't see her (even via FaceTime) for over four years at that point. She has visited me five times in my dreams since she died; The whole thing is just sad. Destiny is not always fun, it was either her or me though, and she drew first blood in this battle. I forgave her so many times, only to be betrayed again and again.

FBI

I started receiving calls from the F.B.I. in December 2019 but ignored them at first, thinking that it was the Triads spoofing their number to play games until they finally left a message and it sounded like a legit white lady. I finally decided that it may be a good idea to call them back rather than risk a B.S. search warrant with my son in the house having to experience it. I called the lady from the F.B.I. back in January 2020 to ask why they are calling me. The F.B.I. Agent told me that she was following up on an international abduction case reported six months prior. I told the Agent that this was a family court issue and that my Ex needed to come here and challenge that. She said, "No, this is something that is under the jurisdiction of the criminal court at the Hague." OK, I said, but I assure you the woman is lying, and not only is she lying, but my son's mother died three months ago on 9/11/2019, and given that the complaint was six months ago, I assume that the F.B.I. wasn't aware of this. I then proceeded to tell the F.B.I. the hospital she died at in Vi Thanh, Vietnam and told her to call me if she has any more questions. Needless to say, they never called me again!

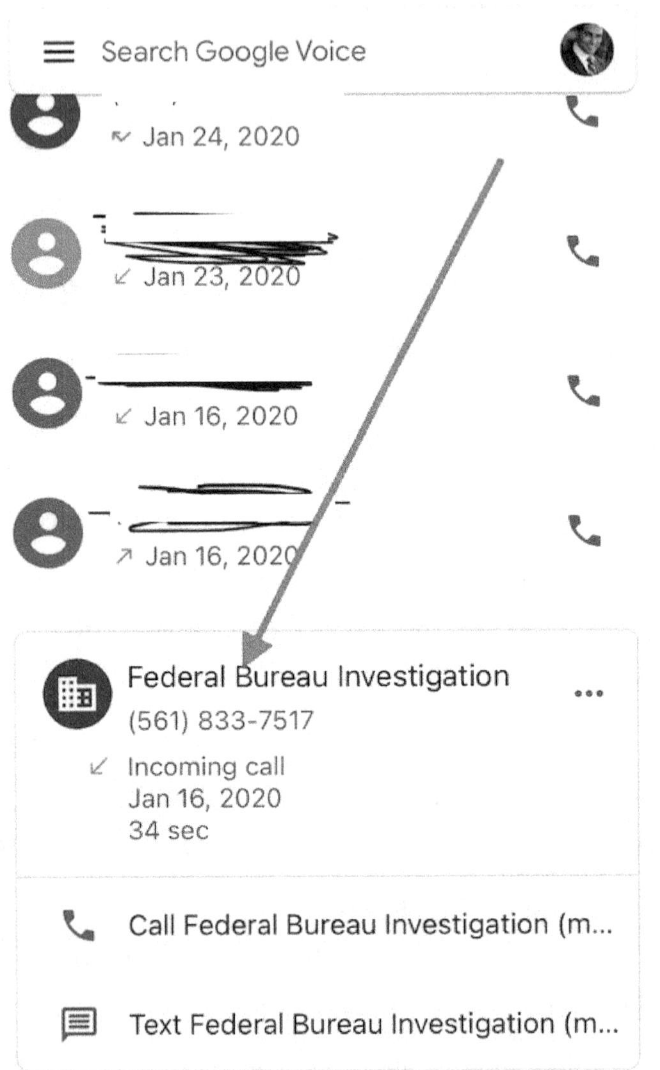
Search Google Voice
Jan 24, 2020
Jan 23, 2020
Jan 16, 2020
Jan 16, 2020
Federal Bureau Investigation
(561) 833-7517
Incoming call
Jan 16, 2020
34 sec
Call Federal Bureau Investigation (m...
Text Federal Bureau Investigation (m...

31 - FINAL THOUGHTS

Jasmine told me dozens of times that this story will be both a book and a huge series on a large network provider like Netflix or Amazon Prime that will span several seasons. I believe that 100%. Everything I discussed in this book is true. Until it becomes a series, as of October 1st 2021, I am looking to speak to large networks only because the story must get told the right way and with the best talent.

If you are an agent (literary or film), large publisher, or work with a big media powerhouse like Netflix, Amazon Prime, or HBO, please feel free to contact me at one of the several contact options below. I highly suggest you use several contact options below if you don't get a response from me within 24 hours in the event my forever nemesis, "the Triads," find a way to stop one or more contact channels.

My son and I on 8/2/2021

Thank you for taking the time to read my story. My battle with the Triads is ongoing and will not end anytime soon. To be kept in the loop about new events that happen because of this saga, please make sure to join my mailing list at www.thedevilprefers.com.

email:
edward@jamisonlawgroup.com
edwardjamison@gmail.com
Telegram Chat: +1-724-640-3713